CURRENT TRENDS IN INDIAN EDUCATION

CURRENT TRENDS IN INDIAN EDUCATION

Ashok Kumar

A P H PUBLISHING CORPORATION
4435-36/7, ANSARI ROAD, DARYA GANJ
NEW DELHI-110 002

Published by
S.B. Nangia
A.P.H. Publishing Corporation
4435–36/7, Ansari Road, Darya Ganj,
New Delhi-110002
Phone: 011–23274050
e-mail: aphbooks@gmail.com

2026

Typeset by
Ideal Publishing Solutions
C-90, J.D. Cambridge School,
West Vinod Nagar, Delhi-110092

Printed at
DIVINE DIGITAL PRINTERS
Ansari road Daryaganj Delhi-110002

Preface

As in any other developing country, in India too, one of the major blocks for educational development has ben the paucity of resources. The implementation of national policy on education has necessitated initiating several new programmes and increasing the tempo of existing ones to meet the broad policy thrusts and priorities. Eventhough the allocation of funds for education of the Central Government level has got more than doubled during th last two years, the magnitude of resources required can not be mobilised, through government sources alone. However the country has, undoubtedly made long strides in terms of quantitative growth in educational facilities. By now, primary education facilities have been provided within easily accessible distance to almost all Children of country. But it has been realised that mere provision of facilities does not ensure education of all children. In fact, a closer analysis of th situation reveals that a large section of the population have failed to benefit these facilities.

Nevertheless, it has been expanding, obviously yielding to be pressures, totally unconnected and without any reference to the manpower needs of the community. However, the direction of the reform, the content of the reform and the objectives to be achieved through our reformed educational system is still debatable. Unless we get rid of the idea that education is some kind of social service performed by Welfare State and substitute it with the idea that education is the most critical input into the entire processes of social, economic, political and cultural transformation of India, the so-called educational reforms would predictably produce explosive social tensions in our country. Reform must begin with some base.

However, question of central importance to the present study is to understand the education from the vantage point of the mid 1980s, compared to how it looked from the earlier perspective. Because the colonial education system emerged on the academic scene outside of and in antiseptic isolation from the historically evolved structure. While the task before free India was to remove the infirmities of the inherited structure of the educational system and transform it into a social force geared to the socio-economics transformation of the Indian polity from colonial underdevelopment of self-reliant development.

A major presentation of the war on poverty and inequality is that education and training are effective ways to bring people out of them. But it is not in India. The affluent class (holding land/asset and upper middle and higher castes) has been constantly accumulating higher education and its returns. The children of the illiterate and poor parents are clearly at disadvantage. The Government's funancial assistance and other facilities have not reached to the poor people in desired manner due to one reason or another. Hence wide range efforts as shown in this study must be considered for developing effective educational planning in the country.

Another factor that needs attention is the lack of proper linkages between education and employment. Several steps have been initiated to tackle this problem. However, the two major parts i.e. economic aspects of educational planning and education employment linkages of the present study attempt to synthesize the building of unique model to necessitate and bring these interdiciplinary developments to the attention of the educational planner. The need for planning arose with the intensified complexities of modern techological society. Problems such as population, manpower needs, ecology, decreasing natural resources and haphazards application of scientific developments all place demands on educational institution for solution. If educational organizations are meet the problems, then planning becomes a necessity and planning competnece becomes mandatory.

In writing and developing this book, I have been helped, directly and indirectly, by many people. But the enthusiastic support given by Prof. Monnis Raza, Prof. J.S. Sodhi, Dr. S.P. Jain and Miss Harish was essential in making the initial idea a reality. I am particularly grateful to Prof. K.S. Sivaswamy, Prof. Ishwari Parashad (JNU) Mr. P.N. Tyagi (NIEPA), Shri M.S. Ramanujam, Shri H.P. Joshi and Shri G.P. Joshi and Shri S.N. Mishra who have been constant source of inspiration to me. A number of colleagues and friends have provided valuable advise and assistance, hence, I shall be failing in my duty if I do not express my gratitude. I must however, make it clear that the views expressed here are exculsively those of the author and not of the institute to which I belong. I hope this work will bear fruit and serve as an eye-opener to the educationist planners and policy makers. Finally,k I, ofcourse, accept responsibility for errors, omissions and the presentation of ideas contained herein.

New Delhi
1990

ASHOK KUMAR

Contents

1 The Background

1.1 Introduction

A linguistic therapy is not in itself enough, though it may constitute an essential propaedeutic. Education aims to transmit aspects of human experience to the as yet uninitiated, and so involves an introduction to modes of behaviour—which certainly include modes of thinking and feeling—relevant to our common life. It is a search for the knowledge of the self, of the meaning of life, of the relationship of man to other beings and to the ultimate reality. It is the foundation on which rests the edifice of society and democracy.

Though the role of education in socio-economic development has been recognised since Adam Smith, it is only during the fifties of the present century that it has been identified as an important instrument of national development. Theodore Schultz's Presidential Address to the American Economic Association (1961) brought about what Bowman (1966) aptly described as a 'human investment revolution in economic thought'. Recently, the role of education in the development of traditional people has been very well stressed by educationists and sociologists.

In India education is at the crossroads. It has to decide its future directions. But it does not seem to be in the mood to nor, unfortunately, does it seem to be qualified to do so. Nevertheless, it has been expanding, obviously irrespectibly yeilding to the local pressures, totally unconnected, and without any reference to the manpower needs of the community. The net result is the massive of an unabsorbable number of graduates from the non-professional facilities of higher education.

What is however, still debatable is the direction of the reform, the content of the reform, and the objectives to be achieved through our reformed educational system. Any educational policy must provide answers to some of the very simple questions. The very first question is : Why Education? The conceptual error committed by us is to look upon education as part of social welfare and social service.

That is why we still have a rest number of citizens of India illiterate after nearly four decades of independence; that is the reason also why our educational system as a whole has no inner consistency as between university education, schooling, the so-called vocational education and continuing education outside the formal system. Unless we get rid of the idea that education is some kind of social service performed by a Welfare State and substitute it with the idea that education is the most critical input into the entire processes of social economic, political and cultural transformation of India, the so-called educational reforms would predictably produce explosive social tensions in our country.

Educational reform must begin with some base. And that base lies in our entire schooling system from its primary stage to the secondary stage. It is on this foundation that the structure of education must be built. To build somewhere in the middle of the pyramid is an architectural absurdity. Unless making everyone educated, in the sense that our children begin to understand their environment and can cope with it through the education in imparted to them, we may have a sensation of doing something, but actually, we would produce agents of destruction rather than of construction. Once we get possessed with the idea that a period of a decade we shall impart education to everyone, nothing really can be achieved. However given that passion, backed by new concept of education as the most critical input in changing or modernising India, financial resources need be no constraint.

Education is the most powerful tool for change and hence it must train the minds of the educated to cope with the change. Equally, the educational system throughout the length and breadth of India must actively promote that value system and outlook which is consistent with the kind of society we wish to establish. Finally, those who are thinking about education must realise that in the fast changing world of today no education system can be frozen into a mould. It would need periodic revision and change to enable the educated to grapple with social, economic and technological changes.

Seen in this perspective, education is increasingly becoming a continuing process stretched over the entire life span of man in terms of the Quaranic imagery 'from the lap to the grave'. It is available to the new generation as the quintessence of the accumulated social experience of mankind before its initiation into the world of work; it would continue to complement and supplement work through leisure time activities through the formal as well as non-formal channels during the working age and it would steer the life of the aged in meaningful directions after retirement. Education of the future is bound to be united intimately with the life of mankind through every fibre of its being.

The implications, however, should not automatically be pressed too hard and too far. It should not be asumed that nothing is beyond redemption before educational systems are overwhelmed with ruin. The evidence does not support any such cataclysmic forecast. Moreover, we have a positive duty, as a simple matter of morale, to remind ourselves that, despite many formindable obstacles and shortcomings, the educational progress has been made throughout India over the past four decades. The task is to grasp the nature of the critical problems that have enveloped the world of education and more to overcome them by altering their underlying causes.

However, question of central importance to the present book is to know how the education in India looks from the vantage point of the mid 1980s, compared to how it looked from the earlier perspective. As will be seen in a moment, the many economic, social and political changes have occurred in the ecology of education.

1.2 Golbal Picture of Education

'To know thyself, compare thyself to others.' It would appear that the educational systems of the four countries—India, England, the USA and the USSR—have developed in their own way in different historical, geographical, economic and social conditions and thus illustrating as well as explaining different national styles. Different aspects of education in these countries bear comparison and reveal a picture of both similarities and contrasts and thus provide a better insight into the system of education of one's own country.

Nevertheless, formal education is only possible where production exceeds consumption. This may be the result of tremendous industrial development or favourable natural circumstances. This will depend upon fertility of soil, abundant natural resources and proper climatic conditions for work. Such conditions will provide men with leisure to persue education. Where there is a subsistence economy and it is difficult to make both ends meet it is a far cry to afford time for formal schooling. Education, by necessity, has to be informal, occurring on the job. This is the reason why poorer and under-developed countries have a minimum education for their children, while industrially advanced countries afford to keep nearly all their children at school and for a longer time. Even in Europe, the countries having large peasant population introduced free compulsory primary education quite late in comparison to the industrially advanced countries. The enforcement laws on school attendance were introduced in 1852 in Sweden.[1] In Spain, the principle of compulsory school attendence was accepted in 1911.[2] In Italy, where primary education is compulsory upto 14 in theory, the children in the poorer southern part of the country often leave school at 11.[3] The climate of Norway is quite rigorous, and the sun rises in winter after 10.00 A.M. It is, therefore, not possible to send children to school before the age of 7. Switzerland having little natural advantages on the skill and craftsmanship of its small manpower.[4] The country is renowned for high quality precision work and attaches great importance to the dignity of skilled labour.

The tremendous impact of science and technology has shaken the old leisurely outlook on life and has created intricate problems of social adjustment. It has engendered an intellectual revolt against tradition and against established institutions, beliefs and social practices. It has marked a progressive rise in the standard of living. It has created demand for greater diversity of new skills for manning the developing network of industry and commerce. It has ushered in a new outlook for appreciating change, demanding adjustment and encouraging reforms. A new emphasis has been placed on literacy. Efforts are made to extend the period of free compulsory education. A growing interest is shown in reorganizing the curricula at all stages. The facilities of technical education are enlarged to the fullest extent. Education to adults and young people takes its rightful place.

However, we have examined the level of literacy in South and East Asian countries separately for male and female. The data regarding this are presented in Table 1.1 which exhibit that the literacy rate is very high in Japan (100) followed by Thailand (88), Sri Lanka (85), and Vietnam (84); on the other hand Bhutan (10), Nepal (19), Afghanistan (20), and Bangladesh (26) are having very low literacy rate. If we have a look at the gross enrolment ratios (%) by sex and level for the World and Regions (Table 1.2) we find that America has got the maximum ratios as compared to the other regions. And same is the case with the developing countries too.

Table 1.1 : *Education in South and East Asia*

Country	Literacy		
	Total	Male	Female
Afghanistan	20	34	6
Bangladesh	26	37	13
Bhutan	10	—	—
Burma	66	76	56
China	66	79	51
India	36	47	25
Indonesia (82)	67	77	57
Japan	100	100	100
Korea (N)	—	—	—
Korea (S)	88	94	81
Malaysia	60	69	47
Maldives	82	82	82
Nepal	19	33	5
Pakistan	24	30	10
Philippines	82	84	81
Singapore	83	92	74
Sri Lanka	85	91	81
Thailand	88	92	84
Vietnam (80)	84	90	79

Source : Statistical Year Book, *UNESCO*.

Financial implications are the important aspects for the development of education in any country. Table 1.3 exhibits that public expenditure is very high in developed countries as compared to those of developing countries. However, it will be more clear when we will examine the expenditure on education as percentage to GNP (Table 1.4). Saudi Arabia is spending maximum (8.9 per cent) followed by Botswana (8.4 per cent). Whereas lower percentage of expenditure to GNP is witnessed in Burma (1.6 per cent), Afghanistan and U.A.E. (1.9 per cent).

1.3 Characteristics of Colonial Education

The Colonial education system was not a modernised transformation of the traditional system of India education with its great chronological depth.[5] It emerged on the academic scene outside of and in antiseptic isolation from the historically evolved structure. While the quintessence of millenea of intellectual experience was frozen into immobility—becoming sterile, atrophied

Table 1.2 : *Gross Enrolment Ratios (%) by Sex and Level for the World and Regions (1960-1985)*

World/Regions	Year	First - Level			Second - Level			Third - Level		
		T	M	F	T	M	F	T	M	F
World Total	1960	77.0	85.0	68.0	26.7	30.4	22.8	6.0	8.0	4.0
	1980	91.3	98.1	84.2	43.0	47.1	38.6	14.3	16.3	12.2
	1985	100.0	NA	NA	44.0	NA	NA			
Africa	1960	44.1	56.2	32.0	5.1	7.3	2.9	0.7	1.2	0.3
	1980	78.1	87.2	69.0	21.0	25.8	16.2	3.2	4.7	1.7
	1985	77.0	NA	NA	14.0	NA	NA			
America	1960	90.5	91.9	89.1	42.8	42.8	42.8	13.5	17.1	9.8
	1980	108.7	109.6	107.7	59.1	58.7	59.5	29.9	31.1	28.6
	1985	107.7	NA	NA	36.0*	NA	NA			
Asia	1969	66.5	80.5	52.1	20.3	26.6	13.6	2.9	4.4	1.3
	1980	84.8	95.5	73.6	34.9	42.1	27.2	8.2	10.9	5.2
	1985	104.0	NA	NA	34.0	NA	NA			
Europe (Including USSR)	1960	103.3	103.4	102.7	45.6	16.5	44.6	9.7	12.3	7.2
	1980	103.6	103.1	103.2	76.4	73.8	79.1	22.2	23.4	21.0
Developed Countries	1960	105.9	106.4	105.4	54.8	55.3	55.4	12.8	16.5	9.1
	1980	106.6	106.9	106.4	78.3	76.6	80.1	30.0	31.7	28.1
	1985	102.0	NA	NA	86.0	NA	NA			
Developing Countries	1960	60.2	72.6	47.6	12.7	18.0	7.3	2.0	3.1	1.0
	1980	85.9	95.1	76.5	31.2	37.3	24.9	7.4	9.5	5.2
	1985	99.0	NA	NA	32.0	NA	NA			

Note : * : Belongs to Latin America and the Carribean
T = Total, M = Male, F = Female, NA =, Not Available

Source : (*i*) Statistical Year Book, UNESCO
(*ii*) World Education At a Glance.

or fossilized in this process—a thin veneer of rootless modernity, imported from across the seas, was super-imposed over this oozing layer of decayed tradition. However, before proceeding futher, it may be worthwhile to identify some of the main characteristics of colonial education.

Table-1.3 : *Estimated Public Expenditure on Education*

World/ Regions	Public Exp. on Edn. in Millions of Dollars		Public Exp. on Edn. as % of GNP			Public Exp. on Edn. per inhabitant	
	1970	1982	1970	1982	1985	1970	1982
World (Total)	159,540	627,736	5.4	5.8	5.8	57	181
Africa	3,138	19,568	4.1	4.9	5.8	9	39
America	77,393	268,468	6.3	6.4	4.0*	152	424
Asia	12,551	103,907	3.5	5.1	3.8	10	67
Europe (Including USSR)	64,501	224,384	5.2	5.6		92	298
Oceania	1,957	11,409	4.4	5.8		108	490
Developed Countries	146,983	535,765	5.7	6.2	6.2	137	455
Developing Countries	12,557	91,971	3.3	4.3	4.1	7	40

Note : * : Belongs to Latin America and the Carribean
Source : (*i*) Statistical Year Book, UNESCO.
(*ii*) World Education At a Glance

Firstly, the system was quantitatively a miniscule with only a marginal section of the teeming millions inhabiting the vast subcontinent within its orbit of influence. Secondly, education in Colonial India responded to the needs of alien administration rather than to those of socio-economic development. Thirdly, the multi level educational system was highly pyramidical with acute angles at the base. The transition rates from the primary to the secondary, from the secondary to the higher secondary, from the higher secondary to the lower tertiary and from the tertiary to the higher tertiary were exceptionally low. Fourthly, education in colonial India—particularly at the higher levels—was concentrated in and around port cities. This enclavisation of education was an important element of the spatial system of underdevelopment wherein newly established ports of Calcutta, Bombay and Madras acted as apex points.

Table 1.4 : *Expenditure on Education in Selected Countries*

Country	Per Student Expenditure 1985 (US $)	Expenditure as % to GNP 1985
Afghanistan	82	1.8
Algeria	644	6.1
Bangladesh	2	1.9
Botswana	292	8.4
Burma	-	1.6
China	42	2.9
Congo	151	5.4
France	2912	6.0
Ghana	67	2.3
India	42	3.7
Iran	609	3.8
Iraq	428	3.8
Japan	2694	5.2
Jordan	207	6.6
Kenya	72	6.7
Kuwait	2658	4.2
Malaysia	535	6.6
Mauritius	181	3.8
Nepal	28	3.0
Pakistan	63	2.1
Papua New Guinea	282	-
Saudi Arabia	3898	8.9
Singapore	1252	4.4
Sri Lanka	47	3.1
Thailand	138	3.9
U.A.E.	2131	1.9
U.K.	2152	5.2
U.S.A.	5220	6.8
U.S.S.R.	1056	6.9
Yemen	288	7.5

Source : World Education at a Glance.

Fifth, the socio-economic base of education in colonial India was extremely narrow. Its gates were closed to the vast majority of the toiling people. Such segments of population, wherein economic and social deprivation were combined with each other as in the case of scheduled caste and tribes, found it almost impossible to enter the sacred precincts of educational institutions. Sixth, education in colonial India was essentially teaching and not learning oriented.

Seventh, the educational system was intended to weaken the forces of national integration which were growing on the basis of the strengthening of the national home market, on the one hand and under the impact of the national movement on the other.

1.4 Education in Free India

The task before free India was to remove the infirmities of the inherited structure of the educational system and transform it into a social force geared to the socio-economic transformation of the Indian polity from colonial under-development to self-relient development. Within such a conceptual frame, education was conceived of as being inter-winded with the developmental process as one of its important components. It took quite some time to clearly outline the following multifaceted tasks :[6]

First, to quantitatively expand the inherited miniscule in such a manner that quality and quantity move together in symbiosis;

Second, to strengthen the linkage between education and the labour market and to bridge the gap between work and knowledge;

Third, to evolve a desirable transition matrix within the educational sector to universalise primary education, to 'vocationalize secondary education and to diversify higher education in terms of sepcialism related to self-reliant development and to import substitution in the world of the intellect.

Fourth, to reduce regional disparities in the spread of education so as to make its benefits available to all regions of the country;

Fifth, to widen the socio-economic base of the educational system through programmes of protective discriminations as well as of proper incentives so as to reduce and ultimately eliminate the differentials between the scheduled and non-scheduled, rural and urban as well as male and female population;

Sixth, to transform the essentially teacher and teaching-oriented education into an essentially learning and learner-oriented education and to emphasize the creativity of the learner rather than the assimilation of 'received' truth; and

Seventh, to develop education meaningfully in such a manner that it contributes to national integration, humanism and love for nature.

Since the advent of independence, this old but rejuvenated country embarked on its tryst with destiny and is currently engaged in modernising itself and building perhaps the largest and the most complex educational system in the world. However, the synoptic view of the developments since independence in the educational sphere, which has been presented above, bring out the nature of the advances made as well as the persisting inadequacies of the system. The Government of India has developed several programmes for the development of education. In the subsequent paragraphs we will have a Book of the major programmes.

1.5 Programmes for Educational Development

A number of attempts were made in the past to relate education to socio-economic development but the success has been very partial. In some respect the two have moved in opposite directions. However, the educational policies should strengthen programmes of long and short-term national development in which the country is engaged. It is observed that the implementation of educational programmes has been far from satisfactory in the past. Concrete and vigorous steps will, therefore, be taken to improve the quality of implementation, especially in the backward States where low level of enrolment in schools and large scale illiteracy among adults are a common problem.

Programme for Elementary Education :

The programmes of qualitative improvement in elementary education should be enjoined with the expansion programme. This will enhance the holding power of the schools. Such programmes as do not require large investments but nevertheless are of crucial significance and can be easily implemented have to be identified. These include upgradation of the competence of teachers, curricular reorientation, strengthening of administration at different levels, strengthening of science education, radio and television support to elementary education etc.

Cultural Exchange Programmes :

Programmes of Cultural Exchange are intended to promote cultural, educational and scientific cooperation between India and other countries and are covered under specific agreements between the Government of India and Governments of other countries.

Programmes connected with higher education are assigned by the Government of India to the UGC for implementation. These programmes relate generally to exchange of visits of teachers for study-cum-lecture, exchange of views, developing contacts, development of bilateral academic links between institutions in the two countries, organisation of joint seminars, assignment of foreign language teachers and award of scholarships/fellowships. Visits under these programmes normally range from four to 12 weeks. In specific cases, these visits could be for a period of upto six months. In the case of assignment of foreign language teachers and award of fellowships/scholarships, these visits are normally for one academic year. These programmes prove useful to the teachers in keeping themselves abreast of advances made in their fields of specialisation and in exploring possibilities of developing collaborative programmes. During 1986-87, such programmes were being implemented by the Commission with 46 countries. During the year, the Commission hosted the visits of as many as 61 foreign scholars from various countries and arranged their programmes at various institutions in India. The corresponding number of Indian scholars who were deputed abroad under these programmes during the year was 60.

An important activity on which the Commission laid greater stress during the year was the development of bilateral institutional linkages in specific areas between indentified departments of universities and institutions of higher education in the two countries. The Commission has not been in favour of comprehensive institutional linkages as these are not considered viable on account of different levels of development of teaching and research of the corresponding departments of the universities. As such, areas of bilateral collaboration have been identified under the Cultural Exchange Programmes with countries like the USSR, FRG, GDR, Bulgaria, Czechoslovakia, Hungary, Poland, France, Yugoslavia, Italy, etc. This programme of bilateral collaboration is reviewed from time to time and additional areas are identified for collaboration. An important development in this respect during the year was the agreement between the University Grants Commission and Yugoslav authorities for the identification of areas of mutual cooperation. The Commission is gradually shifting emphasis in the cultural exchange programmes from the general exchange of scholars to the programmes of developing institutional linkages in specified areas. It is felt that such linkages would strengthen collaboration between India and foreign countries in specified areas. Efforts are also being made to identify areas of possible mutual collaboration with other countries covered under the Cultural Exchange Programmes.

A resume of the various activities included under the Cultural Exchange Programmes for 1986-87 is given in the paragraphs which follow.

Foreign Language Teachers :

The University Grants Commission continued to provide foreign language teachers in Russian, German, Polish, Serbo-Croation, Rumanian, Bulgarian, Mongolian, Korean, Vietnamese, Hungarian, Portugese, Chinese and French languages to the universities having a proper infrastructure for teaching the foreign languages concerned as per the provisions of the Cultural Exchange Programme. The Commission, however, feels that foreign language teachers should support the indigenous Indian Staff and not replace them. With this in view, the Commission has emphasised that the department in the university should develop a proper infrastructure in the teaching of the foreign language concerned with the help of Indian faculty members. During the year 1986-87, 35 teachers in Russian, 11 in German, 10 in French and one each in Polish, Serbo-Croation, Rumanian, Bulgarian, Monogolian, Korean, Vietnamese, Hungarian and Chinese were assigned to universities in India. The Commission has also forwarded a proposal from the German Academic Exchange Service for providing German language teachers for scientific and technical subjects to universities in India.

Joint Seminars :

The UGC with the help of an expert Committee has decided the theme for the organisation of Joint Seminars with the USSR in terms of the provisions of the Indo-Soviet Cultural Exchange Programme. The themes decided by the Commission have already been notified to the USSR side for their approval.

Fellowships and Scholarships :

The following fellowships/scholarships were offered during 1986-87 :

(i) The Soviet Government offered 35 scholarships for Russian language and literature. Nominations made by the Commission against these scholarships have been accepted by the Soviet Government.

(ii) The UGC nominated scholars against the 12 fellowships offered by the German Academic Exchange Service for advanced research in Natural Sciences, Mathematics, Geology, German language and literature and some areas in Humanities and Social Sciences. Two of these fellowships are reserved for German language and literature. Eight nominations were accepted by the FRG side.

(iii) The German Academic Exchange Service offered six short term fellowships for teachers of German language and literature for a period of three months each. The Commission has utilised five of these fellowships.

(iv) Against three short term fellowships of three months' duration for teachers of German language, offered by the German Academic Exchange Service, the Commission nominated one scholar.

(v) Against five short term fellowships of the total duration of 20 man-months, offered by German Academic Exchange Service in German culture and related fields for Ph.D. scholars, one scholar visited the Federal Republic of Germany.

(vi) The Commission nominated teachers and students against the six fellowships and 13 scholarships offered by the French Government for French language, literature and civilisation for 1986-87.

Academic Link Interchange Scheme :

This programme, which is being implemented in collaboration with the British Council, provides for the development of linkages in specified areas between institutions of higher education in India and the UK. It involves the exchange of faculty from indentified participating institutions for a period not exceeding 20 weeks each. The visits have the following objectives :

(a) Joint Research

(b) Joint Publications

(c) Curriculum and Courses Development
(d) Academic/Professional/Administrative staff exchange development.

Of the 25 areas identified for collaboration, programmes have been mutually agreed to in 12 areas for implementation. During the year, 25 Indian scholars visited the UK under the programme while the number of British scholars who visited universities in India was 13. The question of taking up collaborative programmes in additional areas identified is under consideration.

Collection of Source Material of Research Work in UK and other Countries :

Under the scheme, the UGC provides travel and maintenance expenses to senior Indian scholars in Humanities and Social Sciences for their visit to UK for a period of 6-8 weeks to enable them to collect material for their research work which is ordinarly not available in India. The period of 12 man-months available under this programme was almost fully utilised and eight scholars were assisted under this programme during the year.

The UGC continued to provide travel grant to teachers for their visit to foreign countries for collection of material for their research work or to avail offer of a fellowship or assistance from an agency from that country where the scholar has been offered partial or full financial assistance for his maintenance. Seven teachers were provided assistance under this scheme during the year.

Development of Canadian Studies :

Under the scheme the UGC has identified some universities for the development of Canadian Studies in specific disciplines. Although universities have been identified for a single discipline to start programmes in Canadian Studies, the intention is that in course of time they would be developed into multi-disciplinary centres of Canadian Studies. During the year, a scholar from Rajasthan University visited Canada to familiarise himself with teaching and research being done in Canadian universities with a view to introducing Canadian Studies in the area of Political Science in Rajasthan University.

It has been agreed with the Shastri Indo-Canadian Institute that there will be an exchange of scholars between the two countries for a period of two man-months per year. The UGC nominated two scholars for a period of two weeks each for visit to Canada to study problems relating to administration of universities. A Canadian political scientist also visited India under this programme during the year and had discussions with senior scholars in some universities.

Indo-US Fellowship Programme :

The UGC continued to award fellowships under this programme. Against 15 fellowships of 10 months each to American scholars for their post-doctoral research work in India, the Commission received nominations for 13 long-term fellowships of 10 months duration and 6 short-term fellowships of 2-3 months duration. The Commission has already cleared most of the nominations received from the US side for the year 1987-88.

The Government of India has allocated 12 fellowships to UGC for the visit of Indian teachers from universities/colleges and institutes of technology for post-doctoral work in USA. Against 12 fellowships which have been allocated to the UGC, the Commission converted six fellowships into 17 short-term visitorships of 13 weeks each and made nominations against the residual six long-term fellowships of 10 months each and 15 short-term visitiorships of 13 weeks each.

CSIR-CNRS (France) Exchange of Scientists Programme :

Under this programme CSIR allocated 200 man-days for the visit of Indian scientists to France and similarly the UGC allocated 200 man-days to the CNRS for the visit of French scientists to India in connection with their research work during the year. Seven Indian scholars visited France while no French scholar visited India under this programme during the year.

Commonwealth Academic Staff Fellowships & Scholarships :

Under this programme initiated in 1969-70, the UGC coordinates with the Commonwealth Scholarship Commission in UK and makes nominations for the Commonwealth Staff awards (fellowships and scholarships) to enable promising faculty members in universities and colleges in India to work at universities or other institutions in the UK. These awards are not available in the fields of Medicine and Surgery as Commonwealth Medical awards are available separately. During 1986-87, the Commission recommended

21 scholars for fellowships and 13 for scholarships. Out of these, the Commonwealth Scholarship Commission have finally selected 16 for fellowships and 7 for scholarships.

Sepcialised Programmes Organised by International Centres/Agencies :

The UGC provides one-way air fare to teachers in universities and colleges for participation in summer/winter schools on specialised courses organised by centres run by international agencies or professional bodies like the British Council. The remaining air fare and living expenses for the duration of the course are to be provided by the orgainsers of the programme or the institution where the teacher is working or the State Government or any other agency. During the year, the Commission agreed to provide financial assistance by way of one-day air fare to 12 teachers from universities/colleges.

Adult Education :

The current involvement of universities in the adult and continuing education activities is the outcome of the recognition of the importance of extension education programme by the University Grants Commission as reflected in the 'Policy Frame' of the Commission (1978).

The policy statement underlined the need for extension activity as an important dimension of higher education equal in importance with teaching and research.

The Government of India launched the National Adult Education Programme (NAEP) on October 2, 1978. It was intended to impart functional literacy with assured follow up and continuing education within a target-oriented and time-bound frame. Universities and colleges also participated in this national task under the UGC scheme of Adult Education and Extension.

The programme of adult literacy through the students and teachers of universities and colleges, inter-alia, envisaged their involvement in a planned manner, acclerating their inter-action with the community by way of extension work with special emphasis on literacy programmes for women, scheduled castes and scheduled tribes, handicapped and people from the rural, backward and slum areas. The Adult literacy programme was conceived to be implemented in the first phase upto March 1985 covering all affiliated universities and at least 15,000-20,000 centres and thereafter raising the adult education centres upto 50,000 in the second phase till March 1990 by involving all the universities. During the year 1986-87, the Commission continued assistance to 92 universities involving 2121 colleges and 25,824 adult education centres in the country.

Besides, financial assistance was continued to the three Resource Centres located at Srinagar, Chandigarh and Hyderabad for producing literacy material for use by different agencies. In addition, the North Eastern Hill University was requested to establish a resource centre for the North Eastern Council areas. 18 universities received assistance for purchase of audio-visual equipment while 9 universities received 50 per cent assistance for vehicles purchased by them for adult and continuing education programme during the year.

Mass Programme for Functional Literacy (MPFL) :

As part of the Adult Education Programme, a Mass Programme for Functional Literacy (MPFL) was launched from 1st May, 1986. Under the programme, the universities were advised to involve students in the Mass Programme for Functional Literacy on a voluntary basis with the hope of involving two lakh NSS volunteers and one lakh Non-NSS students during vacation in an attempt to eradicate illiteracy. The University could consider giving suitable recognition to the contribution made by the students for participation in the programme. This programme had the following components :

(i) Literacy kits were to be made available free of cost to the learners through the Resource Centres.
(ii) Orientation of programme was to be done in collaboration with the Resource Centres;
(iii) The area plan was to be prepared with sub-area allocation for colleges to eradicate illiteracy;
(iv) Involvement of local organisations, and co-ordination with them as well as the development department was envisaged;
(v) Financial assistance was provided to the universities and colleges participating in the MPFL with the purpose of promoting maximum utilisation of resources in universities and colleges in terms of students and teachers;
(vi) Students, with a view to make a learner literate, could (a) conduct an adult education centre as "Instructors",

(b) involve in 'each one teach one programme', or (c) organize and conduct supporting programmes at adult education centres, as explained below :

(*a*) *Role of students as instructors :*

As instructors, students could initiate a process of awareness among adult learners, introduce developmental activities in the community and help the learners to acquire certain functional skills for tackling their problems. Also, students could enlist learners, decide timing of the teaching in consultation with them, procure learning material, maintain necessary record of learners, send monthly reports and help in evaluation of the programme.

(*b*) *Role of Students under 'Each one teach one' or 'Each one teach family' :*

Under this programme, students are expected to identify adult learners or a family and teach them by fixing mutually convenient time, and submit required information about learners.

(*c*) *Role of students in supporting programmes :*

Under this, students are involved to help in

(i) Survey of selected area and identification of learners, (ii) shramdan activities in consultation with the community and (iii) motivating illiterates for learning and organising simple audio-visual units and mobile libraries.

According to the reports received from 73 universities, as many as 1,47,055 students (both NSS and Non-NSS) were involved in the campaign during the year under report. Sanction for holding a seminar on the concept of M.P.F.L. was also accorded to the Delhi University during the year.

It has been impressed upon the universities participating in the adult education, continuing education and extension programme to give new impetus to the programme and also provide for a project report in lieu of one of the optional papers in degree courses which should be evaluated on the lines of the project report in the faculties of social work etc., and whose marks/grades added alongwith other subjects of examination. Arising out of this, the Bharathidasan University (Tiruchirapalli) has included Adult Education, Extension

Education, Population Education & Community Development as an extra disciplinary subject in the university curriculum for Under-graduate courses. Similarly, the Punjab University has decided to grant incentives to students who are participating in adult education programmes by way of weightage for purposes of admission to other courses of the University.

Keeping in view the importance and the large scale expansion of the above programmes and the fact that extension work has been declared as an important function of the institutions of higher learning, the UGC Standing Committee suggested that allocation of adult education centres be rationalised. It was also suggested that universities and colleges participating in the programmes should adopt specific areas to provide awareness and education on community programmes for purposes of development in an integrated manner covering eradication of illiteracy as well. In order to bring home the processes involved in the change over, the Committee suggested integrating other departmental activities in literacy programme, population education programme and in holding of regional workshops for functionaries in the University Department/Centres of Audlt, Continuing Education and Extension.

Continuing Education and Extension :

The programme of Continuing Education was initiated in 21 selected universities and subsequently spread over to 68 universities and 705 colleges. The objectives of the programme are reported in the annual report for the year 1984-85. The programme is amied at disseminating knowledge by giving priority to the less privileged and under-privileged sections of the society. During the year under report 20 universities and 17 colleges were supported by the Commission for organising different types of programmes under the Continuing Education Scheme.

Population Education :

The scheme of setting up of Population Education Clubs in universities and colleges aims at involving students in the task of educating the community about consequences of population growth at the family and national levels. About 1400 Population Education Clubs were operative till 31st March, 1987 with assistance from the Commission. These clubs orgainsed different types of activities viz.

debates, dramas, essay competitions, group discussions, experts' lectures, extension activities and developing simple audio-visual material etc. In addition, the twelve Population Education Resource Centres created during 1985-86 also started functioning effectively during the year under report. These Centres, set up in order to facilitate the implementation of the UNFPA* - UGC project, would provide support service in population education programme to universities/colleges in a specified area, in terms of training, production and distribution of learning materials in print and audio-visual forms as part of well-formulated curriculum, evaluation, documentation and integration of population education at the undergraduate level. The UNFPA-UGC project formualted in 1985-86 seeks to secure the involvement of the entire system of higher education in the country in institutionalising and spreading awareness of population education and link it with the developmental process of India.

During the year 1986-87, Joint meetings of the Convenors of the Task Forces and the Directors of the Resource Centres were held with the objective of :

(a) assessing the progress made and activities undertaken under the Population Education projects; and
(b) considering measures necessary to speed up implementation of the project.

Some of the significant achievements of the various Task Forces were as under :

(i) the Task Force on Training finalized and circulated to all the Resource Centres a resource book on training to facilitate training programmes for the functionaries of the project and the population Education teachers etc.
(ii) the Task Force on Curriculum Development finalised an approach paper on formulation of curriculum under non-formal approach, and circulated the paper to all resource centres and universities. The Task Force is likely to complete curriculum for under-graduate and post-graduate courses shortly. The Task Force also published a monograph titled, 'Population in the context of Indian Development with special reference to Population Education'.

* Stands for United Nations Fund for Population Activities.

(iii) the Task Force on Learning Material (Print) prepared a hand book for teachers and students. It also completed the identification of the reading material for circulation to the universities.

(iv) the Task Force on Research prepared a bibliography of the select research publications and also completed base line survey format.

(v) Some of resource centres organized training programmes for personnel of different universities and college principals in their services area.

(vi) The resource centres used the audio-visual aid for quick transmission of the messages under the extension programme of Population Education. The resource centres also produced video films, slides, charts and posters on subjects like women education, breast-feeding etc., depicting different themes of population education etc. Some of the video films produced by the resource centres were found to be very useful in communicating the message on population education.

(vii) Two News letters reporting various developments under the Population Education Programmes were issued during the yer under report.

The list of equipment (prepared by Commission in consultation with the Resource Centres) to be bought under UNFPA assistance for the resource centres was aproved by the Government of India during the year and funds were released from the UNFPA for

	Activity	Name of the Organising Resource Centre
1.	Workshop on Planning sample materials for teachers and students.	Gujarat Vidyapith
2.	Training of Resource Centre Personnel	SNDT Women's University
3.	Workshop on Audio Visual material	Poona University
4.	Seminar on Research	Ranchi University
5.	Summer Institute	Kerala University
6.	Seminar on Monitoring and Evaluation Design	Delhi University
7.	Workshop on curriculum for Population Education and Extension Activity	Gujarat Vidyapith

making purchases. The format for reporting progress in the implementation of the project and its evaluation was also analysed. Most of the PERCs prepared their own project documents indicating the yearly programme of activities upto 1990.

Besides, the as tubulated on p. 21 activities were assigned to the Resource Centres for completion during 1987-88.

Planning Forums :

With a view to create an awareness of the need for planned development of the country among the student community and involve them in national development efforts right from the planning, stage, the Commission continued to provide assistance to the universities and colleges for instituting planning formus. The scheme aims to develop plan consciousness among the educated youths in particular and through them among the general public.

During the year under report 19 universities and 24 colleges participated in the scheme and organised various activities. With a view to ensure that Planning Forums work effectively, the universities and colleges have been asked to report the type of activities undertaken by them and send their suggestions to the Commission.

Coaching Classes for Competitive Examinations for Weaker Sections amongst Minority Communities :

The UGC continued to provide assistance to universities and colleges for organising special coaching classes for students belonging to socially an economically weaker sections of the minority communities. The coaching programmes are meant to prepare such students to compete in various competitive examinations for recruitment to services under the Central and State Governments, public undertaking etc. at various levels.

While the main coaching centres are located at the universities, the sub-centres are located in colleges. The universities are largely responsible for organising coaching classes for the all-India services as well as State level services while the colleges are responsible for organising coaching classes for lower categories of examinations.

Suitable guidelines formulated in this regard have been circulated to the universities. A Standing Committee advises the Commission from time to time on the functioning of the scheme. The Standing Committee has constituted a Sub-Committee which studies the working of the coaching centres at the spot and makes suggestions to overcome deficiencies, if any. During the year, 20 universities and 15 colleges were assisted to organise coaching programmes.

National Integration :

With a view to involving the university system in the promotion of the process of national integration through its teaching, research and extension activities, a Committee under the Chairmanship of Hon'ble Justice Mr. M.H. Beg had been constituted in 1985-86 for suggesting measures in this regard. The Committee submitted its report during 1986-87 which was considered by the Commission. The Commission desired to send the report of the Committee to the universities for comments and to deliberate on it after receiving responses through Seminars at different levels. Some of the salient recommendations of the Committee are :

(i) Well organised teaching programmes on languages, literature, philosophy, comparative religion, history of the Indian aesthetics of architecture, sculpture, painting, music, dance and drama play a vital role. It would be desirable to promote greater knowledge, understanding and appreciation of the wide specturm of our cultural heritage in different parts of India by incorporating suitable topics in the teaching curricula.

(ii) In their recruitment policies, universities will be well advised to give fair shares to all regions and communities in such a way as to promote national integration. The persons so recruited should be given housing facilites and travel concessions.

(iii) Every university should have certain number of scholarships earmarked for students coming from distant States and different communities. Students who come from other regions with different mother tongues should be given the facilities of appropriate 'remedial courses', irrespective of their number, without which student mobility will be impeded.

(iv) Travelling has been a great source of learning through the ages and has stimulated the enquiring spirit of man. It has also been instrumental in engendering a broader understanding of India by people from different parts of the world. It should help development of objective scientific approaches for solution of our problems of national integration.

(v) Travel should be give its legitimate place in the syllabi of university courses. A number of credits should be assigned in the university courses for travel by students individually or in small groups and a report thereon covering different aspects of life in the areas visited should be invariably given. This report should reveal what aspect of national integration in the country or parts visited impressed to marker of it.

(vi) While inter-regional mobility of students at the university level should be encouraged in general, it should be desirable to introduce a system whereby students in any university in the country can spend some time in any other university. A suitable provision in the University Statutes and Ordinances should be made so that a university student can join any other university depending on his interests and areas of specialisation in that university for pursuing a few courses for a brief period extending upto a semester. He or she should be able to earn special credits which should be added to overall credits in the university where the student is pursuing his studies substantively.

(vii) A certain percentage of seats in all the educational institutions should be reserved for students from distant regions and different cultural or religious backgrounds. All students who come from outside the State should be given hostel and free travel facilities from their residence to the institutions concerned.

(viii) National integration be introduced in the curricula at the undergraduate level.

(ix) Study tours and educational excursions should be orgainsed to different part of the country. In these tours, the students should be taken not only to cultural and historical places but also introduced to modern projects and industries.

(x) Sports and games will help greatly to bring about integration of people. Hence, they should be encouraged. Greater emphasis should be given to organise such activities on Inter-State basis.

(xi) Students may be encouraged to visit different places of worship of all religions. These should be accompanied by due explanations of special features.

(xii) Activity programmes, such as sports and games, group discussions, debates, and group singing bring the students closer, physically and emotionally, and thus help to understand each other better. Such programmes should be encouraged in universities and colleges.

(xiii) Simple, inexpensive, and healthy dishes, which people from all parts of the country may like, be evolved out of the regional diets. This may foster sentiments of appreciation and unity. Hostels and institutes of Home Science can play a leading role in this.

(xiv) Above all, the Vice-Chancellor of every university should be a person passionately interested in promoting national integration and strengthening secular traditions by every conceivable means in his or her power. This functionary should be capable of inspiring all members of the university comprising teachers, taught, officers, as well its employees to become fine soldiers in the cause of better integration of the nation.

Comments on the report are being received from the universities.

During the year, the Commission financed the construction of a building for Indira Gandhi Centre for National Integration at Visva Bharati. Besides, the Commission has also been encouraging universities/colleges to conduct seminars on themes of national integration.

Distance Education/Correspondence Courses :

Programme of distance education/correspondence courses have been instituted by various universities in India to enable a large number of persons with necessary aptitude to acquire further knowledge and improve their professional competence. Distance education/correspondence course is essentially based on the supply of instructional material for home study, but has to be supported and supplemented by personal contact programmes, radio programmes, audio-visual aids etc. The objectives of the scheme are (a) to meet the increasing demand for education by utilising alternative system of delivery and (b) to bring about equalization of opportunity by providing facilities in backward regions, as also to the weaker sections of the community who have to take up jobs owing to their pecuniary circumstances and for women, many of whom still find it difficult to go to a college as they belong to tradition-ridden families and communities.

During the year, the Commission continued to provide assistance towards staff, personal contact programmes, study centres, preparation of lessons and library facilities etc. to universities for distance/correspondence education. As many as 35 universities in India conduct distance education/correspondence course programmes with the Commission's assistance.

The Commission has requested the universities that the institutes of distance education be given more autonomy both in their functioning and in academic programmes. They may be given the status of university department of an institute with an open approach to admission of students, selection of courses etc. Moreover, the functioning of the Centres of Distance Education should be regularly monitored at the national and state level with a view to ensuring the quality and relevance of courses of study.

The Standing Committee appointed by the Commission on Distance Education has been reconstituted with a view to have large representation of the Experts from the system of distance education. During the year, the Commission received a Status report on distance education, prepared with Commission's assistance. The report is under consideration.

1.6 An Overview on Literature

The available literature so far shows a broad spectrum of aspects which have been covered. They portray the diversity of status of Indian Education from the ancient to the modern time. The major part of this literature comes in books on the various aspects and problems of the Indian education.

Saxena (1979)[7] in his book has analysed the planning process broadly in two parts—theoretical formulation and operational design. The study reveals the weak points in both theoretical formulation including approach, objectives and priorities, and operational design including various stages such as appraisal and analysis of statistical data, formation of policy proposals, projection, programming and project analysis, casting and financing and implementation and evaluation. The achievements and shortcomings of plan operations have been analysed under certain specific criteria. Progress in literacy and in student enrolment, growth of institutions and increase in teachers are mentioned as some indicators of the progress achieved in the post plan era. Attention has been drawn to such shortcomings as the unfulfilled task of providing elementary education upto the age of 14 to all boys and girls, regional imbalances, lack of quality at all levels and increase in the number of educated unemployed. The author has also made some useful and constructive suggestions.

A book by Singh and Shukla (1979)[8] deals with the importance of non-formal education and clarifies the ideas about non-formal education : its purpose; its nature and its methodology etc. This book covers the following contents : (i) Non-Formal Education (Concept, Definition and Scope); (ii) The Role of State and Voluntary organization (with special reference of non-formal education); (iii) Non-Formal Education as Innovation; (iv) Experiences from India and Abroad (A review of literature); (v) Non-Formal Education (philosophy and processes); and (vi) the future prospects.

Saini (1980)[9] has made an attempt to interpret the history of Indian education in the last quarter of the British rule in India, using an inter-disciplinary approach to political, social and economic detriment of education. The book is in five parts; (i) introductory (plan and procedure); (ii) background material (bases and focal points of interpretation); (iii) detriment of development of Indian education (1921-1947); (iv) conclusion (prospect and retrospect); (v) journey ahead. The last part has been specially added because it highlights the major developments in education in the post-independence.

A book by Aikara (1980)[10] explains that the Centre and State Governments have made special provisions for the education of scheduled caste population. What is the outcome of these provisions? How do the beneficiaries of the provisions fare in studies? The present study is stimulated by these questions. It investigates into the factors responsible for dropout and stagnation among the scheduled caste college students vis-a-vis the non-scheduled caste students. The study comes out with findings that have practical implications for the policy on the special provisions.

Tiwari's (1980)[11] book containing a collection of essays by five authors representing different viewpoints, provides an opportunity for evaluating J.P. Naik's treatise, "Education for Our People". It also gives practical suggestions for the eradication of our educational malaise. The authors lay bare the defects of the existing system and place special accent on Pragmatism. This book contains the following essays :

(i) Education for Our People : Some Observations; (ii) Politics of Education for Our People; (iii) Redemption and Resurrection; (iv) Anarchy in Education; (v) Educational Planning for Failure.

Leitner's (1982)[12] book is in five parts. Part one deals with the religious and national foundations of indigenous education; vernacular indigenous education in Punjab; female indigenous education; and opinions of witnesses before the Education Commission on the subject of indigenous schools in Punjab, and notes thereon; Punjab before and on annexation, etc. Part two contains details regarding every ascertained schools in the various districts of Punjab and the names of local SAVANS. Part three gives the number of pupils : Maktabs and Madrassahs, Pathasalas, Gurumukhi schools, Mahajani schools, etc. Part four discusses the Sikhs and the education. Part five provides precise of, and conclusions from, the records of the Punjab department bearing on the subjects of the village school cess and of indigenous schools. At the end, the author has added specimens of the commercial cypher in use in North of India.

A study by Naik (1982)[13] examines the report of the Indian Education Commission 1964-65 and the steps taken to give effect to its recommendations during the last twelve years. It discusses how far the recommendations of the Indian Education Commission 1964-65 have been accepted by the nation. It highlights the efforts made in the past ten years or so, to implement the proposals made by the Indian Education Commission and extent of success or failure of these efforts alongwith the reasons for the same. The study is in ten chapters. Chapter one deals with the Indian Education Commission 1964-66, and its comprehensive approach to educational reconstruction and its attempts to project a blue print of a National System of Education for India. The second chapter describes briefly the mode model of the National System of Education recommended by the Indian Education Commission 1964-66. The other chapters deal with the National Policy on Education 1968, implementation evaluation, recommendations that attracted wide attention, recommendations that were opposed and rejected, the continuing educational crises 1965-66 to 1977-78 and other recommendations.

Sharma (1982)[14] is of the opinion that education in India has been plagued by confused thinking and blurred vision. That is why real progress has been evading the country even after 34 years of independence. He attempts to stimulate fresh thinking on the subject, particularly on informing education with cultural values through the following articles : (i) education and culture; (ii) Indian cultural heritage; (iii) humanisation—a crucial task for education; (iv) wine is considered the wrecker of culture and can play havoc with our lives. Women's Legacy is an article that attempts to restore women to their rightful place in our society by dispelling wrong notions fostered by male chauvinism. The articles : (i) academic freedom in India; (ii) the teacher in India today; (iii) why education has failed us; (iv) text-books—a boon or a bane, seek to provoke the teacher, the student and the educational planner to think how education can be revitalised to enable it to play its legitimate role effectively.

Gupta (1983)[15] has discussed the essential problems of educational administration. Many of these problems might be perennial but they have been interpreted afresh in the light of rapid changes. The contents of this book include the following : (i) Administration-Management Concepts; (ii) Principles of Educational Administration; (iii) Decentralisation of Administration; (iv) The Personnel Aspect of Administration; (v) Leadership in Education Administration; (vi) The Students; (vii) Students' Role in University College Governance; (viii) The Principal; (ix) Continuing Education; (x) Experinentation in Colleges; (xi) Affiliated Colleges and their problems; (xii) Autonomous Colleges; (xiii) College as a Community Centre; (xiv) Student Welfare Service; (xv) Ten Plus Two Plus Three Concept; (xvi) Internal Assessment; (xvii) Open University or Open College; (xviii) Education as a Concurrent Subject and (xix) Education in the Five Year Plans.

Mohanty (1983)[16] attempts to fulfil a long felt need of students, teachers, and teacher educators for a book on educational philosophy and sociology, particularly in the context of curricular changes made by most of the progresive universities of the country. It consists of three parts : (i) Education in the Emerging Indian Society dealing with modern values, trends and precepts; (ii) Some Current Problems in Indian Education, with emphasis on matters of national and international importance and implications; and

(iii) Philosophical and Sociological Perspectives of the New Educations, dwelling on the meaning, aims and 'isms' of education as well as its new concepts.

The contents of Shukla's (1983)[17] book are as follows : (i) General Background; (ii) Legal Base for Education; (iii) Organizing Educational Administration; (iv) District Level Administration of Education; (v) Education Planning; (vi) Administration of Educational Finance; (vii) Supervision and Inspection; (viii) Administration of Higher Education; and (ix) Conclusion, which gives some suggestions.

Mathur's (1983)[18] book contains the proceedings of the First National Conference of Indian Association of Educational Planning and Administration, held in New Delhi on June 12-13, 1982. It gathers together key-one papers and abstracts of papers received from eminent members of IAEPA, as also the Inaugural Address by the then Lt. Governor of Delhi, Presidential Address by M.V. Mathur, President, IAEPA, messages from Emeritus W.G. Walker, President, CCEA, and Madhuri R. Shah, Chairmap, UGC, and highlights of discussions in the form of group reports. The papers focus upon the three themes of the Conference : 'Administrative Leadership in schools' ; 'Management of Higher Education', and Towards improved Educational Planning', which reflect some of he major concerns of educational planning and administration today.

The book by Sethi (1983)[19] contains nine chapters and covers 273 pages. The author feels that the whole structure of higher education should be changed as it is only meant for middle and upper classes and do not touch to the lower masses. It is due to that the policy makers confined themselves always within the Macaulay framework. In this book, the author specially discusses the crisis and collapses exist in higher education. So the author deals with the following topics : (i) the collapse : a cinematic overview; (ii) and (iii) the crisis—I and II; (iv) and (v) faulty assumptions—I and II; (vi) structural duality in education; (vii) thirteen million educated jobless; (viii) the myth of India's scientific manpower; (ix) education and the new international order etc.

Bhatnager (1983)[20] has made an effort to present the problems of education as the author has perceived. Almost every aspect of education is covered in this book. This book is a mass volume, having 736 pages and divided in the following chapters : (i) education in ancient India; (ii) education in the Muslim period;

(iii) education in the British India; (iv) education in free India; (v) Five Year Plans and education; (vi) problems of Indian education; (vii) crisis in education; (viii) primary education; (ix) secondary education; (x) university education; (xi) teacher education; (xii) school organisation and administration; (xiii) social education; (xiv) technical and vocational education; (xv) institutional planning; (xvi) national educational policy 1968; (xvii) national education policy 1979; (xviii) non-formal education; (xix) constitutional provisions of education in India; (xx) nursery and pre-basic education; (xxi) single teacher school; (xxii) rural area and schools; (xxiii) the language problem; (xxiv) the role of education in national emergency; (xxv) women's education and co-education; (xxvi) education for the gifted and handicapped children; (xxvii) adjustment and discipline in higher education; (xxviii) national development and education; (xxix) educational finance and its problems; (xxx) religious and moral education; (xxxi) emotional and national integration; (xxxii) educated unemployment; (xxxiii) student unrest; (xxxiv) population education etc.

A book by Aggarwal (1984)[21] contains documents concerning the development of education in India since 1813. It has 429 pages and covers sixty nine documents. The documents rich in content and singnificant in objectives have been arranged chronologically. Commissions, Committees, Resolutions, Despatches, Seminars have been included in this book. Five Year Plans, First to Sixth have also been dealt with.

An edited book by Raghavan (1984)22 deals with perspectives of higher education, its challenges, constraints and opportunities in the eighties. It contains 10 papers presented at a seminar to critically examine the past experience and the present status of higher education and seek answers for the future. The book also includes other specific issues such as making the university a centre of excellence by introducting suitable changes in its structure to bring into existence authonomous institutes within the system, to facilitate absorption of knowledge, development of suitable organisations and establishing links with society and popular centre.

Some efforts have been made by Paliwal (1984)[23] to present a synthesis of the ideas, educational problems and their solution which have emerged over the last few years from research, studies, reflections and discussions on education in the various regions of the world. The book also covers the various issues, facets, problems and the innovatory practices associated with education in general and teacher education in particular.

Sharma's (1984)[24] book examines the major problems of education faced by schools, colleges and universities and suggestes measures for their solution. Efforts have been made to classify the various concepts of education through suitable examples. The book cover thirteen chapters : (i) Education in Ancient India; (ii) Education during Medieval Times; (iii) Education in British India; (iv) Education in Post-Independence Era; (v) Education under Five Year Plans; (vi) Contemporary Educational Problems; (vii) Primary Education; (viii) Secondary Education; (ix) Higher Education; (x) Technical and Vocational Education; (xi) Women's Education; (xii) Teacher Education; (xiii) Social Education etc. The first three chapters provide a historical perspective that acts as a base in developing proper insight into the problems faced by the authorities in the field of education. The remaining chapters present detailed descriptions of various levels and types of education and their problems.

Aggarwal (1985)[25] in his book covers 32 chapters dealing with the different aspects of education since independence of India. Discussion on different aspects of education in the book is based primarily on the recommendations of : (i) University Education Commission, 1948-49; (ii) Secondary Education Commission 1952-53; (iii) Sri Prakasha Committee on Religious and Moral Education, 1959; (iv) Emotional Integration Committee, 1961; (v) Indian Education Commission, 1964-66; (vi) National Policy on Education, 1968; (vii) National Committee on the Status of Women in India, 1971-74; (viii) Ishwar Bhai Patel Review Committee, 1977; (ix) National Review Committee for the + 2 curriculum, 1978; (x) Draft National Policy on Education, 1979; (xi) Fourth All India Educational Survey, 1980; (xii) Six Five Year Plans. The book reveals the development of Education in the country.

However, survey and studies which cover several aspects of educational problems in India are many and quantitatively extensive. But these studies are sometimes repetitive and often very general in their approach, and the informations cited in that are still uneven and scanty. The unexplored areas indicate that limitations of educational statistics, economic aspects of educational planning and education employment linkages are yet to be properly understood and studied. Within this broad framework of continuity and change this book is concerned with introducing the reader to the major issues related to education in India.

1.7 Frame of the Study

The entire work has been divided into seven chapters for the sake of convenience. A vivid account of various education Commissions/Committees and policies in India especially during post independence period are discussed in chapter two. Having discussed the background of the study in the present chapter, the educational system and sub-system in India are dealt with in chapter three. For formulating any plans/schemes for the development of education, there are some problems with the non-availability of educational statistics. Hence, the sources of educational statistics and their limitations are described in chapter four.

Chapter fifth gives a detailed description of educational development in India at every stage since independence. We have tried to analyse the economic aspects of educational planning and established the linkages between education and employment in chapter sixth.

Chapter seventh concludes the study by pointing out some major findings and forwarding suggestions for further study. Various appendices are presented at the end of the book in order to facilitate their use by other researchers.

Notes & References

1. J.C. Aggarwal (1982), *Development and Planning of Modern Education*, Vikas Pub. House Pvt.Ltd., p. 411.
2. *Ibid*, p. 411.
3. *Ibid*, p. 411.
4. *Ibid*, p. 411.
5. Kuldip Kaur (1985), *Education in India* (1981-1985), CRRID, Chandiigarh, pp. 1
6. *Ibid*, pp. 3-4.
7. Sateshware Saxena (1979), *Educational Panning in India : A study in Approach and Methodology*, Sterling Publishers, New Delhi.
8. R.P. Singh & N. Shukla (1979), *Non-formal Education : An Alternative to Formal System*; NCERT, New Delhi.
9. S.K. Saini (1980), *Development of Education in India Socio-Economic and Political Perspectives*, Cosmo Pub., New Delhi.
10. J. Aikara (1980), *Scheduled Caste and Higher Education*, Dastane Ramachandara & Co., Poona.
11. R.P. Tewari (1980), *Critique of Education for our People*, South Asian Pub. Pvt. Ltd., New Delhi.

12. G.W. Leitner (1982), *History of Indigenous Education in the Punjab since Annexation and in 1882*, Amar Prakashan, New Delhi.
13. J.P. Naik (1982), *Education Commission and After*, Allied Pub. Pvt. Ltd., New Delhi.
14. O.P. Sharma (1982), *Education of National Progress*, Anu Prakashan, Meerut.
15. L.D. Gupta (1983), *Educational Administration at College Level*, Oxford & IBH Pub. Co., New Delhi.
16. J. Mohanty (1983), *Indian Education in the Emerging Society*, Sterling Pub., New Delhi.
17. P.D. Shukla (1983), *Administration of Education in India*, Vikas Pub., New Delhi.
18. M.V. Mathur (1983), *Towards Improved Educational Planning and Administration*, Joy Madathi Kummel for Dialogue, New Delhi.
19. J.D. Sethi (1983), *The Crisis and Collapse of Higher Education in India*, Vikas Pub. House, New Delhi.
20. S. Bhatnagar (1983), *Indian Education : Today and Tomorrow*, Loyal Book Depot, Meerut.
21. J.C. Aggarwal (1984), *Landmarks in the History of Modern Indian Education*, Vikas Pub. House, New Delhi.
22. J.V. Raghavan (1984) (Ed.), *Higher Education in the Eighties : Opportunities and Objectives*, Lancer International, New Delhi.
23. M.R. Paliwal (1984), *Social Change and Education*, Uppal Pub. House, New Delhi.
24. A.P. Sharma (1984), *Contemporary Problems of Education (with Special reference to India)*, Vani Educational Books, New Delhi.
25. J.C. Aggarwal (1985), *Development and Planning of Modern Education*, Vani Educational Books, New Delhi.

2 Various Education Commissions/ Committees and Policies in India

2.1 Introduction

The structure of education in any system conveys something more than merely the thinking on setting time limits for educational prepartion at different levels starting from pre-primary and ending with university degrees. Each level of education has to be relevant to development stage of the pupils.[1] It has implications for the nature and content of the courses. The courses of study need to be formulated bearing in mind the aspirations of pople, national ideals and goals, availability of physical and natural resources and their utilization. Various Commissions, Committees, and Policies etc., discussed in this chapter later on appeared to have been concerned with the pertinent issue of structural reorganisation of education to suggest suitable changes in the educational system.

In spite of various Commissions, Committees and Panels appointed by the Central and State Governments from time to time, Indian education is still at the cross roads. Education has failed to evolve a national pattern so far. The new pattern of education, popularly known as 10+2+3, had raised fresh hopes. It is destined to be the national system of education in due course of time. It has been accepted in principle by almost all the States in India and was actually launched in 1975 in some States and Union Territories and almost in all the Central schools spread all over the country. The classes eleven and twelve under the new pattern have been provided for diversified academic and vocational courses. The first batch of students joined class eleven under the new pattern in July 1977 and the first batch of students was to take the Board's Higher Secondary Examination at the end of class twelve in March 1979[2].

2.2 Kothari Commission

Education Commission 1964-66, popularly known as Kothari Commission under the name of its Chairman Prof. D.S. Kothari, was appointed by a Government Resolution in July 1964 to advise the Government of India on the national pattern of education and on the general principles and policies for development of education at all stages and in all aspects. The Commission began its work on October 2, 1964 and submitted its report on June 26, 1966. Shri J.P Naik was the member-Secretary of the Commission. The publication of the report is an epoch-making event in the history of Education in India. The report is entitled 'Education and National Development'.[3]

Three Facets of Educational Revolution

The Commission identified three important facets of the big programme that would bring about the desired 'educational revolution'.

- Internal transformation so as to relate it to the life, needs and aspirations of the nation;
- Qualitative improvement so that the standards achieved are adequate, keep continually rising and, at least, in a few sectors become internationally comparable; and
- Expansion of educational facilities broadly on the basis of manpower needs and with an accent on equalization of educational opportunities.

Educational Programme

This is a four-fold Educational Programme. For the internal transformation of the system of education the following programmes urged high priority :

(1) Work experience as an integral part of general education; vocationalisation of education at the secondary level; improvement of professional education and research, promoting national consciousness;

(2) Introducing a common school system; making social and national service compulsory; developing all modern Indian languages;

(3) Making science education an integral part of all school education and developing scientific research;
(4) Inculcation of high values—social, moral and spiritual at all stages of education.

Objective of Education

The transformation was considered necessary for achieving the four national objectives: increasing productivity, achieving national integration, accelerating the process of modernisation and cultivating social, moral and spiritual values.

(*i*) *Programmes for improving the quality of education.* The quality of education is crucial for national development and the nation must be prepared to pay for the quality. According to the Commission's recommendations, the major programmes for qualitative improvement include raising the economic, social and professional status of teachers and improving the quality and scope of teacher education and in-service programmes, radical reform especially in Science and Mathematics, vigorous improvement in the method of teaching and evaluation, and providing quality textbooks and other teaching material, search for introduction of a nationwide programme of school and college improvement where each institute finds congenial conditions to strive continually to achieve the best results of which it is capable, the establishment of 'quality' schools to act as pace-setters in their districts and the creation of 5 or 6 'major' universities; revitalising the system of supervision and reorganising the State departments and the reorganisation of the educational structure on the 10+2+3 pattern.

(*ii*) *Expansion programme.* The Commission hopes that 5 per cent of the 3-5 and 50 per cent of the 5-6 age-groups will find places in nursery schools or classes by 1986. It recommends five years of good education for all children by 1975-76 and seven years of such education by 1985-86, and places the highest priority for free and compulsory education up to the age of 14. The problems and policies of expansion at the Secondary stage would differ from those in primary education because on the one hand it would not be financially possible for several years to come to have universal secondary education and on the other hand it would be essential to enlist half the enrolment at the higher secondary stage in vocational education. It is an important recommendation that the expansion of higher secondary and collegiate education should be related to manpower needs and must be selective. The programmes of equalisation of educational opportunities visualised by the Commission include the reduction of the regional imbalances to the minimum, increased provision of free education and scholarships, paying special attention to the education of girls, placing adequate emphasis on the spread of education among backward classes including the Scheduled Castes and the Scheduled Tribes. It is also recommended that a nationwide campaign should be launched for complete liquidation of literacy within 20 years.

Educational Commission's report is an acheivement, a mine of information and wisdom. The report is a synoptic survey of the entire educational situation in all its complexities. It reveals an imagination sweep not found in the excellent report of the past. The achievement was possible partly bacause the Commission had faith in the key role of education in national development implying economic growth and social transformation and partly because it was knowledgeable in the strategy and techniques of prospective planning. The Education Commission naturally hopes that the nation would be willing to pay for the reforms leading to the transformation of education so that fullest possible development of human resources might be possible. The Commission boldly assigns to education the task of tranforming and modernising existing social order so that the desired goal of a socialistic pattern of society might be realised within the foreseeable future. While it may not be possible to engineer the educational revolution envisaged by the Commission with our present resources, we shall have achieved a marked advance even if half the recommendations are implemented.

A survey of such a large magnitude is bound to have omision here and there. The Education Commission, for instance, is not clear and definite enough on the content and courses for elementary stage. A redefinition of basic education and an examination of the merits of earlier eight year composite basic school would have been worthwhile. The division of the primary stage into lower and higher, the nature of work experience, the qualities, aspects of the elementary stage are issues which need explaining. It is doubtful if a teacher can teach if there are rooms in most of the schools which can seat 50 children.

The concept of work experience and vocationalisation of education have been left nebulous. Higher education has received a disproportionate emphasis. Probably, there is anxiety to produce executives, managers, technicians of calibre for the emerging industrial society.

The creation of pace-setting schools and six major universities is a disturbing recommendation. It is bound to create a new caste and deprive the commmon schools of the few good teachers working in them. The recommendation does not seem to be in harmony with those relating to school complexes and neighbourhood school.

Educational Structure proposed by the Kothari Commission

1. The new educational structure will consist of :

(a) One to three years of pre-school education.

(b) A primary stage of 7 to 8 years divided into a lower primary stage of 4 or 5 years and a higher primary stage of 3 or 2 years.

(c) A lower secondary stage of 3 or 2 years.

(d) A higher secondary stage of two years of general education or one to three years of vocational education.

(e) A higher education stage having a course of three years or more for the first degree and followed by a course for the second or research degree of varying durations.

2. Age of admission to class I ordinarily not to be less than 6.

3. First public examination to come at the end of first ten years of schooling.

4. The system of streaming in school of general education to be made beyond class X.

5. Two types of secondary schools, high schools providing a ten years course and higher secondary schools providing a course of 11 or 12 years.

6. Bigger schools and more efficient schools—about one-fourth of the total number to be upgraded and attempts to upgrade every secondary school to the higher secondary stage to be abandoned.

7. New higher secondary course beginning in class XI, to be instituted and classes XI and XII to provide specialised studies in different subjects; existing higher secondary schools with integrated courses in classes IX, X and XI and running satisfactorily to continue until class XII is added.

8. Transfer of the pre-university course from the universities and affiliated colleges to secondary schools by 1975-76 and the duration of the course to be lengthened to two years by 1985-86;

U.G.C. being responsible for effecting the transfer of all pre-university or intermediate work from university and affiliated colleges to schools.

9. Starting of Higher Secondary class or classes in selected schools by State Education Departments, as self-contained units, and assisted with adequate recurring grants.

10. Reconstituting Boards of Secondary Education to accept the responsibility for the higher secondary stage also.

11. Vocationalization at the secondary stage at two points at the end of Class VII and at the end of Class X and provision to be made for the introduction of different types of vocational courses at the lower and higher secondary stages, the duration of these courses to vary from one to three years which would prepare young persons for employment.

General Observations

Favourable comments. The proposed education structure is more scientific. "The proposed system of one to three years of pre-school preparation, a 7-8 year primary stage, a lower secondary stage of 2-3 years, higher secondary of two years, and higher education beginning with a three-year course, will no doubt be considered more scientific than the present system, but unless the proposals are uniformly applied, the existing confusion and imbalance as between States cannot be removed.

Twelve-Year Course—A Very Practical Integrated System (National Solidarity, July 7, 1966). "The Commission has suggested a very practical integrated system consisting of a twelve-years course of Higher Secondary stage, followed by a three-year course of degree and another two-year course for the final degree."

Two-Year Higher Secondary Stage—An Important and Constructive Recommendation. Dr. D.S. Raddi, the Vice-Chancellor of the Osmania University, observed, "The Commssion has shown great wisdom in keeping the first degree stage at the present 3 years." (Deccan Chronicle, July 17, 1966).

"It has been categorical in attempting to strengthen and enlarge education by spreading it over 12 years and in retaining English." (Hindustan Standard, Calcutta, July 12, 1966).

Criticism. "Dr. Anil Chandra Banerjee, veteran educationist and a former President of the Board of Secondary Education, wondered how by merely adding one more year to the present education structure, the quality of education could be improved. This would mean fresh financial burden on the shoulders of the overburdened guardians who would have to foot the bills for their wards in schools. (Amrit Bazar Patrika, July 3, 1966).

Mr G.N. Acharya states: "The period from the primary school to the first Arts of Science degree has been 15 years for a long time. Many variations of intermediate stages have been tried; but eleven years of schooling for matriculation or its equivalent has remained constant.

Now the Commission has proposed a ten-year, common, undiversified, lower secondary, and a two-year higher secondary course, followed by a three-year degree course. This merely combines the last year of the present secondary course and the existing pre-University of first year.

This has the startling effect of lowering the standard of the general course equivalent to matriculation by one year, when the real need is for raising the standard. Secondly, as the upper secondary course examination is to be in the charge of another Board, this will result in a needless multiplication of such bodies." (Blitz, July 9, 1966).

Dr. P. Parija (a veteran educationist of Orissa) felt, "The schooling period was recommended as 11 or 12 years with a primary stage of 4 or 6 years. Who will decide whether the period should be 11 or 12 years ?" "Such indecision is prejudicial to uniformity", he said.

Then the Commission has suggested two types of schools, one providing 12 year course and the other 11 or 12 years course. This is likely to create difficulty. If the students leaving the 10 years school intend, as they certainly will, to enter colleges, will they be debarred or made to come through 11 to 12 year schools ? (Amrit Bazar Patrika, 17 July, 1966).

Implementation of the Recommedations of the Education Commission

1. *National Policy Resolution* (1968). Recommendations of the Education Commission 1964-66 were considered by various education organizations and institutions. These were also discussed by educators all over the country. Many educational conferences were held to think over these recommendations. Meetings of Vice-Chancellors, State Education Secretaries, Directors of Education

were convened. All these discussions and debates resulted in the adoption of a Resolution on the National Policy on Education in 1968.

2. *Introduction of the new pattern of education*. On the recommendations of the Education Commission and in accordance with the National Policy on Education (adopted by Parliament in 1968) the Central Advisory Board of Education adopted a resolution in its meeting held in November 1974 recommending the introduction of the 10+2+3 pattern of Education all over India during the Fifth Plan period. This resolution followed widespread consultation with several educational bodies and other concerned agencies throughout the country. By the end of the year 1978-79 this pattern has been introduced in 22 States/Union Territories, namely, Assam, Andhra Pradesh, Gujarat, Jammu & Kashmir, Karnataka, Kerala, Maharashtra, Sikkim, Timil Nadu, Tripura, West Bengal, Andaman and Nicobar Islands, Arunachal Pradesh, Chandigarh, Dadra and Nagar Haveli, Delhi, Goa, Daman and Diu, Lakshadweep and Pondicherry.

3. *Vocationalisation of higher secondary education*. A Centrally-sponsored scheme for vocationalisation was formed during 1976-77. Under it the State Governments were provided with Central assistance during the Fifth Five Year Plan period and thereafter the programme was run on a regular basis as a State scheme.

Vocational surveys of 150 districts in a phased manner during the Fifth Plan Period were conducted. Out of the districts so surveyed, 40 districts were selected for the introduction of vocational courses at an average of 16 courses per district. On the basis of the recommendations of a National Conference organised by NCERT on 5th June 1976, a document entitled 'Higher Secondary Education and its Vocationalization' has been brought out by the NCERT. The Central Board of Secondary Education Delhi introduced a large number of vocations at the higher secondary stage from the academic session 1977-78. Two other Committees, namely Ishwar Bhai Patel and Adiseshiah Report (1978) also made recommendations regarding vocationalization.

4. *Work experience*. As recommended by the Education Commission, work experience has been made an integral part of the new scheme of studies under the pattern (10+2+3).

5. *Book banks*. About one lakh books have been established in educational institutions which provide books to the students belonging to the weaker sections of the society.

6. *Two Levels of courses*. Under the new pattern of education, provision has been made for the students to select courses in some subjects at two levels, i.e., ordinary and advanced depending upon their capacity to work and comprehend.

7. *Revised pay scale of teachers*. They pay scale of teachers working in schools were revised almost in all the States as a result of the recommendations of the Education Commission.

8. National institute of educational planning and administration, New Delhi. The Working Party on Educational Planning. Administration and Evaluation in the Fourth Five-Year Plan set up by the Planning Commision reiterated the recommendation of the Kothari Commission for the setting up of the National Staff College. The Government of India accepted this recommendation and accordingly initiated at the Asian Instutute an Indian Programme in Educational Planning and Administration as a precursor to the National Staff College. The National Staff College for Education, Planners and Administrators began to function on 1st January, 1971 after it was registered under the Indian Society Registration Act, 1860 on 31st December, 1970. With the expiry of agreement with UNESCO under which the Asian Institute of Educational Planning and Administration was functioning, the staff and activities of the Asian Institute were taken over by the Staff College from 1st March, 1973. The Staff College is located at the premises of the NCERT. Its main function is to provide pre-service and in-service training and professional guidance to the senior educational officers of the Central and State Governments and Union Territories. Staff College was renamed as National Institute of Educational Planning and Administration in 1980.

2.3 10+2+3 Pattern of Education

On the recommendations of the Education Commission 1964-66 and in accordance with the Resolution on National Policy on Education (1968), the Central Advisory Board adopted a resolution in its meeting held in November 1974 recommending the introduction of the 10+2+3 pattern of education all over the country during Fifth Plan period. The Resolution followed widespread consultation with several bodies and other concerned agencies throughout the country. By 1980, this pattern had been introduced in 15 States and 8 Union Territories. The States of Haryana, Himachal Pradesh, Madhya Pradesh, Meghalaya, Punjab,

Rajasthan and Uttar Pradesh have also accepted the new pattern in principle.[4]

Objectives of the 10+2+3 Pattern

The new pattern envisaged that by providing work experience and vocational courses education will be linked with productivity. It will prepare students for entry in gainful employment after completing higher secondary education. It was expected that students will not rush for university degrees. It aimed at making students more mature and knowledgeable. It was intended to avoid specialisation at an early age.

Salient Features of the 10+2+3 Pattern

1. *Ten-year common course*. The pattern envisages a common course of general education for all students at this stage. There is an undifferentiateed course of general education for all without any diversification of courses. The main emphasis has been on providing a wide spectrum of knowledge relevant to life and to develop different aspects of personality, especially at the secondary stage comprising classes IX and X. Courses at this stage include the following subjects :

(i) Science, (ii) Mathematics, (iii) Languages, (iv) Social Studies including History, Civics, Geography, Economics and Commerce, (v) Two Languages, (vi) Work Experience, (vii) Health and Physical Education, and (viii) Additional Language — Optional.

2. *Higher secondary education* (Classes XI and XII). A broad-based general education at the secondary stage to be followed by two years of diversified and vocational education will have 2 types of courses i.e. Academic and Vocational.

It was visualized by the Education Commission (1964-66) that at the end of the ten years of school education a proportion of students would step off the school system and enter working life (about 40 per cent); some more would step off the stream of general education and enter voctional courses whose duration would be one to three years (about 30 per cent); and the remaining would continue further in the stream of general education whose duration will be one, and ultimately two years.

Main Characteristics of the 10+2+3 Pattern

1. It envisages 10 years of schooling with common and undifferentiated courses in classes IX and X.

2. It provides for 12 years of Higher Secondary Education in place of the 11 year, the usual school pattern.

3. The first degree course to be of three years after 12 years of schooling.

4. The first degree to be attainable after 15 years of education.

5. It provides for the compulsory teaching of science, mathematics, social studies, two languages, work experiences.

6. It provides for various vocational courses in class XI and XII.

7. It provides for two levels of courses in some subjects.

8. It provides for specialization after 10 years of schooling.

9. It provides for a core course in classes XI and XII.

New Education Pattern—Revolutionary Implications

A publication of a State Department contains the following observations, "Never before, either in the past or during the contemporary period, has there been a more relevant and realistic step in the field of education than the introduction of the 10+2+3 pattern. It has a lot of merit, promise and potential. Those incapable of appreciating new reform have raised their eyebrows. But the new pattern of education has such strong credentials and its sweep to wide-ranging, productive and positive that its results are bound to please the votaries as well as critics. The thrust of the new pattern is an honest attempt not only to improve the standard of education but also to make it employment oriented."

"The new pattern of education" according to the same publication "will give a new complexion (a new meaning), a new purpose. The new pattern, in fact admirably fits into two fundamental objectives — national integration and social purpose."

The new pattern is seen as a happy marriage between education and vocational skills which will now go hand in hand.

The new pattern of education is the culmination of the labours and wisdom of several committees, conferences and commissions.

The new system has been in vogue in some of the States for about 2 to 4 years and a stage has now come when we must give a fresh look to this new pattern. Searching enquiries have to be made at various levels to find out as to what extent we have been successful in reaping the benefits of the new pattern. The most important factor in the implementation of the new pattern was the introduction of Science and Mathematics, Work Experience and Vocational Courses. A glance at the implementation on the pattern reveals that we have failed to provide the facilities needed for its successful implementation. The critics of the new pattern argue that it was a great blunder on the part of the educationists to accept this new system of education. They point out that no where in the world such a large scale programme of reforms has ever been taken up without any try-out on some areas. The USSR introduced a new scheme of National Reforms in education after experimenting on a large scale. Many practising teachers and experts were associated with these experiments and a fair trial was given.

The education system which was meant for the children of the country was never discussed with them. The parents were never consulted while introducing the 10+2+3 pattern of education. We all know that educational system must meet the needs and aspirations of the students for whom it is a service. After all it is the student community who is the consumer of the educational institutions and it must be convinced that the courses of study and various curricular and co-curricular programmes which they are expected to follow are really very beneficial to them. It is common knowledge that during the last 2 years we have never tried to find out the reactions and responses of the students. It would be very worthwhile if students are asked to express their views openly about their experiences of the new system. Sometimes elders forget that the children can understand better though they consider them devoid of any insight. Students have their own views on certain aspects. They are 'thinking beings'. It is not fair on our part to think that we can do as we like with the children.

2.4 Ishwar Bhai Patel Review Committee

With the formation of the Janata Government in March 1977 the Education Minister appointed this Committee. The Education Minister had received many letters and comments from different sources regarding the introduction and the implementation of the new pattern of education. The Education Minister desired to have a review of the new pattern. [5]

In the 1968 National Policy Resolution, it was outlined that the Government of India will make a review of the scheme every five years. It was also envisaged that other recommendations of the Kothari Commission as well as various guidelines issued for implementation of the recommendations would also be reviewed. Since no such review had been done so far, it was considered very appropriate to have this review. This Standing Committee of the Central Advisory Board of Education had expressed grave doubts in that there was not enough allocation for education in the Fifth Plan and the Committee felt that the state of affairs might possibly be worsened at the end of the Plan.

The Kothari Commission had not recommended that education should be placed on the concurrent List but with the 42nd Amendment of the Constitution, education was placed on the Concurrent List. The Janata Government wanted to consider legal and educational aspect of the issue.

Major Recommendations of the Review Committee

1. *Formal and non-formal arrangement for education.* The learning system should be organized through formal and non-formal arrangements — some institutional, some partly personal — and that the institutional arrangements should not be so rigid as to exclude those learners who wish to make use of them.

2. *Flexibility of the curriculum.* Linked with such flexible arrangements within the learning system, the content of learning must also be flexible and arranged so as to suit the needs of individual learners of groups.

The curriculum too must be capable of catering to the requirements of a wide range of learners and learning circumstances.

3. *Minimal core.* The curriculum has to be built round local situations, though there must be a core of basic content for comparability of educational attainment and the acquisition of further skills and knowledge. This core should be minimal.

4. *Work education.* The principles of Basic Education as evolved by Mahatma Gandhi and accepted in the Kothari Commission Report with the stress on work education need to find a central place in the educational system.

5. *Various sources of learning.* The classroom is not the only place or source from which children learn. The environment and society are also sources from which children acquire attitudes and knowledge. Educational programmes must be so arranged that all these factors are fully utilized and hence rigid uniformity of educational programmes is neither desirable nor sound.

6. *Socially useful productive work.* We also prefer the term 'Socially useful Productive Work' to that of 'Work Experience' as it

is not only more expressive but it focusses attention on the practical aspect of this area of education.

7. *Increased allocation of time.* In order to implement socially useful productive work effectively, the Review Committee has recommended more time. As against about 3 hours for middle and secondary classes recommended by the NCERT framework, the Review Committee recommends about 6 hours, i.e., the double time.

8. *Educational structure.* (i) Primary classes I to IV/V. (ii) Middle Classes IV/V to VII/VIII. (iii) Secondary classes VIII/IX to X.

The scheme envisages flexibility in view of the different existing schemes in the States.

9. *Less instructional hours.* $2^1/_2$ to 3 hours of formal instruction is sufficient for classes I to IV/V.

10. *No rigid time table in classes I to IV/V.* At this stage a rigid distribution of time into class periods is educationally unsound.

11. *Textbooks.* Except in the case of language there is no need for textbook for languages, one book in Mathematics and one for Environmental Studies are sufficient.

12. *Teachers' guide books and teaching aids.* Teachers' guide books and teaching aids are necessary and these should cover the whole range of activities for all classes and that in the preparation of guide books principle of correlation should be the basis.

13. *Ban on home work in classes I* to *IV/V.* One of the most unethical educational practices, at present, is giving children unlimited home work. A child works four to five hours in school and is then faced with the prospect of two to three hours of home work. Thus a child is a prisoner either in the four walls of the school or in his house for the greater part of the day. A majority of children are, therefore, unable to take part in activities that make life joyful.

We are, therefore, constrained to condomn the practice of prescribing home work and we call for a complete ban on home work from classes I to IV/V.

14. *Self-study.* Arrangement for self-study will be more beneficial as it can be done under the supervision of teachers.

15. *No rigid academic year.* The school session should be scheduled according to local needs in view of the fact that more than 80 per cent of the primary schools are in rural areas.

16. *Alternative courses in mathematics and science*. It is necessary that courses in these subjects should be so framed that they take into consideration the availability of teachers, the needs of childern and in addition, in science, the extent of laboratory facilities and apparatus available. Therefore, alternative courses are recommended.

17. *Alternatives and not higher or lower courses*. We would, however, stress that the alternatives in mathematics and science must be considered alternatives and not higher or lower courses.

18. *History, civics and geography*. We are of the view that one area in which the present scheme is over-loaded is 'social studies' or 'social science'.

The Committee, therefore, recommends the inclusion of courses in history, civics and geography and excludes subjects like economics, commerce and psychology.

19. *Syllabus frames*. We believe that there is an advantage in not giving detailed courses of studies as they will not be immediately operatable. The advantage is that the Education Departments, Examining Boards and Schools will have an opportunity of studying the main topics and then deciding the details of the content, in relation to their particular needs and in keeping with the facilities available.

20. *Freedom to develop textbooks*. We recommend that NCERT should concentrate on the production of instructional material and that State Governments, Examination Boards, schools and other educational agencies must be given freedom to adapt and develop this material to suit their particular need.

21. *Multiple entry*. We wish to reiterate that opportunities through formal and non-formal educational arrangements must be made so that drop-outs are enabled to re-enter the stream of education without any difficulty at any stage.

22. *Staffing pattern*. We do not propose to suggest any formula as the constraints of finance and availability of teachers are important variables which make the application of a single formula generally impracticable.

We suggest two principles to appraise the needs of each area separately and where the teaching conditions are most difficult, to provide extra teachers and provide also the best available teachers.

23. *Experimentation on creative work, remedial instruction*. We feel that if teaching conditions are made even reasonably congenial,

creative and experimental work will develop and thrive and individual attention and remedial work will follow.

24. *Funds on priority basis.* Funds must be collected on a priority basis.

2.5 Adiseshiah Review Committee

In October 1977, the then Union Education Minister, Dr P.C. Chander, in his capacity as President of the NCERT, appointed a National Review Committee under the Chairmanship of Dr Malcolm S. Adiseshiah, the then Vice-Chancellor, University of Madras, to review the curriculum of the +2 stage of school education with special reference of Vocationalization of education. The Committee submitted its report in February 1978.[6]

Major Recommendations

Mojor recommendations of the Report may be listed as under :

1. *Work-based learning.* Learning must be based on work either through what the Ishwar Bhai Patel Committee calls socially useful productive work or through vocationalised courses.

2. *Agriculture-oriented vocational courses.* Vocational courses should be in agricultural and related rural occupational areas and in managerial, commercial, health and para-medical vocations and not through opening vocational courses at this level in the manufacturing, industrial and engineering occupations.

3. *Flexible streaming.* There should be no rigid streaming of courses into the General Education and Vocationalised Educational Spectrums. Each school should be allowed to offer such General Education and Vocationalised Courses in accordance with the facilities available and the demand in the region.

4. *Two spectrums of the higher secondary stage.* The Higher Secondary Stage should comprise of a General Education Spectrum and a Vocational Spectrum.

5. *Curriculum.* The curriculum should be so structured that the courses lend themselves to imparting instruction in terms of well connected modules to enable the students to choose and combine them according to their needs.

6. *Suitable text-books.* In order to impart instruction in vocational courses, in agricultural and related subjects, books be written on a priority basis to suit local conditions and made available

to the schools. In some general education and commercial subjects where textbooks produced in other countries are suitable, these books may be adopted and translated in Indian languages.

7. *Semester pattern and credit system*. In some States where the Universities have already adopted the semester system the same may also be introduced in classes XI and XII. The other States may study the experiences of the States which have already introduced the semester system and take suitable steps for the orientation of teachers, and preparation of modules of learning and textbook for adopting the semester pattern, at a later and appropriate time.

8. *Counselling and placement*. As vocationalisation is extended Counselling and Placement Officers be appointed in clusters of 3 or 4 schools, particularly in rural areas to start with.

9. *Teachers for vocational courses*. At the start there should not be insistence on post-graduate qualification in respect of teachers of vocational courses. What is needed is means of developing the required skills and competencies in particular vocations and for this, services of persons who have had actual experience of on-the-job may be fruitfully utilised to teach vocational courses. Part-time teachers may also be appointed wherever necessary.

10. *Pre-service and in-service training of teachers*. Both pre-service and in-service teacher education should be so organised as to bring about the proposed changes at this stage of education. The Universities, the Teachers Training Colleges, State Councils of Educational Research and Training (SCERTs), State Institutes of Education, State Institutes of Science Education, NCERT, Boards of Secondary Education, Agricultural Universities, institutions like ICAR and all others who are engaged in the preparation of orientation of teachers should be activety involved in this task.

11. *Vocational survey*. With regard to the offering of vocationalised courses in rural or urban schools, a vocational survey of the area—metropolitan, block, taluk, district or state—be undertaken, such surverys being done even in cases where the vocational courses have started.

12. *Location of schools in the rural sector*. In the selection of schools, it is recommended that the location of schools in the rural sector be given priority. Since little or no vocationalised education facilities are readily available for rural students, it is recommended that all the new schools should be constructed in rural areas and should be adequately equipped.

13. *Use of available facilities*. To economise on the financial investment on infrastructural facilities, it is recommended that the spare capacity in all these schools be used and the enrolment be increased through running double shifts wherever it is feasible and whenever further demands for technical skills and competencies arise in neighbourhood, including as necessary (adding) new courses and strengthening the existing facilities.

14. *Apprenticeship facilities.* Apprenticeship facilities should be extended to all the students who complete education in vocational streams if they desire to benefit from such training.

15. *Recruitment policy*. The recruitment policy of the government as well as public sector organizations should be revised and job requirements should replace the university degrees as essential qualifications. Vocationally qualified persons should be preferred to graduates, and be entitled to the pay scales available to the graduates as long as the jobs performed are the same or similar. Also such persons should be eligible for the higher positions in the ladder, either on the basis of departmental tests or improvement of qualifications through correspondence or evening course or block-time training.

16. *Vertical mobility*. The apprenticeship and recruitment policy are part of a package recommended to improve the prospects of the majority of those who enter the plus 2 stage and terminate their formal schooling after acquiring some vocational skills.

17. *Organisation of national council of vocational education*. One of the most important pre-requisite for the successful implementation of the vocational spectrum of the plus 2 stage is to bring about cooperation and co-rodination for the purposes of employment and recognition, among all agencies and departments of the government. Such co-ordination will also economise on our scarce financial resources by preventing replication of efforts in various departments offering vocational education and making a well-planned effort possible to achieve the National Education should be set up and all the agencies such as the Indian Council of Agricultural Research, All India Council for Technical Education, the Nursing Council, the Dental Council, the Pharmacy Council and the National Council for Training in Vocational Trades should be members of this apex body.

18. *State council for vocational education*. At the state level, State Councils for Vocational Education be created to perform

similar functions under the general guidance of the National Council of Vocational Education.

19. *Local support*. The programme of vocationalisation of education requires constant support of local community and other agencies. Agencies, such as Panchayat Union, Agricultural and Rural Cooperatives, the Small-Scale Industries Corporation, Khadi and Village Industry Commission, local branches of Nationalised and other banks, Financial Corporations, Krishi Vigyan Kendras and various voluntary organisations, held in identification of vocation and in training for entrepreneurship, provisions of loans and credit facilities, marketing of product and services.

20. *Evaluation of the programme*. It is not only adequate planning and preparation but also a continuous process of evaluation of the programme that is necessary for the success of the plus 2 stage and its vocationalisation sector. There should be an in-built machinery for such evaluation of the programme at various levels i.e., the National, the State and the local and appropriate follow-up action taken.

21. *Financial resources*. (i) No large scale of ambitious expenditure be incurred on equipment, unless it is ascertained that it will be needed for a long period and even so not in the area of manufacturing, industrial or engineering skills which are left to existing vocation/technical education institutions.

(2) In fact with the short-term emphasis in the report on agriculture, managerial and health and para-medical vocations attempts should first be made to identify and exploit locally available resources.

(3) In view of the immense stakes in the programme of vocationalisation and in the interest of national economic development and social transformation, some additional resources will be needed. Any expenditure on vocationalisation should be considered as a national investment for the future. Where necessary, provision for additional financial resources must, therefore, be made ungrudgingly. Such an expenditure will generate new capabilities in the human wealth of our country,. which will in its turn return the investment multiplied over the years.

2.6 Educational Policies in India

The Education Commission (1964-66) provided an opportunity before the country to declare a comprehensive national policy on education. The Report of the Education Commission (1964-66) provided a blue-print of educational development spread over 20 years. The Education Commission advised the Government on the general principles and policies and for the development of education at all stages and in all aspects. Hence, in 1967 the Government of India constituted the committee of Members of Parliament on Education to prepare the draft of a statement on the National Policy on Education. Thereafter the Government of India issued the Resolution on National Policy on Education in 1968. Since then the Resolution has become the basis of educational reconstruction in India.

2.6.1 THE 1968 EDUCATION POLICY :

The National Policy of 1968 marked a significant step in the history of education in post, independence of India. It aimed to promote national progress, a sense of common citizenship and culture, and to stengthen national integration, It laid stress on the need for a radical reconstruction of the education system, to improve its quality at all stages, and gave, much greater attention to science and technology.[7]

Since the adoption of the 1968 Policy, there has been considerable expansion in educational facilities all over the country at all levels. More than 90 per cent of the country's rural habitations now have schooling facilities within a radius of one kilometer. There has been sizeable augmentation of facilities of the other stages also. The Government of India accordingly resolves to promote the development of education in the country in accordance with the following principles :

(i) Free and compulsory Education for all children upto the age of 14;

(ii) Status, Employments and Education of Teachers;

(iii) Development of Languages: (a) Regional languages, (b) there Language Formula : (Includes the study of a modern Indian language preferably one of the southern languages, in the Hindi-speaking states, and of Hindu along with the regional languages and English in the non-Hindi speaking states);

(iv) Equalisation of Educational Opportunity: Strenuous efforts should be made to equalise educational opportunity;

(v) Identification of Talent;
(vi) Work-Experience and National Service;
(vii) Science, Education and Research;
(viii) Education for Agriculture and Industry;
(ix) Production of Books;
(x) Examination; and
(xi) Secondary, university, part-time, correspondence courses, spread of Literacy and Adult Education etc.

Perhaps the most notable development has been the acceptance of a common structure of education throughout the country and the introduction of the 10+2+3 system by most states. The higher secondary stage of two years being located in schools, colleges or both according to local conditions.

However, a variety of new challenges and social needs make it imperative for the Government to formulate and implement a new Education Policy for the country.

2.6.2 The 1986 New Education Policy

Realising the fact that the country has reached a stage in its economic and technical development, a major effort must be made to derive the maximum benefit from the assets already created. To ensure that the fruits of change reach all sections, education is the highway to that goal. With this aim in view, the Government of India announced in January 1985 that a new Education Policy would be formulated for the country. A comprehensive appraisal of the existing education scene was made, followed by a countrywide debate.

The Cardinal principles contained in the National Education Policy, 1986, may be stated here in brief. Some principles are old but these have been stated in new spirit and perspective. These cannot be described as mere old wine in the new bottle as some people sarcastically opine.

(i) *Universalisation of Elementary Education* : The National Policy on Education (1986) has laid great emphasis on universalisation of elementary education, Assuming that the universal elementary education is achieved by 1990, out of the total age-specific population of 17.4 crores, 11 crore pupils should be in primary stage and the remaining 6.4 crores in the middle stage. It may be noted that this achievement implies that the primary education will be 1.5 times and the middle 3.2 times of its present size. It seems that it may not be achieved due to the grim reality prevalent in our socio-economic system. However, many things in the proposed policy are vague. Unless large scale wastage is reduced to minimum and other objective conditions are fulfilled the target of universalisation of elementary education by 1990 will remain a pious will.

(ii) *Adult and continuing education* : Half of the total illiterate population of the number of illiterates in Indian was 30 crores. In 1981 it was 43 crores and 70 lakhs. Now it is about 45 crores. In 2000 A.D. it will be 50 crores. Thus the number of illiterates is increasing instead of decreasing though some laudable measures were taken in the past. However, it is realised that Government efforts alone cannot solve this problem effectively. Hence, all private and voluntary agencies should join hands with the Government in successful tackling of this national problem.

Another important principle of the proposed national policy is the increased emphasis on :

(iii) Secondary Education;
(iv) Establishment of model schools or centre of excellence;
(v) Social relevant and radical transformation of the curricula;
(vi) Vocationalisation of Higher Education;
(vii) Delinking of degrees from jobs;
(viii) Development of technical education and its social relevance;
(x) Role of voluntary agencies in education. Privatization of Education;
(xi) Value oriented Education;
(xii) Teachers' education—pre-service and in-service training of teachers;
(xiii) Physical and Health education—facilities for games and sports;
(xiv) Examination system;
(xv) Education of girls;
(xvi) National integration and Education;
(xvii) International understanding and cooperation;
(xviii) Language policy in Education;
(xix) An Integrated Strategy of Education

Keeping above points in view, now it should be possible to intensify the nation-wide effort in Human Resource Development, with Education playing its multifaceted role.

Intra-sectoral Resource Allocation in Education

Percentage of plan outlay as a whole has ranged between 8 per cent (first plan) and 2.59 per cent (sixth plan) — the highest and the lowest respectively. They average share of education in total plan during the last four five year plans (Fourth, Fifth, Sixth and Seventh) of 3.61 per cent (3.63 per cent excluding the Seventh Plan), has, in fact, turned out to be one-half of the average share of 6.85 per cent during the first three plans.

It has been argued that elementary education should account for a minimum of 50 per cent of the resources denoted to education. However, it was only in the First Plan that its share was 56 per cent. Thereafter, it has remained in the vicmity of one-third.

There is a substantial fall in the average share of elementary education. Because the average for the first three plans was around 42 per cent and for the next three plans the average share was approximately 34 per cent.

It is felt that the actual amount spent is less than that provided in the Plan. For example, in the Fifth Plan, as against the provision of Rs. 7.43 crore for elementary education, the actual expenditure incurred was Rs. 410 crore. In contrast, the average share of secondary education in both the periods has remained fairly constant at 17 per cent to 16.7 per cent upto 1956-66 and 17 per cent thereafter. The position of the higher education sector looks enviable.

Despite all talk of vocationalisation of education, the Plan allocation between general and technical education tells a different story. In each Plan, the share of general education was more than four fifth (86.6 per cent on the average). Thus, education in India has yet to become 'mass' education in the real sense of the term.

2.7 Summing-up

In spite of various commissions, committees and panels appointed by the Central and State Governments from time to time, Indian education is still at the cross-roads. Education has failed to evolve a national pattern so far. However, the new pattern of education popularly known as 10+2+3 had raised fresh hopes. It is destined to be the national system of education in due course of time. It has been accepted in principle by almost all the States of India.

The report of Kothari Commission is a synoptic survey of the entire education situation in all its complexities. The Education Commission, for instance, is not clear and definite enough on the content and courses for elementary stages. A redefinition of basic education and an examination of the merits of the earlier eight year composite basis school would have been worthwhile. The division of the primary stage into lower and higher, the nature of work experience, the qualities, aspects of the elementary stage are issues which need explanation.

The new pattern 10+2+3 introduced Science and Mathematics, work experience and voctional courses. A glance at the implementation on the pattern reveals that we have failed to provide the facilities needed for its successful implementation. It would be worthwhile if students are asked to express their views openly about their experiences of the new system.

In the New Educational Policy emphasis has been laid on the need of linking the education planning with the manpower planning. Some of the priority areas identified for attention for implementation of new education policy are, as manpower planning and demand forecasting and by strengthening the data base, monitoring and evaluation system. Even the Steering Groups on Education of the Plan Commission are giving stress on planning, monitoring, evaluation and data base in connection with the formulation of 8th Five Year Plan.

Notes & References

1. Kuldip Kaur (1985), *Education in India (1781-1985) Policies Planning and Implementation,* CRRID, Chandigarh, p. 109.
2. *The Tribune,* May 17, 1977.
3. J.C. Aggarwal (1982), *Development and Planning of Modern Education* Vikas Pub. House, New Delhi, p. 118.
4. *Ibid*, p. 137.
5. *Ibid*, p. 149.
6. *Ibid*, p. 157.
7. National Policy on Education—1986, Ministry of HRD, Govt. of India, New Delhi, May 1986.

3 The Educational System and Sub-System in India

3.1 Introduction

It is easier to appreciate the potentialities and limitations of education in the task of structuring a society which is just, egalitarian, democratic, socialist and secular. It is a truism to say that education and society are intrinsically related. The connection is universally recognised. And yet educational reformers, in their desire to achieve progressive changes in education, tend to give the impression as if it existed in a social vacuum. The subsystem cannot exist outside the system. Although education is a part of the larger social aggregate, its independent dynamism does not get curtailed. In fact, it generates and sustains progressive social change. Evidence of the contributions made by education to the development of human societies and to the making of civilisations is available in abundance. But not all the hypotheses on which the above faith is based are equally tenable. The fact that education functions and has functioned as a double edged weapon goes to prove the operation of social purpose which give it specific twists and turns. Depending on the nature of social organisation and the propensity of the ruling elite, education through the mediation of suitable technologies has been used for war and peace, for murder and self-defence, for subjugation of people and for releasing them from bondage. However, even as the old society reproduces itself through education, a dissenting consciousness, itself a reflection of elements of dissent objectivity existing in society, also grows.

There is no doubt that we have a wide range of analysis of the system and system with theories of culture saturation, cultural production, reproduction, socialisation and transmission. In making such analysis there is an increased interest in understanding the ways, implied or explicit, in which culture and education may act on each other. In nearly all the analytical models, the powerful role of education in modifying human behaviour and in reshaping the human environment is admitted. Education—and particularly its tertiary segment may have played only a marginal role in the early years of the Industrial Revolution with an endless series of innovations acquired through intensive R&D endeavours. Moreover, the role of education as an essential input in the re-organisation and modernisation of societies in the developed countries of today has been even more far reaching. Education played a crucial role in the acquisition of the knowledge base of their people and in the setting up of their exceedingly efficient communications network. Education and socio-economic development are inseparably inter-linked through bi-directional consation. They feed, support, sustain and strengthen each other. The fact is that this obvious relationship needs to be often reiterated, particularly in the developing countries, either to the persisting naivette of the misguided or the consistent efforts of those in this unequal world who have a vested interest in keeping the poor societies poor. Therefore, educational policies must be intrinsically interwined with the basic structural changes without which the new international order would remain an idle dream. It must correct the perspectives of those who search solace in the spurious spirituality of poverty as well as those who seek meaning and purpose of the consumerist counters of affluence.

Since the acceptance of educational responsibility of the Indian people by the East Indian Company in 1813, a large number of incidents and developments have occurred in the avenue of Indian Education. Quite a few commissions and committees have been set up to shape the Indian education from different angles. Many conferences and seminars have been held to steer the Indian education in right direction and to fulfil the national ideals and goals.

This section paper attempts to focus the opinions of the commissions and committees appointed so far and consider the valuable opinions expressed by educational experts. The present state of modern Indian education has a chequered career and originated through the vicissitudes of divergent socio-economic and political factors. We tried to focus the structural pattern of education during pre and post independence. We have also tried to trace the position of social, and adult-non-formal education in India. On the whole, on attempt has been made in this section to give an account of the educational system and point out burning educational problems and solution in suggestive manner.

3.2 Role of the Centre in Education

As per the constitutional provisions, the Central Government is expected to play a significant role in the field of education. Though

Ministry of HRD, Department of Education, Government of India, discharges the major responsibility in the field of Education on behalf of the Government of India, yet there are other Ministries of the Centre which also perform functions in the field of Education. Broadly, following are the major functions performed by the Ministry, Government of India :

— The Central Government determines targets and prepares the educational plan to be implemented by the country as a whole, because educational planning is a part and parcel of the total planning.

— For carrying out educational plans, Government of India has set-up institutions like All-India Council of Technical Education and the National Council of Educational Research and Training which provide guidance to the States in the field of Education.

— From time to time the Government of India has set up Commissions which have gone into the various aspects of Education at different levels and have provided valuable recommendations and suggestions. These recommendations have further been considered by the experts and the states requested to implement the recommendations of the expert bodies.

— The Central Government also directs and guides the State Government, local and private enterprise so as to encourage education on right lines. This is being done by the Ministry through the Central Advisory Board of Education.

— The Central Government allocates suitable grants to the states, local bodies and private agencies.

— Government of India is wedded to the establishment of an egalitarian society and therefore has taken many steps to provide equal education opportunities to the weaker sections of the society.

— A large number of pilot projects have been undertaken by the Union Ministry which aims at providing enlightened leadership.

— Centre is directly responsible for education in various union territories and other central administered areas.

— From time to time it brings out useful information on various aspects of education. The Ministry also publishes a few educational journals/statistical informations which have proved to be very helpful in disseminating information in the country.

— It carried out some programmes in cooperation with UNESCO.
— The Ministry is directly responsible for the running of a few universities, national libraries, museums, art galleries and central schools.

In addition to this, the following more steps are to be taken at the Central level :

— To establish institutions of scientific and technical education as well as of social sciences and humanities. Such institutions are to be established in close collaboration with the universities and are to be an integral part of university system.
— To undertake a measure for talent in different fields and to make this talent available to the states ;
— To expand the Central and centrally sponsored sectors in education.

3.3 Role of the States in Education

The Education Commission observes, "As we visualise, the responsibility for school education will rest squarely on the State Government. The local authorities will, no doubt, have a good deal of initiative and we should like the State Governments to encourage them by adopting flexible policies. But, by and large, they will act as agents of the State Governments and exercise delegated powers." Thus, the State Education Departments which are the principal agency of the State Government take following steps :

— Periodical revision and upgrading of curricula, preparation of textbooks, teachers guide and other teaching and learning materials, and improvement in methods of teaching and evaluation.
— Prescribing the standards to be maintained in schools in consultation with professional bodies.
— A Statutory Council of Education should be created at the State level with the State Education Minister as the Chairman. Its members should include representatives of the universities in that state, all Directors of Education and some eminent educationists. Its main function will be to advise the State Government on all educational matters upto the school level, to review the progress of education and evaluate such programmes from time to time.

— Supply of teachers, for fixing their remuneration, retirement benefits and conditions of work and service and for organisation teacher preparation both pre-service and in-service on proper lines and for establishing, conducting or aiding training institutions of high quality with adequate intakes and outputs.

— State management of education implies that the educational institutions in the state are brought into existence by the state, are financed by it through the government offices and are also adminitered by persons directly appointed by government. There are no educational institutions other than government ones.

However, State Control of education means overall control exercised by the State over educational institutions. There are educational institutions financed and managed by bodies other than the government. These bodies may be educational trusts, religious bodies, local boards, etc. The private institutions have greater chances of going in for educational experimentation for the heads of these institutions and their masters are always ready to decide upon things in a quicker and better way.

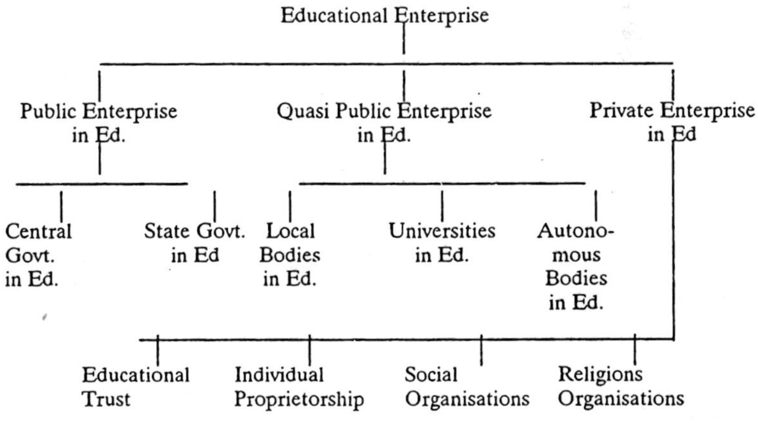

(After Aggarwal, 1982)

3.4 Organisational Set-up of the Education System in India :

Since independence the Central Government, the State Governments, local authorities and the voluntary organisations have been providing educational facilities in the country. The role played by these agencies in the administration of education has been changing from time to time. The Indian Education Commission 1964-65, viewing the administration as an element in the improvement of standards, laid stress on the co-ordinating functions of the Central and State Governments. The Commission pointed out the following perceptible trends in the Indian education administration.

- A pyramid-type organisation is gradually being replaced by a flat organisation ;
- Administration is being academicised day-by-day ;
- There is no end to the improvement of the administrator nor to his specialisation. So he needs periodical orientation, in-service education, resulting in more and more of decentralisation ;
- Democratic attitudes are developing, may be slowly, in the participants in the administrative process.

The Central Government lays the general educational policy and is responsible for the educational development in the Union Territories and the area governed by it. The Central Government has the following structure of educational administration :-

1. Education Minister
2. Minister of State for Education
3. Deputy Minister of Education
4. Education Secretary
5. Advisor, Deputy Advisor, Programme Department
6. Director
   (1) Project; (ii) Adult Education (iii) Statistics and Information
7. Joint Secretary
   (i) Programme Controller ; (ii) Education Advisor (iii) Deputy Secretary (School Division) ; (iv) Deputy Secretary (UNESCO Division) ; (v) Assistant Educational Advisor (Publication unit).
8. Director (Internal Finance)
9. Joint Secretary
   (i) Director (Administration) ; (ii) Deputy Secretary (Book Improvement) ; (iii) Deputy Secretary (Hindi Section) (iv) Special Officer (Sanskrit) ; (v) Sub-Education Advisor ; (vi) Deputy Secretary (Youth Services).

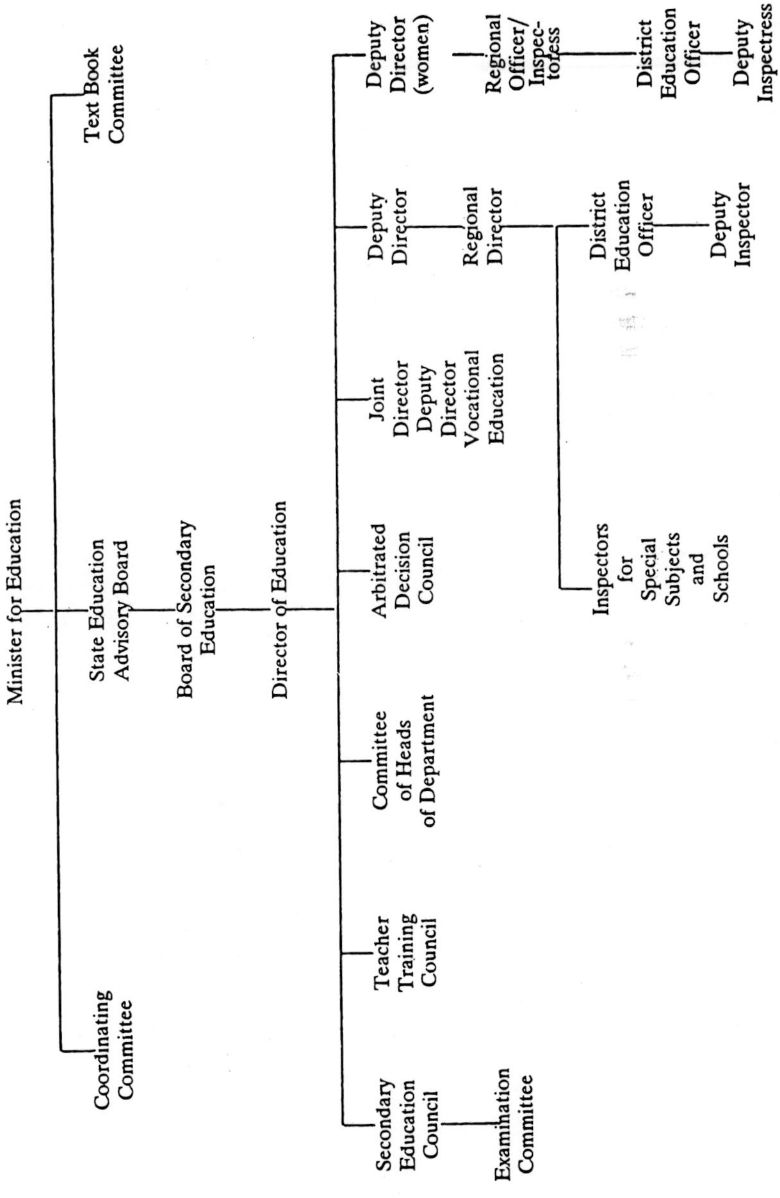

Minister for Education
Text Book Committee
State Education Advisory Board
Coordinating Committee
Board of Secondary Education
Director of Education
Deputy Director (women)
Deputy Director
Joint Director Deputy Director Vocational Education
Arbitrated Decision Council
Committee of Heads of Department
Teacher Training Council
Secondary Education Council
Examination Committee
Regional Officer/ Inspectoress
District Education Officer
Deputy Inspectress
Regional Director
District Education Officer
Deputy Inspector
Inspectors for Special Subjects and Schools

10. Joint Educational Advisor
    (i) Sub-Advisor (Higher Education) ; (ii) Deputy Secretary (Foreign Scholarship) ; (iii) Sub-Advisor (Union Territories)
11. Educational Advisor (Technical)
    (i) Sub-Advisor (Technical Education Division).

The administrative set up for the states was proposed by the Secondary Education Commission according to which the State Education Department* was to be structured as shown in the Chart (p. 59).

The Education Commission did make several other proposals for the strengthening and reorganisation of the Ministry at the Centre and States. Among the proposals that the posts of the Secretary to the Ministry and the State Education Secretary should be filled by educationists rather than from the Cadre of IAS officers was also turned down. The creation of District and Municipal School Boards was one of the most important proposals made by the Education Commission regarding decentralisation of authority in educational administration. The other recommendations of the Commission were really minor, because of the assumption that the creation of the IES cadre would take care of most problems. Consequently, the present position is that the Education Commission has not been able to make any contribution to the improvement of the educational burecucracy, either at the Centre or in the States.

The State Administrative Machinery Schools** was to be structured as follows :

1. *At the State level* :

	Minister of Education	
	|	
State Board of Vocational Education	Education Secretariat	State Board of School Education
	|	|
	Directorate of Education	Higher Secondary Committee/Board
	|	|
State Evaluation Organisation	Deupty Director School Education	Examination Committee/Board
	|	

* (Quoted in '*Indian Education : Today and Tomorrow*' by S. Bhatnagar, p. 366)

** As suggested by Indian Education Commission 1964-66. Quoted in *Current Problems in Indian Education* by R. Safaya, p. 182.

2. *At the District Level* :

	District Education Office	District Education/ School Board
3. *At the Local Level* :	Block Education Office	Block Education/ School Board

3.5 Structural Pattern of Education

3.5.1 During Colonial Period

During British period education was colonial, imperialistic and bureaucratic in character. It served the purpose for which it was intended. It served to the advantage of the upper and middle strata of the society. The common people were not benefited by it. But emphasis we laid on the importance of mass education based on the tradition of the nation and its needs and aspirations. Education was regarded as a tool for national emanicipation. The Indian Education Commission (1882-83), the first in the series, was set up under the chairmanship of William Hunter to enquire into the manner in which effect had been given to the principles of the Despatch of 1854 with particular emphasis on elementary education. The second and the third commissions, viz., the Indian Universities Commission (1902) under the chairmanship of Mr. Releigh, a member of the Viceroy's Executive Council and the Calcutta University Commission (1917) under the chairmanship of M.E. Sadler, Vice-Chancellor of Leeds University education. With the recommendations of the first Education Commission of 1881-82 education expanded at all levels quantitatively at the cost of quality. Its weaknesses and defects were exposed with the rapidly growing consciousness particularly after the birth of the National Congress in 1885. The national leaders laid great stress on national education under national control and based on national ideals and tradition.[1] As a result National Education Movement originated. It had sure impact on the development of primary, secondary and collegiate education.

The National Council of Education was set up in June, 1906.[2] The curriculum of the National Council of Education was broad-based and comprehensive. Its scheme of studies was to be imported in three stages[3] : (3+7+4).

(a) Primary—3 years Course (6-9)

(b) Secondary—7 years Course (9-15)
(c) Collegiate—4 years Course (16-19)

In the *Primary* stage both Literacy and Scientific education was to be given including rudimentary technical education. Teaching at this stage was mostly oral. The scientific and technical subjects included the use of simple tools, clay modelling, cardboard modelling, paper cutting, vernacular, object lessons, drawing, Geography, Arithmetic, Health Education and English Primer.

In the *Secondary* stage also literacy and scientific education was imparted with some technical subjects vocationally biased. Education at this stage was both theoretical and practical. Workshop practice and laboratory expreiments were introduced. At this stage education was truly three dimensional—Literacy, Scientific and Technical and the course was obviously a mixed course. The subjects included Arithmetic, Workshop Practice, Drawing, Object lessons, Classical languages (Sanskrit, Arabic or Persian), Vernacular, Geography, History, Mathematics (from 3rd year), English (from 1st year), Physics, Chemistry and Biology (from 5th year).

In the collegiate stage (4 years) education was also Literacy, Scientific and Technical. Both theoretical and practical subjects were taught with more proficiency. The literacy course included Indian languages, English language and literature, Comparative Philosophy, History, Economics, Political Science, Philosophy, Comparative Religion etc. The scientifice and technical courses included both theoretical and practical subjects such as Pure Mathematics, Mixed Mathematics, Physics, Chemistry, Agriculture, Forestry, Mining, Medicine, Engineering, Pedagogical Science, Botany etc. These subjects were taught for higher technical education.

This system of education was condemned as academic and too literacy.[4] Therefore, after independence it was felt that in the filed of education a change in pattern and content of the educational set-up is must.

3.5.2 During Post-Independence

All the five earlier commissions (two in pre-independence and three in post-independence) did not deal with education as a whole but focused attention on different levels of education. The first dealt with some aspects of primary, secondary and college education (excluding university education), the second, third and fourth with university education and the fifth with secondary education. The unique feature of Education Commission (1964-66) (popularly known as Kothari Commission) was to limit its enquiry to specific sectors or aspects of education, but to have a comprehensive review of the entire educational system. And then unique feature of the commission was its conviction that education is the most powerful instrument of the national development. The crucial role of education in national development appears in all its vividness on every page of the report. The report concludes : 'We must either build a sound, balanced, effective and imaginative educational system to meet out developing need and respond to our challenging aspirations or be content to be swept aside by the strong currents of history.' Never before was it conceived aspirot of national honour and the prosperity as revealed in the pages of the Commission's Report.

One of the novel experiements in the field of modern Indian Education is the restructuring of the educational set up or pattern. Pattern and content are the two most important components or ingredients of education. The new structural pattern as proposed by the Education Commission and as it exists in India has tremendously affected the entire field of education—secondary, higher secondary.[5] A change is made in the expectation of progress but every change does not produce desirable progress. The present experiment has not been introduced all of a sudden but it is the product of historical developments. Rather it is the result of successive experiments before and after independence.

The prevailing education system in India comprises of both recognised and unrecognised institutions and includes formal education. According to the constitution, education is a state subject. The Union Government functions only as a coordinator of educational activities and helps to maintain uniformity in pattern and standards of education.[6] It also act as clearing house in respect of the educational statistics.

In 1974 (November) the C.A.B.E. strongly recommended the introduction of the 10+2+3 pattern of education all over the country during the fifth plan period. The National Education Policy was announced in April, 1979 and has suggested 12 years school education and 3 years undergraduate course. Where a university desires, it could have a two-year Pass course and three years Honours course. By 1980 this pattern had been introduced in 15 states and 8 Union Territories.[7]

However, the entire period of formal education has been divided into two main stages, viz., school education and higher education. Education is further classified into two major categories, viz., (a) General Education and (b) Vocational/Technical/ Professional Education.[8]

3.5.2.1 *General Education*

A proposed reorganisation of educational structure (general) is given in Statement-I. However it is provided through school education and college/higher education, according to the stages mentioned below :

(i) *Elementary Stage I to VIII*

The education at school state is divided into pre-primary, primary and secondary. This is based mainly on two considerations. Firstly, the three stages of education are regarded as corresponding to the three stages in the development of a child—infancy, childhood and adolescence. Secondly, from the social point of view, primary education is meant for the masses and secondary education for the selected few. The primary or elementary stage of general education with eight years duration covers mainly the primary stage with five years of schooling and middle stage with VI-VIII years of schooling.

(ii) *Secondary State IX-XII*

The recommendations of the Secondary Education Commission resulted in the development of a national pattern of school education covering eleven years—five years of lower primary, three years of upper primary and three years of higher secondary to be followed by a three years course for the first degree and further two years course for the second degree. The Education Commission placed highest emphasis on the transformation of education system with radical changes in content and structure in such a manner as to make it a powerful instrument of social and economic changes and relating it to the needs of development and aspirations of the people.

The system of education that is now emerging is likely to be on uniform pattern throughout the country. The minimum age at the entry into the present educational system is 5 years. The first ten years of schooling, of the present education, "are treated as an integrated unit of general undifferentiated education which would emphasise, inter-alia, the use of socially useful productive work (SUPW) as the medium of education, the development of scientific attitudes and temper among the children and the freedom of the child and a living contact with nature". A significant feature of this higher secondary stage is the provision of a separate stream of vocation education providing a large variety of vocational courses to meet the development needs of the economy and the varied needs and aptitudes and capacities of youth.

Statement - I

Proposed Reorganization of Educational Structure

	First Degree	20	III
	General	19	II
		12	I
	Higher Secondary	17	XII
		16	XI
Secondary Stage	Lower Secondary	15	X
		14	IX
		13	VIII
	Higher Primary	12	VII
		11	VI
		10	V
Elementary Stage	Lower Primary	9	IV
		8	III
		7	II
		6	I
	School Stage Begins	5+	-
		4+	-
		3+	-

After Purkait (1987)

(iii) *College/Higher Education*

Higher education starts after senior secondary education comprising of three stages of university (i) graduate (ii) post-graduate, and (iii) research/doctorate degree. According to the new pattern of secondary education, the higher education now starts from 13th class and the duration of graduate and post-graduate courses remains the same.

3.5.2.2 *Vocational/Technical/Professional Education*

The second stream of education prepares the students for vocational/technical/professional courses. It starts at the school level and is followed by courses upto graduation, post-graduation and research. At school levels after VIII and X classes, vocational/technical education of certificate/diploma courses of one to two years duration is given to students in the branches of industrial trades, teachers' training, engineering, medicine etc. The post-secondary vocational/technical education starts from XI class with two to three years duration of studies in relevant subjects. This type of education is imparted in Industrial Training Institutes and Polytechnics. The graduate and post-graduate courses are provided in technical and professional colleges

Parallel to the above formal system of education, the non-formal system of education/training also exists in the country. There are a number of institutions providing skill development in vocational/technical trades like engineering, agricultural extension para-medical services, crafts etc. and their training is recognised by the respective departments/ministries of Centre/State Governments.

The new pattern no doubt was a philosophy of its own. Education has to be related to the life. It must fulfil the needs and aspirations of the people and become a powerful instrument of social, economic and cultural transformation. With this end in view, the Education Commission has recommended the prevailing structural pattern.

Although the present educational structure has been introduced after a much thought, discussion and deliberation in different meetings, conferences and seminars at national level yet the system has inherent loopholes. The entire educational areas has been seriously affected by the change in structural pattern because secondary education is the pivotal stage in the academic system.

3.6 Women's Education

The role of education in the development of the traditional people has been very well stressed by educationists and sociologists. Education is needed for a cultural revolution as brought out by Iran Illich. According to Bane and Jancks, and Colemen, schools provide equal opportunities for children from unequal groups. Wynee has observed that it is through education alone that better socialization take place. Freire says that education is essential for creating awareness among the people. However, much of rural women's education depends upon the general conditions in the villages. Mridula, Ahuja and Bhatty have made certain useful comments on women's education in Indian situation. The education of girls and of women was regarded as the legitimate responsibility of Indians : it neither suited nor interested the rulers to take much initiative in this area. However, disparities in male-female literacy rates have clearly been pointed out by Mazumdar and Pandey.

Education is one of the most important factors which determines the status (both social & economic) of a person. For the purpose of getting any job the level of education plays a very significant role in determining one's suitability or otherwise. Literate women force constitutes an important input in the process of socio-economic development of a nation ; but the literacy among women in India still appears like a far fetched cry. However, the literacy rates in regard to males and females are given in Table 3.1 on next page.

It can be observed from the table (3.1) that literacy amongst women has gone up from 0.69 per cent in 1901 to 24.82 in 1981. The progress, statistically, is no doubt substantial but still in absoulte terms it is far from satisfactory. That is, still three-fourths of women are illiterate. Further, the pace of increase in percentage of literacy amongst females has been less than that of males. During the last 80 years the increase in percentage of literacy amongst males had increased by 37 percentage points whereas in case of females it had increased by 24 percentage points.

The literacy rates by sex and by rural and urban areas after independence are presented in Table 3.2 on next page.

It would be seen from the table (3.2) that the literacy amongst females in rural areas in only 17.9 per cent as against 47.8 per cent in Urban areas. This indicates that more efforts in regard to increasing

Table 3.1 : *Progress of Literacy Rates in India*

Census Year	Percentage of Literates to total population			
	Males		Females	
	%	Increase in a decade	%	Increase in a decade
1901 *	9.83	—	0.69	—
1911 *	10.56	6.73	1.05	0.36
1921 *	12.21	1.65	1.81	0.76
1931 *	15.59	3.38	2.93	1.12
1951 +	24.95	9.36	7.93	5.00
1961	34.44	9.49	12.95	5.02
1971	39.45	5.01	18.72	5.77
1981 + +	46.89	7.44	24.82	6.10

* For undivided India,
\+ Excludes Jammu & Kashmir
\+ + Excludes Assam.
Source : Census of India 1981, Key pop. stat.

Table 3.2 : *Literacy Rate (per cent) by sex and Locationtis India, 1951-81*

Location	Male				Female			
	1951	1961	1971	1981	1951	1961	1971	1981
Total	23.5	34.5 (46.8)	39.5 (14.5)	46.8 (18.6)	7.6	13.0 (17.1)	18.7 (43.8)	24.8 (32.7)
Rural	19.0	29.1 (53.1)	33.7 (16.0)	40.7 (20.8)	4.9	8.6 (75.5)	13.1 (52.1)	17.9 (37.3)
Urban	45.1	57.5 (24.4)	61.2 (6.5)	65.8 (7.5)	22.3	34.5 (54.7)	42.0 (21.8)	47.8 (13.7)

Note : Figures in brackets are percentages.

the literacy are required in the rural areas. However, a comparison of the sex ratios of literates in the age groups will indicate that the gap between the literacy rates of males and females is being steadily bridged. In the rural areas the sex ratio among literates, or the number of females per 1,000 males who are literates steadily increase towards the younger ages.

In view of the above discussions, it can be stated that the women lag far behind so far as the educational achievements of the women force in India are concerned. However, in the proceeding Chapter-5 we will review the progress of education made by both men and women at different levels of education i.e. elementary, secondary and higher education as well as in professional education and try to identify the tasks ahead.

3.7 Social Education in India

In India social education corresponds to adult education. But in the progressive countries it is more than adult education. In those countries, even the educated receive social education. For fullest development of an individual, social education is essential, Education is a life long process. At the end of formal education, social education can make an individual a true dutiful and responsible citizen.

By Social Education we mean education for the complete man. It gives him literacy, so that the knowledge of the world may become accessible to him. It will teach him how to harmonize himself with its environment and make the best use of physical condition in which he subsists. It is intended to teach him improved crafts and modes of production so that he can achieve economic betterment. It also aims at teaching him the rudiments of hygiene both for the individual and community, so that our domestic life may be healthy and prosperous. Lastly, this education should give him training in citizenship.

However, the Central Ministry of Education defined social education in 1963 in the following ways :

— Social Education is adult education. It means functional literacy.
— Social Education is education for desirable social changes.
— Social Education is education for the betterment of the individual's social economic, political and moral life.
— Social Education is education which enables a community to assure direction of its own development.
— Social Education is education for better work, better rest, better use of leisure and recreation.

INESCO named Social Education as fundamental education and defined it as—'The only means to elevate mankind emotionally, intellectually morally and materially'.

The Indian Education Commission (1964-66) has given three essential ingredients of social education[9] :

(i) It must be work based and aimed at creating attitudes and interests and imparting skills and information for efficient doing of a work.

(ii) It must create interest in the illiterate to participate actively in vital national problems and in the social and political life of the country.

(iii) It must impart such skills in reading, writing and arithmetic as would enable him, if he so wishes, to continue his education either on his own or through other available avenues of informal education.

Social Education Agencies in India :

— Literacy classes : They impart knowledge in SR's only

— Community Centres : They organise social survey, information processing, group discussion, crafts, hobbies etc.

— Youth Clubs : These clubs organise community living, games and sports etc.

— Mahila Samitis : They undertake such work as tailoring, knitting, child care, maternity welfare, mutrition, balanced diet, household skills.

— Janata Colleges : These are like popular colleges in Denmark. There are such colleges in Tripura, Manipura and Kalimpong. They train people in SUPW (socially useful productive work).

— National Social Service Scheme : Universities and colleges undertake this scheme. Various social service activities are organised under this scheme such as Adult Education, Population Education, Social Survey, Cleaning, Health Programme etc.

— Youth Festival and Film Festivals : They play a great role in promoting social education.

— Mass media of communication like Radio and T.V. also impart social education.

— NCERT : It has a department of Adult and Social Education which undertakes a large number of Social Education programmes.

— National of Adult Education

— Directorate of Adult Education attached to the Ministry.

The Union Ministry of HRD (Dept. of Ed.) initiates social education schemes. It does this work in co-operation with the Planning Commission. The different Central Ministries like Labour, Industry, Defence, Railway have their own social education programmes. The function of the Education department is mainly that of co-ordination, guidance and financial assistance. These works are conducted on the basis of the Reports of the State Governments and through the Central Advisory Board of Education which conducts conferences and meetings. The Union Ministry also gives financial assistance to voluntary organisations and State Governments for their social education work. It normally gives grants to run social education programmes for the production of books and teaching materials for adults and to conduct seminars etc. Each State Government has organisations at the state level as well as at the district levels. Most of the State Governments have either Directorates of Social and Adult Education or Social Education Boards. Each district has a District Officer and an Advisory Committee.

3.8 Adult Education in India

A literate person has greater access to knowledge, which will assist his personal improvement, than an illiterate one. From the national point of view the existence of a substantial proportion of illiterate adults in the manpower potential of a given country can be a bottleneck in its development.[10] Therefore, Adult Education is one of the most important and formidable issues in Indian education. The most urgent national need to our country today is the education of the adults who form the bulk of the population. More than 60 per cent of the fellow countrymen still live in the darkness of ignorance and illiteracy. In 1947, literacy in India was about 14 per cent and according to 1981 census it is 36 per cent. That means 64 per cent in India are illiterate. This is the highest percentage of illiteracy in a country in the world.

An adult falls within the age group of 15-45. But for all practical purposes importance is given to the age group 15-35. The term adult education is defined in different ways in different countries. Adult education also refers to some other connotations such as adult literacy, functional literacy, social education etc.

Adult education is imparted in two ways : Adult literacy and continuing education. Adult education is education for those adults who never had schooling before. Continuing education is education for those adults who have had some schooling or education before. Whereas in adult education, more stress is given on personal enrichment, in social education, social and civil efficiency and community development are emphasised.

However, the Government of India has given a very high priority to adult education. A National Adult Education Programme was launched in October, 1978 to cover 65 million (650) illiterate persons, in the age-group 15-35. About 7 lakhs adult education centres have been set up throughout the country.

A very high priority has been given to adult education in the sixth plan proposals. The total allocation proposed is Rs. 200 crores or 10 per cent of the total educational outlay. It was only 1.4 per cent in the fifth plan (18 crores). Different participating agencies employer groups and project authorities are also expected to finance adult education programme. The plan outlays for agriculture and rural development, includes provisions for Farmer's Function Literacy programmes.

3.9 Non-Formal Education in India

Non-formal education has been defined as organised and systematic education activity carried on outside the framework of the formal school system to provide selected types of leaving situations to particular subject groups in the population, adults as well as children. Non-formal education includes programmes such as agriculture, extension, farming community development, technical and vocational training etc. Such programmes are meant for youths, adults and for whom formal school education has either been inappropriate or unavoidable.[11]

The main objective of non-formal education is to ensure life oriented basic literacy and skill for the children of the age group 6-14 who are either unschooled or drop outs. Non-formal education aims at building up awareness, competence and confidence in the learners not only to solve their own problems but also to develop an attitude of critical thinking to be in a position to face life situation problems with necessary solution.[12] However, non-formal education is not a substitute for formal education. It supplements and reinforces formal education. It removes the rigidness inherent in the education system. For successful implementation non-formal education requires prior careful planning.

A number of agencies are at work in non-formal education programmes. These include both formal educational institutions like schools particularly, primary, colleges and universities, and special institutions for non-formal education. The former have tremendous potential for non-formal education. The latter are unique in character and specially suited for non-formal education.

Since the sixth plan there is a central sponsored scheme for running of non-formal education centres in the nine educationally backward states, viz., Uttar Pradesh, Jammu & Kashmir, Rajasthan, Madhya Pradesh, Andhra Pradesh, Bihar, Orissa, West Bengal and Assam. Under this scheme, assistance has been given to state Governments and voluntary agencies for setting up about 1.50 lakh centres.[13] In addition to the nine educationally backward states it is proposed to extend this scheme on the above pattern to all states in urban slums, hilly, desert and tribal areas and in projects for education of working children. The expenditure pattern in the scheme has been revised keeping in view the emphasis in the Education Policy on upgradation of the quality of NFE and the deficiencies observed in the evaluation of the programme undertaken by the Ministry.

However, the success of non-formal education programmes depend to a great extent on the degree of motivation on the part of the learners. Crores of illiterate people with some amount of education are to be educated through non-formal channels. Only the government in a developing country like ours with its limited resources cannot do this enduous task within a specified time.

3.10 Student Unrest

Since the 1960s, the effect of education explosion has been felt seriously, with the result that much has been written on various aspects of education. Student unrest being the most important problem has attracted the attention of the educationists and many seminars and symposiums have been held on this vital subject during this decade.

Education in the sense in which it is commonly understood is rarely imparted. The only concern of students is to pass their final examinations because without a piece of paper that entitles them to some mystic alphabets after their names, there is usually not even the prospect of a clerk's job. The piece of paper is usually granted not on fair test, on intelligence but of memory, and yet assumes an importance that is totally unrelated to its real worth. To obtain that piece of paper—a passport for a job—it would be seen students are willing to rob, cheat and kill. As the Education Commission recognised a long time ago, this is a problem that cannot be tackled without a radical overhaul of the entire educational structure and the social values that go with it.

Commenting upon the student unrest, strikes and violence in the country, the Hindustan Times observed in its editorial on 24th April, 1971 under the caption 'Murder is a matter of degree', "Human sacrifice has been banned in the country for several decades now. But rituals die hard, and substitutes are easily found. The recent substitute is the ritual of students sacrificing principals of colleges and invigilators in examination halls in their relentless pursuit of the externalia of higher education. On Monday there was one more instance of this. The Principal of Rajendra College, Chhapra (Bihar), was killed by a group of students in his office in broad daylight, while an invigilator who tried to do the job for which he was being paid escaped with minor injuries. No doubt this is meant to go out as a warning to all invigilators and principals. If you care for your skin, do not try to stop us from cheating. And if cheating in examinations does not produce the required results, no doubt a similar fate awaits those who mark examination papers."

A variety of causes has been suggested for student unrest since independence. Some of these are historical and are related with the events preceding independence. It is difficult to assign any one key cause to student agitation in the post independence period. In most of the cases the local grievances stimulated a demonstration or protest. However, based on an analysis of some 200 strikes and demonstrations the following causes of student unrest are listed :

I. *Academic* : This includes the following :

(i) Lack of proper academic atmosphere
(ii) Defective examination system
(iii) Bookish and un-inspiring curriculum.
(iv) Raise in tuition fees
(v) Lack of individual contact between the teacher and student.
(vi) Defective admission and attendance rules
(vii) Lack of amenities
(viii) Lack of hostel facilities

(ix) Lack of library facilities
(x) Lack of motivation among students.

II. *Administration*

(i) Double standards of the authorities and corruption at the highest echelons of administration.
(ii) Lack of sympathy for students
(iii) Non-involvement of students in University affairs.

III. *Political*

(i) Political interference in admissions, appointments etc.
(ii) Political interference in Union elections.

IV. *General*

(i) Lack of ideals in the society.
(ii) Lack of commitment on the part of university teachers.
(iii) Teachers in-fighting.
(iv) Ideological frustration.
(v) Lack of respect for authority—parental, governmental and educational.
(vi) Increase in bus fare etc.
(vii) Inadequate transport facilities and lack of mutual understanding between the bus crew and the students and the police.
(viii) Lack of employment opportunities.

In solving the student problems the following remedial measures may be discussed under the following heads :

— students participation in administrative and other matters.
— curriculum reform
— examination reform
— employment opportunities and other related problems.
— role of student advisory bureaus.
— national services scheme.
— role of student organisations in university life.

However, we need to treat the students as adults, give them respect and channelise their latent potentialities for the reconstruction of the nation. Students' involvement in matters relating to welfare activities, hostel management, sports and union affairs should be encouraged. But in academic matters teachers should help them and guide them. We should treat the university as a unit. Any attempt at polarisation and conflict between teachers, students and the administration should be avoided. What is needed at this critical juncture is to generate a climate of fraternity among students, teachers and administrative staffs based on mutual respect and understanding.

3.11 Summing-up

During colonial period education served to the advantage of the upper and middle strata of the society. But emphasis was laid on the importance of mass education based on the tradition of the nation and its needs and aspirations. The National Council of Education (1906) was broad-based and comprehensive. Its scheme of studies was to be imparted in three stages, viz., (a) primary—3 years course (6-9), (b) Secondary—7 years course (9-15) and (c) collegiate—4 years course (16-19). On the whole this system of education was condemned as academic and too literary.

After independence it was felt that in the field of education a change in pattern and content of educational set-up is must. The present experiment has not been introduced all of a sudden but it is the product of historical developments. Rather it is the results of successive experiments before and after independence. However, the entire period of formal education has been divided into two main stages, viz., school education and higher education. Education is further classified into two major categories, viz., (a) General Education and (b) Vocational/Technical/Professional Education. The C.A.B.E. strongly recommended the introduction of the 10+2+3 pattern of education all over the country during the fifth plan period. The National Education Policy has suggested twelve years of school education and three-year undergraduate course. Where a university desires, it could have a two-year pass course and three-year honours course. By 1980 this pattern had been introduced in almost all states and Union Territories of India. This structural pattern of education has tremendously affected the entire field of education—secondary, higher secondary, collegiate and university education.

At the end of formal education social education can make an individual a true, dutiful and responsible citizen. For fullest development of an individual social education is essential; however, the Union Ministry of HRD (Department of Education) initiates social education schemes in co-operation with the Planning Commission. The different Central Ministries like Labour, Industry, Defence, Railway have their social education programmes.

A little less than two-third or 64 per cent people in India are illiterate. Therefore, the Government of India has given a very high priority to adult education. About 65 million (650 lakhs) illiterate persons in the age-group 15-35 have been covered through National Adult Education Programmes, and 7 lakhs adult education centres have been set-up throughout the country.

To ensure life oriented basic literacy and skill for the children of the age group 6-14 and to supplement and reinforce formal education, non-formal education has been initiated in the nine educationally backward states since the sixth plan. In this scheme, assistance has been given to state governments and voluntary agencies for setting up about 1.50 lakh centres. Later on, it is proposed to extend this scheme to ten more educationally backward states.

However, the success of both, non-formal and social education programmes, depends to a great extent on the degree of motivation on the part of the learners.

Problems and Suggestions

The pattern of education which India inherited at the time of its independence did not suit its need. Each stage in education is linked to the next one without any terminal stage. As a consequence there has been an ever increasing pressure for the provision of university education. A developing country like India can ill afford expansion of expensive university education when it has not been able to provide universal primary education to its children in fulfilment of the constitutional provisions.

The products turned out by the educational system are not in tune with needs of the country. The educated persons have looked down upon manual work and held white collar jobs in greater esteem ; they have preferred wage employment to self employment. Consequently expansion of educational facilities has been accompanied by an increase in educated unemployment which the government is finding it difficult to solve by creating more white collar jobs and wage employment opportunities.

Therefore, instead of solving unemployment problem the educational system is accentuating it. The change in attitude of the students, the dignity of manual work and a preference for self-employment can be brought about though introduction of vocational bias in education.

Another question is whether education should be narrow based vocational education in secondary schools or be balanced between theoretical learning and practical experience in all branches of educational system.

In order to provide education and training and developing skills, provision of vocational education is essential. Besides the development planning envisages an increase in productivity of labour engaged in different sectors of the economy. This can come about only by providing vocational education to the people engaged in work or who are to join the work.

Notes and References

1. B.R. Purkait (1987). *New Education in India*. The Associated Publishers, Ambala, p. 49.
2. *Ibid*, p. 64.
3. *Ibid*, p. 66.
4. *Ibid*, p 226.
5. Y.L. Ahuja, S. Kulkarni & H. Sharma (1988). *Active Education Policy for Skill Development*. Theme Paper of the Seminar, IAMR, New Delhi, Unpublished, p. 7
6. Purkait, *op. cit*, p. 73
7. *Ibid*, p. 73.
8. *Ibid*, p. 226.
9. Report of the Education Commission, 1964-66. *Education & National Development*. Ministry of Education, Govt. of India, p. 425.
10. J.C. Aggarwal (1982). *Development and Planning of Modern Education*, Vikas Publishing House, New Delhi, p. 308.
11. An interview Report of the Non-formal Education Centre, Kilkevi, Delhi, for the year 1977-79. Dept. of School Education, NCERT.
12. Status Reports of Non-Formal Education from some states in India, Dept. of School Education, NCERT, 1978, p. 88.
13. Govt. of India, Min. of HRD, Dept. of Education. *Non-formal Education*, New Delhi, 1988, p. 3.

4 Source of Educational Statistics and their Limitations

4.1 Introduction

For proper appraisal and an effective planning of the educational system, it is imperative to have a strong and up-to-date information system. There is not only the need for generation of statistics but their presentation in a systematic manner to facilitate decision-making for the decision makers like, government officials, technocrats and employers of labour. All these people are likely to be helped by having information relevant to their action in the educational sphere.

Availability of reliable quantitative as well as qualitative data for purposes of planning hardly needs to be emphasized. That such data should be available on time is also of equal significance. However, modern goals raises a multiplicity of problems for the educational planners/policy makers and leads to demands for particular pieces of information. The major problem areas where information is vital and required are :

— For the objective of literacy, one needs to know not only the age and educational attainment by regional distribution of the population but also the cost-effectiveness of different available technologies for improving literacy.

— For the objective of economic growth and manpower needs, one must have good knowledge of the links between education and the economic system, plus a host of other parameters depending on the particular methodology one wishes to follow (e.g., manpower forecasting or rate of return etc.).

— For the objective of employment, one must know the labour force participation and unemployment rates of the educated.

— Social demand satisfaction necessitates through knowledge of population dynamics and people's responses to economic and other incentives (e.g., fellowship, grants, tuition fees and educational loans).
— Regional concerns require disaggregation of many national statistics by geographic area.
— The objective of democratization and equality of opportunity presupposes disaggregation of national statistics by sex, by socio-economic categories and population (e.g., tribal or ethnic) groups.

Most of the statistical information in terms of the modern goals of manpower and educational planning are not readily available in our country. However, keeping in view the relevance and importance of statistical information, an attempt has been made in this section to give an account of organisational arrangements for the collection of data, gaps and deficiencies in the collection of data, and suggestions for improving the existing situation. The major sources of data on education system are listed below :

4.2 Source of Educational Statistics and their Limitations

Data Availability

The data about the total stock, its classification according to various characteristics and for both school and collage level are available with a number of sources. These are :

(i) Ministry of Human Resource Development, Department of Education
(ii) University Grant Commission (UGC)
(iii) National Council of Educational Research and Training
(iv) Census of India
(v) Directorate General of Employment and Training (DGE&T)
(vi) National Sample Survey (NSS) and
(vii) Technical/Professional Bodies

On all the sources, the Ministry of HRD, Department of Education is the most important and is the head of information on a variety of educational items. It is the oldest and the most comprehensive source of information. Since 1949-50, the Ministry has been collecting and publishing comprehensive and detailed statistics of the entire educational system on an annual basic with certain changes and improvements from time to time. As regards university and college education, detailed statistics are available from U.G.C. report since 1961-62. However, above mentioned sources adopt varying concepts and reference periods and differ in coverage and described below separately.

4.2.1 MINISTRY OF HRD, DEPARTMENT OF EDUCATION

The Planning Monitoring of the Ministry has been collecting information on all types of educational institutions including those of higher education through the State Education Department. The State Education Departments collect these statistics from various institutions. Thus, the levels of aggregation are :

(a) Block Level
(b) District Level
(c) State Level
(d) National level which is done by the Ministry

It brings out annually the publications entitled—

— Education in India
— Selected Educational Statistics and
— A Head Book of Educational and Allied Statistics

'Education in India' surveys the progress of education in country annually. It deals with almost all aspects of education and educational institutions. It gives detailed statistics likely to be of interest to planners, educationists, educational administrators and students of education. The last report was published* for the year 1982-83 and it provides data on:

(*a*) *Educational Institutions*

 (i) Number of Institutions by Management
 (ii) State/Union Territory
 (iii) Male/Female
 (iv) Level/Stage
 (v) Rural/Urban

(b) *Enrolment* (General, Professional, Vocational and other education)

* Education in India, Vol. I upto 1982-83, Vol. II upto 1979-80 and Vol. III upto 1979.

(i) Male/Female
(ii) State/Union Territory
(iii) Level/Stage
(iv) Type of Award
(v) Rural/Urban
(vi) Age

(*c*) *Number of Teachers*

(i) State/Union Territory
(ii) Male/Female
(iii) Level/Stage
(iv) Type of Institution
(v) Trained/Untrained
(vi) Teacher/Pupil ratio
(vii) Rural/Urban
(viii) Faculty/Discipline

(*d*) *Cost of Education*

(i) Expenditure by items and types of institutions.
(ii) Income by sources and type of institutions.
(iii) Recurring/Non-recurring expenditure/income by item and states/U.Ts.

'Selected Educational Statistics' publishes summary results on provisional basis in its annual publication. This brochure replaces the previous publication entitled 'Educational Statistics at a Glance'. It provides data on :

(A) *Number of Institutions*

(i) State/Union Territory
(ii) Male/Female
(iii) Levels of General Education
(iv) Trained/Untrained teachers

(B) *Enrolments*

(i) State/Union Territory
(ii) Stages/Classes.
(iii) Enrolment ratio in classes I-V and VI-VIII of Schools of General Education
(iv) Enrolment by Type of Institutions

(C) *Budget Expenditure on Education & Other Departments*

The third source i.e. 'A Hand Book of Educational and Allied Statistics'* is the first one in the series which is brought out by the Ministry periodically. The important statistics covered by this publication are as follows :

(*a*) *Number of Institutions*

- (i) State/Union Territory
- (ii) Time Series
- (iii) Level/State
- (iv) Type of Institution
- (v) Male/Female

(*b*) *Enrolment and Teachers*

- (i) State/Union Territory
- (ii) Stages/Sex
- (iii) Type of Institutions
- (iv) Enrolment in General and Professional Education
- (v) SC/ST
- (vi) Teacher-Pupil Ratio
- (vii) Growth by Stages
- (viii) Trained/Untrained Teachers
- (ix) Retention Rate

(*c*) *Other Information*

- (i) Information about infrastructural facilities
- (ii) Expenditure on Education
- (iii) Plan Outlay and expenditure on education during various plans.

Limitations :

As mentioned earlier the Ministry of Human Resource Development, Department of Education collect a variety of educational items but there are some limitations of the available data. These are :

— Data on institutions by management are not available for the period 1971-72 to 1975-76.

— Data on enrolment by levels of education, age and sex for vocational education are not available for the period 1971-72 onwards.

* Available upto 1986-87.

— Data on teachers by age-group and subject of specialisation are not available.
— Sanctioned strength and actually filled for reserved categories of teachers is not available.
— Data pertaining to teachers engaged in informal sector are not available.
— Data on emigration of teachers are not available.
— Time gap in the actual collection and publication of data is substantial.
— Number of teachers by different manage is not a available.

4.2.2 UNIVERSITY GRANTS COMMISSION (U.G.C.)

University Grants Commission started collection of educational statistics on a systematic basis from the academic session 1961-62. The Commission published report entitled 'University Development in India—Basic Fasts and Figures' Part I and provides information annually, latest 1983-84, on higher education, i.e., University level. The following information are available in the report:

(*a*) *Institutions classified by :*

(i) Type of Institution and State/Union Territory
(ii) Location (Rural/Urban)
(iii) Type of course
(iv) Management

(*b*) *Enrolment by :*

(i) University and State/Union Territory
(ii) Faculty, University and State/Union Territory
(iii) Levels/Stages, Faculty and State/Union Territory
(vi) Class and Faculty
(v) Women enrolment in University by Levels and Faculty
(vi) Subject-wise enrolment at post-graduate level (M.A. & M.Sc.)

(*c*) *Outturn by :*

(*i*) University and State/Union Territory
(*ii*) Level/Stages and Faculty
(*iii*) Class and Faculty
(*vi*) M.A./M.Sc. results/subject-wise and university-wise
(*v*) Outturn by type of institution.

U.G.C. Publication 'University Development in India—Basic Facts & Figures' Part II provides information for college level teacher's training facilities by individual universities/institutions, their enrolment and outturn also.

The U.G.C. collects statistics directly from Principals of colleges and Registrars of Universities through a proforma designed for the purpose. So far as Registrars of Universities are concerned, information is collected only in respect of university departments and colleges directly under the control of the universities.

Limitations :

— Subject-wise enrolment data at post-graduate level by sex are not available.
— Speciality-wise data in professional education and separate examination results for private and regular students are not available.
— U.G.C. do not provide data on teachers by age-group and subject of specialisations (in the absence of which demand arising out of attrition cannot be worked out correctly).
— Experience profile of teachers is not available.
— Information on salary group of teachers is not available.
— Data on Rural/Urban and Inter-state migration of teachers are not available.
— Data for sanctioned and strength of reserved seats of actually filled-in is not available.

4.2.3 National Council of Educational Research and Training (NCERT)

Educational surveys play an important role in the planning of educational facilities. The NCERT has conducted four surveys in collaboration with the Ministry in different span of time which is mentioned below :

— First All-India Educational Survey was in 1957.
— Second in 1965
— Third in 1973
— Fourth in 1978 and
— Fifth in 1989

Realising the importance of the teacher in the educational process and in the national efforts to improve the quality of education, detailed information has been collected regarding the qualification, both general and professional, teachers working in schools and also age and experience of untrained teachers working in schools at primary, middle and secondary levels. The first and second All India Educational Survey collected limited information about teachers. The Third All India Educational Survey was conducted in 1973 with a view to provide useful information to educational administrators and academicians who are concerned about the supply of qualified teachers to the ever-increasing number of primary, secondary and higher secondary schools in the country.

In this survey a large amout of factual data about teachers in primary, middle, secondary and higher secondary schools have been collected on various dimensions such as male/female teachers working in rural and urban areas, management of schools, teachers' qualification, training status, age, experiences, emoluments, participation in service education programme, tenure and mobility, their competence and its utilization, particularly with reference to science teaching etc. Special efforts have been made to study the status of teachers belonging to SC/ST. In addition, the Third All India Educational Survey also covered technical and vocational education of school level. The NCERT has also conducted the Fourth All India Educational Survey in 1978 on :

— Teachers in schools for general education in India by states and organisation and training status.
— Percentage of female teachers to teachers in school for general education.
— Teachers in schools for general education in India by status and SC/ST.

The reference date for most of the data except where it is explicitly mentioned is 31st December of survey year. The source of data collection about the teachers was the information supplied by the teachers themselves in a specially designed proforma.

Limitations :

— In all the four surveys data have been collected only for school education.

4.2.4 Census of India

As a part of decennial census, information on education is available through this source. In 1981 census, the data on teachers are available at three digit level of occupation and one digit level of industrial categories for total and urban India by sex and states. It provides distribution of persons holding degree in teaching by broad age-groups, state and sex for urban areas only based on educational details collected through individual slips. Broadly, the decennial census of 1961, 1971 and 1981 provides data on education by :

(i) Levels of education
(ii) Type (in case of college education)
(iii) Rural/Urban
(vi) Sex
(v) State/Union Territory

Limitations :

— Detailed information by educational levels is not available for rural areas as is available for urban areas.
— Data on trained/untrained teachers are not available.
— Separate information pertaining to diploma holders and certificate holders in teaching is not available.
— Data on graduate and post-graduate degree holders in teaching is not available.
— Data on teachers by subject of specialisation are not available.
— The information on length of experience of teachers is not available.

4.2.5 Directorate General of Employment and Training (DGE&T)

The DGE&T has been collecting data on educational institutions and intake capacity since 1958-59. The DGE&T published 'A Handbook on Training Facilities' (Institutional Training) annually and latest handbook available is for 1982, which provides data on :

— Number of institutions by trade, State/Union Territory and Management.
— Sanctioned/intake capacity by institution, trade and course of each State/Union Territory and course duration and minimum admission requirement.

Its second publication 'Employment Review' provides information for all the categories of teachers according to NCO at three digit level who are seeking employment and are registered with Employment Exchange. The following data are available for 1982-83.

(i) Type of Occupation
(ii) State/Union Territory
(iii) Male/Female
(iv) Vacancies outstanding/modified/filled.

Limitations

— Enrolment and outturn data are not available.
— Since the registration with the Employment Exchange is voluntary, all the unemployed persons especially in rural areas might not have registered with the Employment Exchanges.
— Some registered persons might have been working already and they are registered only for better jobs.
— Changes of double counting is there as a person can get himself/herself registered at more than one place.

4.2.6 NATIONAL SAMPLE SURVEY ORGANISATION (NSS)

The National Sample Survey Organisation has been conducting survey in its various demands and collecting some basic information on education. The latest report of 1983 provides data at all India level on :

(i) Level of education
(ii) Sex
(iii) Age
(iv) Rural/Urban

4.2.7 TECHNICAL/PROFESSIONAL BODIES

The following technical and professional bodies also provide some relevant information:

(*a*) Indian Council of Agricultural Research (ICAR)

(i) number of agricultural veterinary colleges by state
(ii) enrolment
(iii) Outturn for different courses

(*b*) Directorate General of Health Services (DGHS)

(i) number of colleges by state
(ii) students admitted
(iii) outturn of medical colleges

(*c*) Medical Council of India

(i) number of students admitted in the medical colleges
(ii) outturn of MBBS doctors by state.

(*d*) Dental Council of India.

(i) number of dental colleges by states
(ii) intake (in the bachelor of dental surgery course by state).

(*e*) India Pharmacy Council

(i) number of pharmaceutical colleges
(ii) intake data in degree and diploma courses in pharmacy
(iii) outturn data on degree and diploma courses in pharmacy

(*f*) Indian Nursing Council

(i) number of institutions of different types of training.
(ii) enrolment in training institutions for different nursing courses, e.g., ANM and Health Visitors course by state.

Non affiliate institutions shall provide consistency checks on the data being generated by the two sources. In addition there are some significant gaps in the existing statistics on education which are as follows:

— Time lag in the collection and publication of data
— Variation in the reference period of different sources
— Variation in concepts.

4.3 **Related Issues**

An analysis of the existing data sources reveals that there are a number of issues which need to be sorted out so as to build a sound data base for planning purposes. These issues are :

— Non-availability of a speciality-wise data on educational institutions in the formal sector;
— Lack of data on intake for each class for course/subject with further break-up as freshers and repeaters;

— Non-availability of data on number of attempts made by students appearing privately and of certain examining bodies;
— The Ministry and UGC mainly collect data on education but there is no uniformity in their coverage and concept;
— Lack of data on teachers by specialization in various categories of institutions operating in the informal sector;
— Lack of data on teachers leaving teaching profession;
— Lack of information on rural-urban migration of teachers; and
— Lack of information on the cost of education, specially in the institutions operating in the informal sector.

4.4 Suggestions and Recommendations for Improvement of Statistical Information

A number of sources and publications provide information on education even though they adopt varying concepts and reference periods and differ in coverage too thus making the data quite often uncomparable. The need for comprehensive up-to-date data is becoming increasingly imperative in the context of formulation of policies and developmental programmes, while the collection of educational statistics has become a complex and time consuming process. The following suggestions/recommendations may be given under different heads for the improvement of the data.

(*i*) *Institutions :* Separate data for teaching institutions which prepare students and conduct examinations leading to award of degree, diploma, certificate and non-teaching institutions which simply conduct examination should be given.

(*ii*) *Intake/Enrolement :* Enrolment data for professional and technical courses should be published individual course-wise and subject-wise each year. Secondly, intake data should be given for each class for course/subject which further break up as freshers and repeaters. Thirdly, intake capacity as well as actual intake may be made available for each course and subject of each discipline/faculty at various stages/levels for different types of institutions whether recognized/not recognised for formal/non-formal sector. Further details such as rural/urban sex, SC/ST etc. may also be given.

(*iii*) *Outturn :* (a) There are certain examining bodies, whose outturn is not recorded by the Ministry of HRD, Department of Education or any other agency, for instance, Institution of Engineers, Institute of Chartered Accountants of India etc. The same should be made available; (b) Age-wise outturn data should be made available for different stages and levels of education; and (c) Separate information about number of students appearing privately and casually in High//H.S./Degree/Diploma examinations and passing out should be available by course, sex, type of education and State/Union Territory.

(*iv*) *Concept & Coverage :* The Ministry of HRD, Department of Education—(i) Find Arts, Music and Dancing, Painting and Sculpture (ii) Modern Indian Languages, Oriental Learning as professional education and other education. UGC, however, treats all these courses of items (i) and (ii) as General Education Course, and UGC also includes commerce under professional education. Both the sources should adopt uniformity in coverage and concept.

(*v*) *Teachers :* Data on teachers should be available by educational qualification, subject of specialisation and experience for each State/Union Territory.

(*vi*) *Cost of Education :* Data on cost of education (both recurring and non-recurring) by item and type of institutions for informal sector should be made available.

(*vii*) *General :* (a) The NCERT should concentrate on the collection of data for the informal and non-formal system of education. It should collect details of erolment and outturn by type and levels of education. (b) Since the information an enrolment and examination results of University teaching departments, colleges and institutions deemed to be universities is collected by the UGC, so the same should not be collected by the Ministry. This will remove duplication of effort and reduce the delay in the publications of data. (c) Data on non-formal education imparted by unrecognised institutions in trades, viz., typing, stenography, book-keeping etc. should be collected and published by the Ministry. (d) There should be a Data Bank for collection, storage and retrieval of the entire educational statistics covering both the General and Vocational/Professional/Technical education whether imparted under the formal or the non-formal system. The Data Bank can be a part of the Ministry of HRD, Department of Education, which as a centralised agency will also take care of the statistics maintained by various technical/vocational/professional councils/bodies.

It may also be added have that while trying to increase the flow of additional data to fill up the data gaps, it must be ensured that the comparability and consistency in data is maintained.

5 Educational Development in India

5.1 Introduction

The expansion of educational facilities during the last four decades of planned development has been the impact of education phenomenal, although encouraging. The failure on this front is generally recognised as an outcome, on the one hand, of the distortions introduced during the colonial period and of the infirmities and limitations of the current development strategies, on the other. With the beginning of development planning, India entered into a new era of educational development attended by unprecedented social response. The system gradually recovered from the impact of stagnation of two centuries of colonial rule. However, the process of educational development like economic development, in its true character was neither homogeneous in regional spread, nor neutral to social formation. The disparities in educational development may be seen with the help of literacy rate. The literacy rate in 1981 (census data) is as high as 69.17 per cent in Kerala and as low as 20.09 per cent in Arunachal Pradesh.

However, ever since independence various high level commissions and committees, one after other, recommended the need for the minimisation of regional disparities and value orientation of education. The Education Commission mentioned that the balance has to be struck between knowledge and skills which science and technology bring with the values and insights associated with ethics and religion at its best, namely to quote the poetic language of the commission "a search for the knowledge of the self, of the meaning of life, of the relationship of man to other beings and to the ultimate reality".

Education is the foundation on which rests the edifice of society and democracy. Illiteracy constitutes a major hurdle in the way of rapid social, political and economic developments of the country.[1]

The role of education in the development of the traditional people has been very well stressed by educationists and sociologists. Education may mean formal or non-formal education. Formal education means learning in the structured school setting. It is necessarily organised and the vast bulk of formal education either receives state support or is organised by the state itself. Non-formal education would be learning in any organised setting which takes place apart from the specific school programme.[2] Which of these two systems is more utilitarian is a matter of opinion. It all depends upon the conditions under which the people receive education. For those who have already crossed the normal age-limits for formal education, non-formal education is the only alternative. 'Non-formal education specially if viewed as a set of alternative to the formal systems of education, offers a way to devise as effective approach of learning and education'.[3]

The National Policy on Education pointed out that the greater lenders of the Indian freedom movement realised the fundamental role of education and stressed the unique significance of education for national development.[4] And the New Education Policy (1986) has been acclaimed to facilitate social, economic and academic life of our country.[5] Apart from other issues the government has also focused its attention on the student's unrest—causes, type of students involved and its impact on national development.[6]

The present exercise is a response to the need for an authentic aid to the persons who are engaged in educational development, policy making and planning in India.[7] This exploration of the educational development, policies and planning will eventually pave the way towards a serious search for explanatory models.[8]

5.2 Growth of Educational Facilities

Since independence, the growth of education has been phenomenal. A massive quantitative expansion is evidenced at all levels. The number of recognised institutions has increased from 2,31,000 in 1951 to an estimated 7,55,000 in 1984-85. The total enrolment over the same period in these institutions increased from 24 million to nearly 132 million.[9] The national stock of educated manpower is estimated to have increased from less than 4 million to about 48 million. The facilities have not only increased but also diversified at all levels. The enrolment for post-graduate studies, for instance, has grown from a mere 20,000 in 1951 to over 300,00 by

1984-85. The enrolment in science subjects only has increased from 4,400 to about 7,300. Extensive facilities are also available for education in different branches of engineering and technology.[10]

The regional inbalance in respect of educational facilities has been correct and progress towards equality of educational opportunity has been achieved to some extent. The Central and State budgets on education have increased more than fifty times over the last 35 years, from Rs. 114 crores in 1950-51 to more than Rs. 6,000 crores in 1984-85.[11] In order to remove all the imbalances and disparities in all the sectors of education, a National System of Education is created. The National System of Education envisages a comman educational structure of 10+2+3 that has already been implemented in all the states. Adequate provisions have been made in the policy for education of scheduled castes, scheduled tribes, minorities and handicapped; the idea being to bring them at the pace with the rest of the population. However the other priority areas comprise of elementary education, secondary education, vocationalisation of education and adult education.

Educational development in terms of number of institutions, enrolment and expenditure incurred on plan and non-plan outlay from 1950-51 to 1984-85 is presented in Table 5.1 & 5.2. It is evident that between 1951, the number of primary schools increased from approximately 210 thousand to 550 thousand and the number of upper primary schools from 30 thousand to 130 thousand, yet there are large number of habitations without primary schools and one-third of schools in rural area have only one teacher. The emphasis has been on enrolment of approximately 95 per cent children in 6-11 age and 50 per cent in 11-14 age group are enrolled in schools. However, nearly 60 per cent children drop out between classes I-V and 75 per cent between classes I-VIII. It shall be ensured that all children who attain the age of about 11 years by 1990 will have had five years of schooling or its equivalent through non-formal stream. Likewise by 1995 all children will be provided free and compulsory education upto 14 years of age.

There were approximately 60 thousand secondary/higher secondary schools and 140 thousand upper primary schools in 1984-85 giving a ratio of 1 : 2.5. There are unserved areas in the country where there is no school within the range of 10 to 20 kilometers.

Table 5.1 : *Educational Development from 1950-51 to 1984-85*

Sl. No.	Item	Year				
		1950-51 (Actual)	1960-61 (Actual)	1970-71 (Actual)	1980-81 (Actual)	1984-85 (Provisional)
A.	*Institutions* (Number)					
(i)	Primary	2,09,671	3,30,399	4,08373	4,85,538	5,50,000*
(ii)	Middle	13,596	49,663*	90,621	1,16,447	1,40,000*
(iii)	High/Higher Secondary	7,288	17,257	36,738	15,594	60,000*
(iv)	College					
	(*a*) Art, Science & Commerce	548	1,161	2,587	3,393	3,500*
	(*b*) Professional	147	381	1,017	1,382	1,500*
	(*c*) Universities & Deemed Univ.	28	44	93	123	135
B.	*Enrolment* (in '000)					
(i)	Primary (I-V classes)	19,155	34,994	57,045	72,688	85,377
		(42.6)	(62.4)	(76.4)	(83.1)	(91.84)
(ii)	Middle (V-VII classes)	3,120	6,705	13,315	19,846	26,729
		(12.5)	(22.5)	(34.2)	(40.0)	(50.07)

(iii) High/Higher Secondary/Intermediate	1,481	3,483	7,167	11,281	16,800
	(5.3)	(10.6)	(19.0)	(25.2)	(33.2)
(iv) University & Above (Ist Degree)	174	557	1,956	2,752	3,442*
C. *Expenditure* (in crores of Rs.)					
(i) Plan	20	90	115	520	800
(ii) Non-Plan	94	254	1,003	3,226	5,200
Total	114	344	1,118	3,746	6,000
Proportion of GNP (%)	1.2	2.5	3.1	4.6	—

*Estimates,

Source : (*i*) For School Education & Expenditure—Min. of HRD, Deptt. of Education & Planning Comm.
(*ii*) For Higher Education. UGC, Reports.

Note : Figures in brackets indicate Gross Enrolment Ratios, as %age to total population in each category.

Table 5.2 : *Growth* in Educational Institutions, Enrolment and Expenditure Since Independence*

Sl. No.	Item	Becenial Growth			
		1950-51 over 1960-61	1960-61 over 1970-71	1970-71 over 1980-81	Growth in 35 years
A. *Institutions*					
(i)	Primary	57.57	23.59	18.89	162.31
(ii)	Middle	265.27	82.47	28.49	929.71
(iii)	High/Higher Secondary	136.78	112.88	40.43	723.27
(iv)	College (*a*) Art, Science Comm.	111.86	122.82	31.15	538.68
	(*b*) Professional	159.18	166.92	35.88	920.40
	(*c*) Univ. & Deemed Univ.	57.14	111.36	32.25	382.14
B. *enrolment*					
(i)	Primary (I-V classes)	82.68	63.01	27.42	345.71
(ii)	Middle (VI-VIII classes)	114.90	98.58	49.04	756.69
(iii)	High/Higher Secondary/Intermediate	135.17	105.77	57.40	103.43
(iv)	University & above (1st Degree)	220.11	251.16	40.69	187.81
C. *Expenditure*					
(i)	Plan	35.00	27.77	352.17	3900.00
(ii)	Non-Plan	190.47	294.88	221.63	5431.91
	Total	201.75	225.00	235.06	5163.15

* Calculated by Author.

The policy relating to secondary education implies extension of the school education in the unserved areas consolidating the existing facilities and providing special arrangements for the gifted children and the high achievers.

For this the State Governments would be persuaded to open secondary schools in unserved areas taking blocks as a unit, having lower ratio than 1 : 2.5 duly considering the present distance of habitations. It is proposed that by 200 A.D. the unserved areas will be fully served. The programme of vocationalisation of higher secondary education was initiated in 1976 and has been implemented by all the states. The intake in the vocational stream was about 72 thousand in 1984-85 covering only 2.5 per cent of students population entering higher secondary stage. It is proposed that vocational courses would cover over 10 per cent of higher secondary students by 1990 and 20 per cent by 1995. For achieving these targets, steps will be taken to see that a substantial majority of products of vocational courses are employed or become self employed.

In higher education science teaching and research have been accorded high priority. The New Policy has proposed to give greater autonomy to the educational institutions. The rigidity of the university system will be smoothened and appropriate linkages will be provided between government, industry, research organisations and universities.

The National Policy on Education, 1986, envisages that adult education would be a means for reducing economic, social and gender disparities. The main objective of the new National Programme of Adult Education is to provide education including literacy to the population in 15-35 age-group, which numbers about 100 million. The programme of literacy, however, can become meaningful only when they come along with a package comprising practical information and skills relevant to day-to-day needs of learners.

The educational facilities in the country have increased tremendously. It is evident from the Table 5.3 that growth over the period of 35 years in number of institutions is maximum (929.71) at middle stage followed by 920.40 in professional institutions. Whereas the minimum growth is witnessed in primary institutions i.e. 162.31. The maximum growth in middle institutions resulted in growth in the maximum enrolments (756.69) of pupils in classes VI-VII. But same is not the case with college levels enrolments.

As far as growth in expenditure is concerned over the period of 35 years, it has been changed tremendously. The growth in expenditure is high (5431.91) in non-plan sector as compared to plan.

The decenial growth of number of institutions on the whole, is higher in first and second decades after independence (i.e. 1950-51 over 1960-61 and 1960-61 over 1970-71). And same is the case with enrolments. But in case of expenditure it is high in the last decade i.e. 1970-71 over 1980-81. (Fig. 1).

However, looking at growth table one can conclude that in general educational facilities in the country have increased. But the same time it is also observed that quality-wise it has not been able to serve the requisite purpose. Still the country is facing acute problem of massive illiteracy, failure to universalise elementary education, slow progress with vocationalisation of education and unemployment among the educated persons.

After independence, the spread of literacy has been one of the most important programmes launched by the Government. As a result, between 1951 and 1981 the percentage of literacy improved from 16.7 per cent to 36.2 per cent. The literacy rates of females had no doubt improved during this period from 7.9 per cent to 24.8 per cent but they are much lower than that of males (Table 5.4). However, in absolute number of illiterate persons have increased during this period from 300 million to 437 million. Women comprise of 3.57 per cent of the illiterate population. According to the UNESCO[12] illiterates (in the age group of 15-59 years) will continue to grow to reach 41.9 million in 2000 A.D. compared with 26.4 million in 1970 unless political, economic and social factors prove enough to reverse the trend.

To achieve the ultimate goal of literacy and universalisation of elementary education, the major problem is of retaining the students upto a standard that a minimum knowledge of literacy and numeracy is attained at which they do not further lapse into illiteracy. This phenomenon refers to the problem of dropout. The dropout rate for girls and boys in the year 1979-80 is noted to be 63.7 per cent and 57.3 per cent from classes I to V and 81.7 per cent and 73.5 per cent from classes I to VIII. It is observed that dropout rate among girls at primary and middle stages is more than among boys. To have

Fig. 5.1

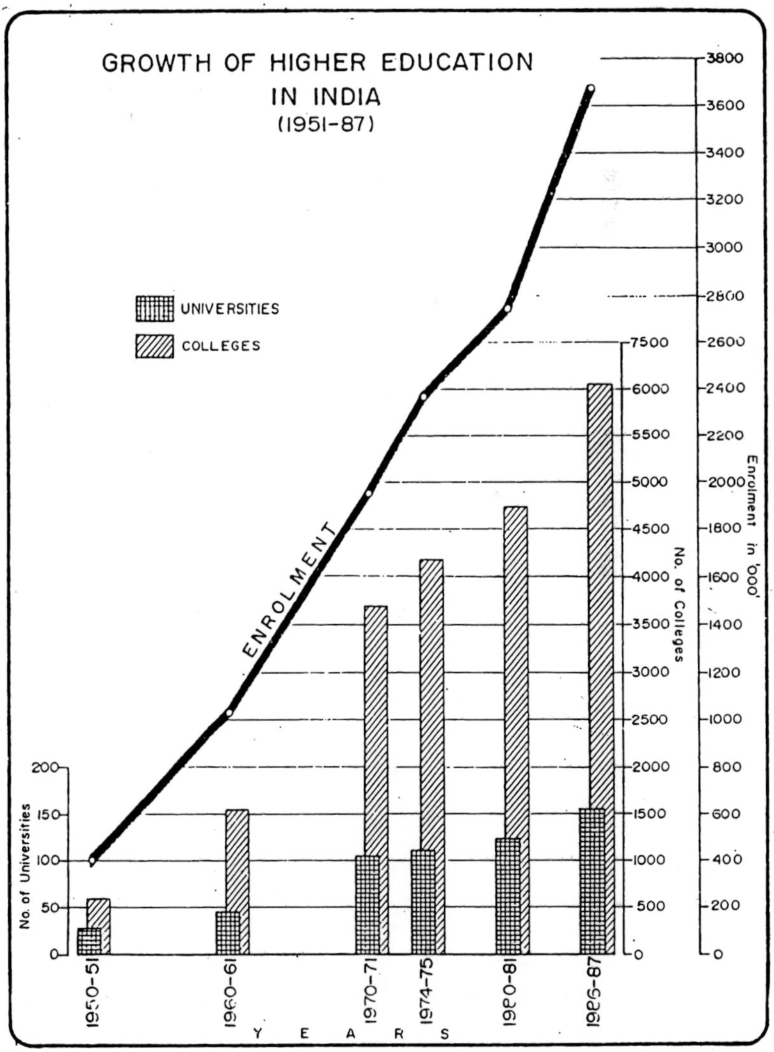
GROWTH OF HIGHER EDUCATION
IN INDIA
(1951-87)
UNIVERSITIES
COLLEGES
ENROLMENT
No. of Universities
No. of Colleges
Enrolment in '000'
1950-51
1960-61
1970-71
1974-75
1980-81
1986-87
Y E A R S

Table 5.3 : *Development of Literacy from 1950-51 to 1980-81*

Item	Year			
	1951	1961	1971	1981
Total	16.7	24.0	29.5	36.2
Male	24.9	34.4	39.5	46.9
Female	7.9	15.0	18.7	24.8
Rural	—	19.0	23.7	29.6
Male	—	29.1	33.8	40.8
Female	—	8.5	13.2	17.9
Urban	—	47.0	52.5	57.4
Male	—	57.5	61.3	65.8
Female	—	34.5	42.1	47.8
Scheduled Castes	—	—	14.6	21.4
Male			22.4	31.1
Female			6.4	10.9
Scheduled Tribe			11.3	16.3
Male			17.6	24.5
Female			4.8	8.0

Source : Indian Census Reports.

Table 5.4 : *Intra-Sectoral Resource Allocation in Education in the Five Year Plans (Percentages)*

Education Level	First Plan	Second Plan	Third Plan	Plan Holiday	Fourth Plan	Fifth Plan	Sixth Plan	Seventh Plan
Elementary	56	35	34	24	30	35	36	29.0
			(30.2)	(20.2)	(18.2)	(31.9)	(31.0)	
Secondary	13	19	18	16	18	17	16	—
Higher (college & university)	09	18	15	24	25	22	19	40.5
Other General	09	10	12	11	14	14	18	19.8
Total General	87	82	79	75	87	88	89	89.3
Technical	13	18	21	25	13	12	11	10.7
Grand Total (Rs. in Million)	155	273	589	322	823	1286	1900	63.8
	100.0	100.0	100.0	100.0	100.0	100.0	100.0	100.0
	7.86	5.83	6.87	4.86	5.04	3.27	2.59	3.55

Source : (i) Brahm Prakash & Yash Aggarwal (1986), 'Selected Issues for Implementing New Education Policy, Indian Journal of Public Administration, Vol. XXXII, No. 3, July-Sept., pp. 476-498.

(ii) Malcolm. S. Adiseshiah (1986), 'Some Thoughts on the Seventh Five Year Plan-1985-90' (Particularly figures in brackets and grand total figures), Dialogur Publication, New Delhi.

satisfactory progress in girls' education, it is desirable to first teach their parents and make them aware about the significance of the problem. But since the majority of such people come from economically backward class of the society, mere education without entailing any improvement in their income standard will not matter much.

5.3 Indicators of Educational Development

There are numerous indicators which can show the educational development of a particular region. Out of these literacy rate and enrolment rate are the two most basic indicators and that is why data on these indicators is easily available for almost all the countries and states.

In order to measure the educational development of various states, in this paper we have taken literacy rates and enrolment figures at primary and middle levels. The enrolment at Secondary/Higher Secondary and Tertiary levels has not been taken into account.

At the national level nine states have been identified as the educationally backward states by the Government of India. These are Andhra Pradesh, Assam, Bihar, Jammu & Kashmir, Madhya Pradesh, Orissa, Rajasthan, Uttar Pradesh and West Bengal. The criteria adopted to define the educational backwardness was enrolment at elementary level. So the states where enrolment ratio at elementary level (i.e., class I-VIII) is below the national average are termed as educationally backward states and thus the states having elementary level enrolment ratio above the national average are the educationally advanced states and are : Gujarat, Haryana, Himachal Pradesh, Karnataka, Kerala, Maharashtra, Punjab and Tamil Nadu. Table 5.5 gives the list of educationally backward and other states with their respective literacy rates for 1981.

The table shows that Rajasthan is educationally most backward while Kerala is most advanced state and the literacy rate of latter is nearly three times that of former. The literacy figures show that in all the educationally advanced states the literacy rates are above the national average with exception of Haryana whose literacy rate almost coincides with the national average. On the other side the literacy rate of all the educationally backward states is below the national average except West Bengal whose literacy rate is 4.7 per cent points above the national average.

Table 5.5 : *Literacy Rates (1981) of Educationally Backward and Other States*

States	Literacy Rates (1981)	Deviation from National Average
Educationally Backward States		
Bihar	26.2	−10.0
Orissa	34.2	−2.0
Madhya Pradesh	27.9	−8.3
Uttar Pradesh	27.2	−9.0
Assam	N.A.	N.A.
Rajasthan	24.4	−11.8
Andhra Pradesh	29.9	−6.3
Jammu & Kashmir	26.7	−9.5
West Bengal	40.9	+4.7
Other States		
Kerala	70.44	+34.2
Tamil Nadu	46.8	+14.6
Karnataka	38.5	+2.3
Himachal Pradesh	42.5	+6.3
Gujarat	43.7	+7.5
Maharashtra	47.2	+11.0
Haryana	36.1	−0.1
Punjab	40.9	+4.7
Literacy Rates of India (1981)	36.2	

Tables 5.5 and 5.6 present the economic development and educational attainment of the 17 selected states separately. In the following pages we will present the state in the cross-tabulation of educational variables with the per capita income. These tables would perhaps give the idea of possible correlation between economic development and educational attainment of various states.

It seems necessary here to note the limitation of methodology adopted in the coming tables. Whereas the average per capita income is calculated for the year 1980-81 to 1984-85, the literacy figures are presented for 1981 and enrolment figures as well as per capita expenditure on education are taken for the year 1984-85. But as the reference year is same for all the states, it would not affect their relative position.

Literacy

One of the basic indicators on which one can measure the educational attainment is literacy. In spite of the progress made during the last 40 years in India and despite the thrust imparted by programmes of universalisation of primary education and adult education, the absolute number of illiterates has progressively increased since independence (National Literacy Mission, 1987) in India. Though the literacy rate has more than doubled i.e. from 16.67 in 1951 to 36.23 in 1981 there were 437 million illiterates in 1981 as against 300 million in 1951 (Fig. 2 & 3). Table 5.6 presents the rank of average per capita income of the 17 states with their respective literacy rates.

The cofficient of rank correlation (*r*) calculated for total literacy shows a value of +0.7036 while the same for female literacy is 0.6882. It can therefore be inferred from these values (of *r*) that there is a high positive correlation between per capital income of the states and their literacy rates both for total population as well as for females. A quick glance at the data in Table 5.6 reveals that many of the poor states (i.e. states having per capital income below the national average) are having literacy rates which are below the national

Table 5.6 : *Rank as per Average Per Capita Income (1980-81 to 1984-85) and Literacy Rate (1981)*

State	Average Per Capita Income Rank	Literacy Rates			
		Total	Rank	Female	Rank
Bihar	1	26.2	2	13.6	2
Orissa	2	34.2	7	21.1	7
Madhya Pradesh	3	27.9	5	15.5	4
Uttar Pradesh	4	27.2	4	14.0	3
Assam	—	N.A.	—	N.A.	—
Rajasthan	5	24.4	1	11.4	1
Andhra Pradesh	6	29.9	6	20.4	6
Jammu & Kashmir	7	26.7	3	15.9	5
Kerala	8	70.4	16	65.7	16
Tamil Nadu	9	46.8	9	35.0	15
Karnataka	10	38.5	10	27.8	9
Himachal Pradesh	11	42.5	13	31.5	11
West Bengal	12	40.9	11.5	30.3	10
Gujarat	13	43.7	14	32.3	12
Maharashtra	14	47.2	15	34.8	14
Haryana	15	36.1	8	22.3	8
Punjab	16	40.9	11.5	33.7	13
India	—	36.2	—	24.8	—

Note : Rank 1 is given to the lowest and rank 16 to the highest value.

Fig. 5.2

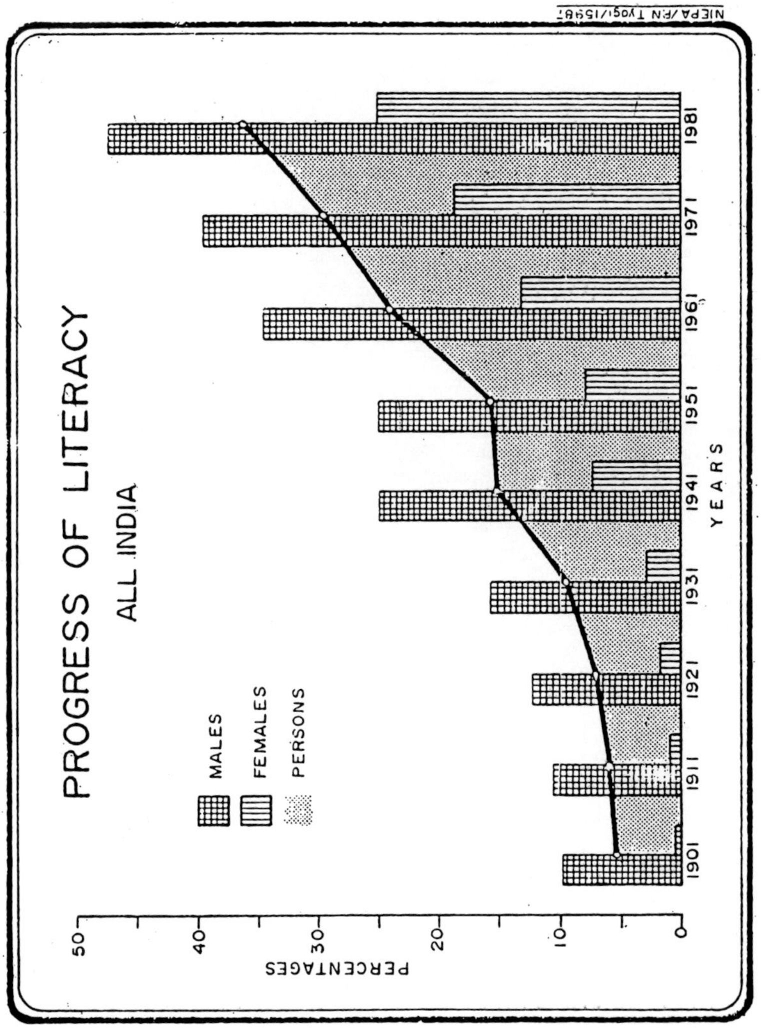
PROGRESS OF LITERACY
ALL INDIA
MALES
FEMALES
PERSONS
1901
1911
1921
1931
1941
1951
1961
1971
1981
YEARS
0
10
20
30
40
50
PERCENTAGES

Fig. 5.3

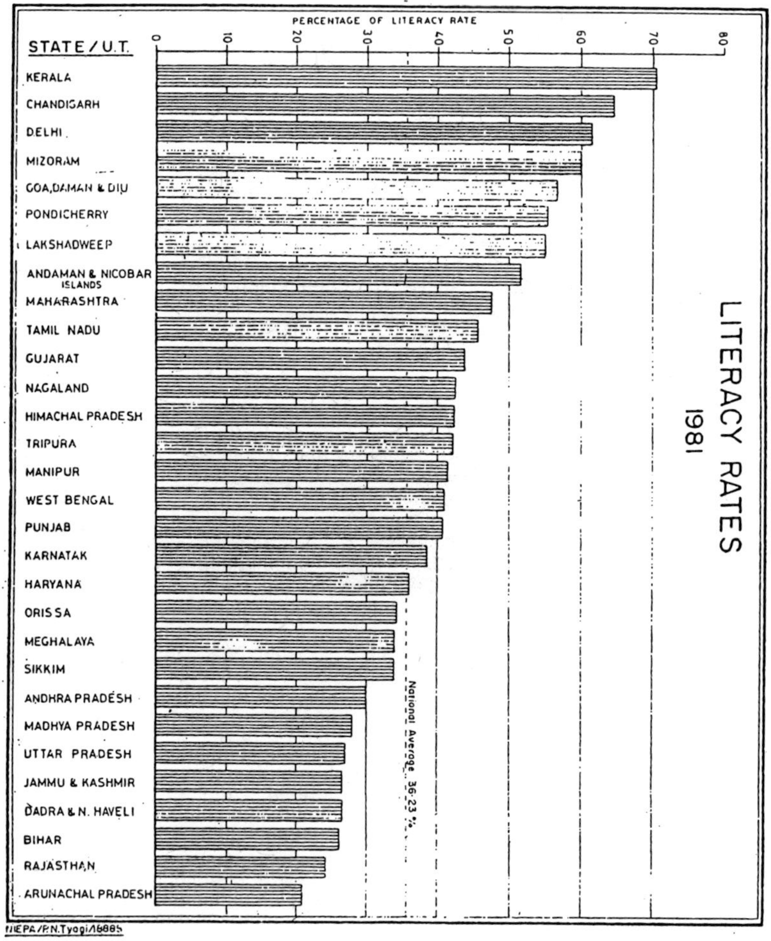

NIEPA/P.N.Tyagi/16885

average. On the other side all but one of the prosperous states has literacy above the national average. Barring these four states (viz., Karnataka, Kerala, Tamil Nadu and Haryana), the data shows the trend that poor states are poor in literacy also and economically advanced states are better in the literacy also.

However, there are some distinct exceptions to this pattern. Whereas most of the other states have followed the main trend of "low income, low literacy" (or its converse "high income, high literacy"). States like Kerala, Tamil Nadu and Karnataka among the "low income, high achievers in literacy" and Haryana in "high income, low literacy" category are cases which do not fall in the pattern. After reviewing evidence on the other dimensions of income education nexus, we will make some specific observations about these states, subsequently.

5.4 Enrolment at Primary Level

The enrolment at primary level is another indicator of educational attainment after literacy. In India, the goal in universalisation of elementary education (UEE) has not been achieved so far and that is why progress in enrolment at primary and middle level is an important indicator of our concern.

Instead of taking enrolment ratios as such, the enrolment in primary classes per lakh of population has been calculated. With a view to focus on the enrolment of female, separate ranks have been given for them. Estimated population of mid-1985 and enrolment of 1984-85 has been taken for these calculations. Table 5.7 presents rank order as per the average per capita income of the states with their respective primary level enrolment per lakh population

The coefficient of rank correlation for total enrolment is +0.4926 which shows that primary enrolment of the states is positively correlated with their average per capita income. The value of coefficient of rank correlation of girls' enrolment is even higher (+0.646). It shows that girls' enrolment at primary level in various states is positively correlated with their average per capita income.

It may further be observed that for total population as well as girls, Uttar Pradesh has the lowest and Kerala has the highest enrolment at primary level per lakh population. As far as the poor states are concerned, enrolment at primary level per lakh population for all is below national average except Kerala and Tamil Nadu which,

Table 5.7 : Rank as per Enrolment at Primary Level Per Lakh Population (1984-85)

State	Average per Capita Income Rank	Enrolment per lakh population			
		Total	Rank	Female	Rank
Bihar	1	10,366	4	6,824	3
Orissa	2	10,906	8	8,604	6
Madhya Pradesh	3	10,951	9	8,538	5
Uttar Pradesh	4	9.906	1	6.789	2
Assam	5	10,885	7	9,890	9
Rajasthan	6	10,205	3	5,860	1
Andhra Pradesh	7	11,323	11	9,620	8
Jammu & Kashmir	8	9,980	2	8,299	4
Kerala	9	11,756	12	11, 261	14
Tamil Nadu	10	13,837	17	13,286	17
Karnataka	11	10,403	5	9,940	10
Himachal Pradesh	12	13,685	16	12,409	15
West Bengal	13	13,204	13	11,255	12
Gujarat	14	13,378	14	11,259	13
Maharashtra	15	13,631	15	12,494	16
Haryana	16	10,566	6	9,018	7
Punjab	17	11,131	10	11,176	11
India	—	11,488	—	9,397	—

as has been mentioned earlier, are above the national average. But among the economically advanced states, Haryana and Punjab (i.e. the two most prosperous states) have enrolment below the national average. With a few exceptions, the same relationship holds for the girls' enrolment at primary level also.

5.5 Enrolment at Middle Level

The elementary level of education includes primary as well as middle classes. Table 5.8 presents ranks of the average per capita income of the states with their respective ranks as per the enrolment at middle level.

The values of coefficient of rank correlation for total enrolment and girls are +0.6397 and +0.6409 respectively. The order of correlation is quite high for both total children as well as for girls.

The data given in the table shows that middle level enrolment is highest in Kerala while it is lowest in Bihar. This is true for total enrolment but for the girls' enrolment is lowest in Rajasthan. Out of 11 poor states, the performance of Assam, Kerala, Karnataka and Tamil Nadu is better than the nation as a whole as their middle

Table 5.8 : *Rank as per Enrolment at Middle Level Per Lakh Population (1984-85)*

State	Average Per Capita Income Rank	Enrolment per lakh population			
		Total	Rank	Female	Rank
Bihar	1	2390	1	1176	2
Orissa	2	2499	2	1629	4
Madhya Pradesh	3	2932	5	1693	5
Uttar Pradesh	4	3150	6	1609	3
Assam	5	4073	12	3502	11
Rajasthan	6	2622	3	1134	1
Andhra Pradesh	7	2923	4	2073	6
Jammu & Kashmir	8	3430	7	2420	7
Kerala	9	6432	17	6133	17
Tamil Nadu	10	4555	15	3789	15
Karnataka	11	3730	9	3228	10
Himachal Pradesh	12	5815	16	4420	16
Kerala	13	4197	13	3635	13
Gujarat	14	3520	8	2693	9
Maharashtra	15	4375	14	3397	14
Haryana	16	3899	10	2475	8
Punjab	17	3956	11	3594	12
India	—	3580	—	2568	—

enrolment per lakh population is above the national average Rest seven poor states' enrolment at middle level is below the national average. Among the six states having per capita income above the national average—Gujarat (for total children) and Haryana (for girls) seem to have lesser middle level enrolment.

5.6 Higher Education in India

In recent years, efforts have been made by the Commission to regulate the growth of higher education as well as the establishment of new universities and colleges with a view to ensuring that higher education grows to meet the genuine needs of the society for trained manpower with appropriate level of professional training, skills and specialisations or general educational attainments. As envisioned in the National Policy on Education (1986), institutions of higher education are expected to possess a modicum of facilities by way of basic infrastructure such as class rooms, libraries, laboratories, hostels, staff quarters, teachers' hostel and other inputs like technical and research support and resources for purchase of equipment, books and journals etc. and the Commission's endeavour in this regard is in harmony with the New Education Policy (NPE).

In the context of the growth of higher education in India during the last three decades or so, three important facts need to be emphasised. First, enrolment at the level of higher education as a proportion of the relevant age-cohort is hardly adequate in spite of the unprecedented growth that has taken place (fig. 4). Second in spite of the fact that there is a need to regulate expansion in view of the limitations of resources, it is not easy to deny expansion altogether. The weaker sections of the society have looked upon higher education as the only means for vertical social and economic mobility and, to deny them access to higher education would be against all canons of social justice and equity. Third, it would not be proper to determine the demand for education from the point of view of the labour market alone without due consideration to the social, cultural and humanistic aspects of education.

The development of higher education in India thus faces the challenge of quantity versus quality and a strategy has to be evolved to arrive at an acceptable balance between the two demands. An adequate realization of this objective requires concerted efforts, careful educational planning and coordination of resources and constant vigil as well. This calls for identification of priorities and regional needs and, above all, determination of relevance and excellence in higher education. This section of the report presents in numerical terms the higher education scenario of the country over the past decade as reflected by the growth in enrolment, staff and the number of institutions.

The following four universities came into being during the year 1986-87, raising the total number of universities in the country to 136 as on 31st March, 1987.

S.No.	Name of the State/ Union Territory	Name of the University
1.	Andhra Pradesh	University of Health Sciences, Vijaywada
2.	Gujarat	North Gujarat University, Patna.
3.	Karanataka	University of Agricultural Sciences, Dharwad
4.	Madhya Pradesh	Indira Gandhi Krishi Vishwavidyalaya, Raipur.

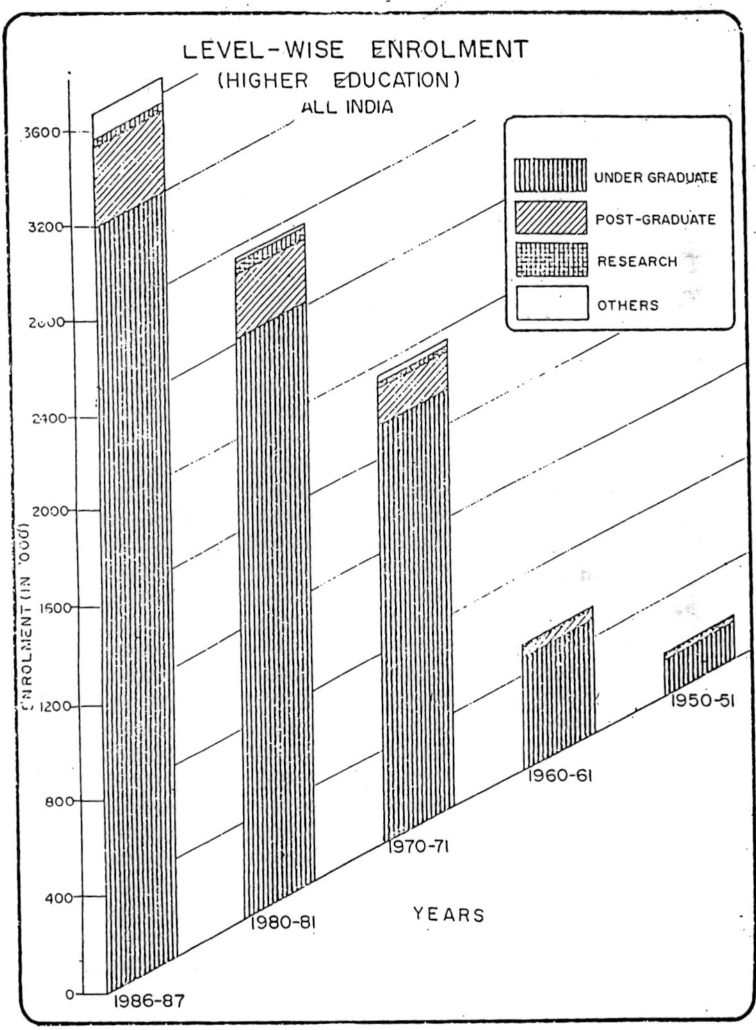
LEVEL-WISE ENROLMENT
(HIGHER EDUCATION)
ALL INDIA
UNDER GRADUATE
POST-GRADUATE
RESEARCH
OTHERS
ENROLMENT (IN '000)
3600
3200
2800
2400
2000
1600
1200
800
400
0
1986-87
1980-81
1970-71
1960-61
1950-51
YEARS
NIEPA/P.N. Tyagi/04289

Fig. 5.4

The following universities were declared fit to receive Central assistance including assistance for institutional development in terms of the rules framed under section 12(B) of the UGC Act.

S.No.	Name of the State	Name of the University
1.	Andhra Pradesh	Andhra Pradesh Open University, Hyderabad
		Shri Padmavati Mahila Vishwa-vidyalayam, Tirupati.
2.	Bihar	Birsa Agricultural University, Ranchi.
3.	Himachal Pradesh	Himachal Pradesh Krishi Vishwa-vidyalaya, Palampur.
		Dr. Yashwant Singh Parmar University of Horticulture and Forestry, Solan.
4.	Karanataka	Gulbarga University, Mangalore Mangalore University, Mangalore.
5.	Tamil Nadu	Algappa University, Karaikudi.

In addition, the Goa University, Panaji was declared fit to receive central assistance for all approved schemes except for Institutional Development in terms of the rules framed under Section 12(B) of the UGC Act. The general development grant will be given after the University gives a report on the action taken by it in implementing the recommendations of the Committee on various academic and other matters and after the position regarding filling up of the teaching positions is made known.

The Cochin University, Cochin (Kerala) was converted into a full-fledged Science and Technological University of a Unitary type for the promotion of postgraduate studies and advanced reasearch in applied science, technology, industry and management by an Act of the State Legislature.

New Institutions Deemed to be Universities under Section 3 of the UGC Act.

The Government of India, on the recommendation of the UGC, declared the following institutions as institutions deemed to be universities under Section 3 of the UGC Act.

1. Birla Institute of Technology, Mesra, Ranchi (Bihar)
2. Rajasthan Vidyapeeth, Udaipur (Rajasthan)

With these the number of institutions deemed to be universities rose to 19 as on 31st March, 1987.

During the period under report, the Commission also recommended to the Government of India, Ministry of Human Resources Development, the conferment of 'deemed to be university' status on the following institutions on the basis of the recommendations of the committees which visited these institutions :

1. Shri Avinashlingam Home Science College for Women, Coimbatore (Tamil Nadu)
2. National Institute of Mental Health & Neuro-Sciences, Bangalore (Karnataka)

The Commission at its meeting held in July, 1986 considered the report of the Committee appointed by it for examining the report of the Committee appointed by the Chancellor, Jamia Millia Islamia to determine the Jamia's present status vis-a-vis its future requirements and desired that the Government of India be informed that the Commission has no objection from the academic angle to Jamia Milla Islamia becoming a statutory university. However, the regulations for the establishment of the university should be in accordance with well established norms reflecting the points made in the Central Universities Review Committee Report, specially regarding (i) the objectives which are to be pursued by the university and (ii) its governance. The above decision of the Commission was communicated to the Government of India for further necessary action.

Student Enrolment :

In terms of absolute numbers, there has been a consistent increase in enrolment as well as institutions over the years as reflected in table 5.9 below. It will be seen that in 1977-78, the number of students enrolled was 25.64 lakhs spread over 105 universities, 10 institutions deemed to be universities and 4,375 colleges whereas in 1986-87 there were as many as 36.81 lakh students enrolled in 136 universities, 19 institutions deemed to be universities, and 6040 colleges.

Table 5.9

Year	Number of Universities	Number of Colleges	Number of Students
1977-78	105 + 10 Institutions deemed to be universities	4,375	25,64,972
1978-79	108 + 10 Institutions deemed to be universities	4,460	26,18,228
1979-80	108 + 11 Institutions deemed to be universities	4,558	26,48,579
1980-81	112 + 11 Institutions deemed to be universities	4,722	27,52,437
1981-82	118 + 13 Institutions deemed to be universities	4,886	29,52,066
1982-83	120 + 13 Institutions deemed to be universities	5,039	31,33,093
1983-84	124 + 15 Institutions deemed to be universities	5,246	33,22,939
1984-85	125 + 15 Institutions deemed to be universities	5,590	34,04,096
1985-86	132 + 17 Institutions deemed to be universities	5,813	35,70,897*
1986-87	136 + 19 Institutions deemed to be universities	6,040**	36,81,870*

Note : 1. The number of colleges given above excludes junior colleges and those offering diploma certificate courses.

* Estimated

** Provisional

Growth Rate of Enrolment :

The average decadal growth rate of enrolment during 1977-78 to 1986-87 was about 4.2 per cent as compared to the average decadal growth rate of 7.5 per cent recorded in the earlier period viz. 1967-68 to 1976-77. A look at the year-wise growth rates of enrolment during the ten-year period 1977-78 to 1986-87 also brings out the fact that there was no definite trend in the growth rate which rose in on year and fell in the other. While the lowest growth rate recorded during this period was 1.2 per cent in 1979-80, the highest was 7.3 per cent in 1981-82. In 1986-87, the growth rate was 3.1 per cent.

The all-India average annual compound rate of growth of enrolment during the five year period 1982-83 to 1986-87 was 4.1 per cent. It will also be seen from the Appendix that there were wide deviations from this average growth rate between different States. Jammu & Kashmir, for instance, recorded the highest average annual compound rate of growth of enrolment of 9.9 per cent during the period while, on the other extreme, Gujarat recorded average compound growth rate of a mere 1.8 per cent. As many as 11 States (including Gujarat) and the Union Terriory of Delhi had average growth rates lower than the all-India average, with Jammu & Kashmir recording the highest growth rate of 9.9 per cent followed by Bihar (7.6 per cent) and Manipur (6.6 per cent).

5.7 Problems and Prospects of Expansion

(a) *Problems*

The quantitative expansion of higher education has led to many problems such as : (i) The pattern of education which India inherited at the time of independence did not suit its needs. Each state of education is linked to the next one without any terminal stage. As a consequence there has been an ever increasing pressure for the provision of college/university education. A developing country like India can ill afford the expansion of university education when it has not been able to provide universal elementary education to its children in fulfilment of the constitutional provisions.

The products turned out by the educational system are not in tune with the needs of the country. The educated people have looked down upon manual work and held white collar jobs in greater esteem. They have preferred wage employment to self employment. Consequently, expansion of educational facilities has been accompanied by an increase in educated unemployment, which the Government is finding it difficult to solve by creating more employment opportunities. Therefore, instead of solving the problem of unemployment the educational system is accelerating it. The change in the attitudes of the students towards manual work and self employment can be brought about through the vocational bias in education. While education should be narrow based vocational education at secondary schools be balanced in the theoretical learning and practical exerience in all the courses.

(b) *Prospects of Expansion*

In view of the above mentioned problems which our country is facing due to the liberal policy it had followed for expansion of institutions (colleges/universities) and the admissions the following are the suggestions.

(i) *No new Colleges/Universities*

It is suggested that the improvement of standards in existing institutions should be given priority over staring of new institutions. A policy decision should be taken whereby, except to meet the educational needs of backward/tribal areas, no new colleges or universities should be started. In recent years it has been a tendency in many states either to take over the management of privately managed colleges or opening of new colleges to cater to the needs of the political pressures and demands. This haphazard and unplanned increase in the number of colleges, especially Arts and Commerce, has worsened the situation and thrown into the employment market thousands of general graduates with very little skill or knowledge required for jobs available. Hard decisions on the part of the state Governments and strong disincentive measures on part of the bodies like University Grants Commission are needed.

(ii) *Vocationalisation*

The action in the sphere of vocationalisation needs to be accelerated. More and more colleges and university centres of continuing education should offer courses and training in job oriented courses.

(iii) *Diversification of Courses*

Understanding the society is an instrument for changing it. We shall have to keep on constantly analysing and understanding society in its totality so that we change it speedily and surely. Hence there is a need for diversifying the courses with emphasis on relating theory to real life situation.

As early as in 1977, the UGC has suggested (a) a set of foundation courses designed to create an awareness of our history and culture ; (b) a set of core courses to make students acquainted with the chosen discipline and study in depth ; (c) some applied studies though not professional, but relevant to the community including project work; and (d) involvement in a programme of national and social services for the first two years at the undergraduate level.

At the undergraduate level courses having practical importance like journalism, public relations and marketing are not given due importance. There is too much stress on the 'academic' content of the courses. As the economy makes progress, new employment opportunities will be available and this factor should not be forgotton while prescribing course for our college youth. In rural areas, the courses such as agriculture and allied activities should be prescribed.

In most colleges, the library facilities are inadequate. Of course, even those limited facilties are poorly utilised. This is due to the fact that our examination system is so defective that a student can get through examination even without using the library. When the present courses are restructured to meet the growing needs of the economy, a well equipped library becomes indispendsable.

There is also need for coordination of various stages of education. The universities are better placed than colleges and colleges are better placed than schools. There should be mutual help and each higher stage of education should take the responsibility for improving standards at the lower stages.

(iv) *Devising Tests at National Level*

As far as possible all admissions to institutions of higher learning in the field of professional and technical education should be on the basis of an appitute test. Vocational guidance facility in schools and other educational organisations need to be strengthened.

5.8 Planwise Educational Achievements since Independence

Though it has been generally recognised that education is the basic condition for social and economic progress, it is a hard reality that in our national plan we cannot give it a high enough priority. The first four years of independence witnessed great educational expansion *one year to budgetary planning* till the inception of the National Planning Commission in 1951. Education is a concurrent subject and educational planning, therefore, is done at two levels—Central and State. At the Central level, the Planning Commission and the Ministry of HRD, Department of Education prepare a national plan of educational development which consists of two parts : first a Central plan dealing with the direct responsibilities of the Government of India in Education and second an integrated summary of the State plans of educational development.

Five Year Plans

The Planning Commission so far has formulated seven Five Year Plans, i.e.,

—	The First Plan	(1951-1955)
—	The Second Plan	(1956-1961)
—	The Third Plan	(1961-1966)
—	The Fourth Plan	(1970-1974)
—	The Fifth Plan	(1974-1979)
—	The Sixth Plan	(1980-1985)
—	The Seventh Plan	(1985-1990)

The three years (1967-69) are known as the Annual Plan Years during the period, the Five Year Plans were substituted by annual ad hoc plans to meet the national draught and financial recession.

First Five Year Plan[13]

This Plan made a provision of Rs. 151.66 crores (35.02 crores for the Centre and 116.64 crores for the States) for educational development or of Rs. 3033 crores per annum. The provision was no doubt inadequate. The following broad targets were made to achieve :

— at the conclusion of the Five Year Plan, educational facilities should be provided for at least 60 per cent of all the children of the school-going age within the age-group 6-11.

— at the secondary stage, the target should be to bring 15 per cent of the children of the relevant age-group into educational institutions.

— in the field of social education at least 30 per cent of the people (and 10 per cent women) within the age-group of 10 to 40 should receive the benefit of social education.

The areas of education selected for development during the plan period were : (i) pre-school education, (ii) primary (including basic) education, (iii) secondary education, (iv) university education, (v) social education (vi) professional education, (vii) women's education and (viii) other educational programmes.

Second Five Year Plan[14]

The Second Plan laid emphasis on linking education with economic development. In this plan Rs. 307 crores had been provided, Rs. 95 crores at the Centre and Rs. 212 crores in the States. The Second Plan made a provision of Rs. 2 crores for rural higher education including establishment of 10 Rural Institutes. In the Second Plan Rs. 17 crores had been provided for increasing training facilities for teachers.

During the Second Five Year Plan, 1956-61, the programmes of Basic Education began to be implemented effectively for the first time. In 1955-56 the number of children going to basic schools accounted for less than one per cent of the total number of children at the elementary stage ; the proportion increased to nearly four per cent by the end of the First Year Plan and was expected to rise to 11 per cent by 1960-61. However, the enrolment progress in secondary and higher education reached to 19.8 lakhs and 7.4 lakhs respectively. It shows that various programmes, in regard to the development of education were undertaken.

Third Five Year Plan

The Third Five Year Plan proposed to continue the work started under the first and second plans. It referred to education as the most important single factor governing the economic and technological growth of the country.

The Third Plan postulated an increase in the number of children in the age-group of 6-14 years about equal to that achieved during the proceeding decade. For girls the proportion in the age-group was to go up to about 46 per cent and for boys to about 73 per cent, the overall proportion increasing to nearly 60 per cent. In the Third Five Year Plan, arrangements were made for the education of the children in the age-group of 6-14 years. Housing facilties and other allowances were provided to the lady teachers, especially in rural areas. Sixty thousand primary schools were converted into basic schools. In this plan, Rs. 209 crore were spent on primary education. During this plan the number of high/higher secondary schools in the age-group 14-17 years was expected to increase from 22 lakh to 26 lakh or to per cent of the population in the age-group.

As far as higher education in the Third Plan is concerned, one of the main tasks was to expand facilities, social demand and availability of financial, material and human resources.

Enrolment target in elementary classes in 1973-74 was 86-88 million (Boys—53.44 million and girls 33.24 million). This was 67-76 million (43-68 million boys and 24.08 million girls) in 1968-69. The trend of expansion of facilties at the secondary stage has shown a positive increase. A total of 6.58 million pupil were enrolled in 1968-69, out of which 4.95 million were boys and 1.63 million were girls. The target for the year 1973-74 was 70 million for boys and 2.69 million for girls.

There had been a steady expansion of teachers training facilties both at the elementary and secondary stages. During the Fourth Plan period the number of elementary trained teachers increased from 0.71 million to 1.24 million. At the secondary stage, the number of teachers in 1968-69 was estimated at 0.525 million of whom 0.381 million were trained.

In higher education, the additional enrolment in the Fourth Plan was estimated to be about one million. Of this, 0.15 million students were facilities of science. The number of universities increased from 27 in 1950-51 to 32 in 1955-56 and to 46 in 1960-61 and about a dozen more universities were likely to be added during the Third Plan. The number of colleges role from 772 in 1955-56 to 1050 in 1960-61. During the Third Plan about 70 to 80 colleges were to be added every year. Student enrolment in all subjects in the universities and colleges went up to 15.28 lakh in 1964-65, recording an increase of 10.4 per cent over the 1963-64.

Aspects of the First Three Plans

— Adoption of the 'comprehensive' as against the 'selected sector' approach.
— Great emphasis was laid on quantitative expansion. This resulted in a comparative neglect of quality.
— They were not rooted in any long-term plan and hence lived mere by from day to day.
— Lack of emphasis on evaluation—both of results and of techniques.

Fourth Five-Year Plan

Educational programmes in the Fourth Plan were related to social and economic objectives of the country. It was *a persepective plan based on manpower needs*, provided education through correspondence courses, evening colleges and part-time classes. During the Fourth Plan, the main emphasis was on consolidation and improvement of higher education. Technical institutions had been planned for an annual admission capacity of 25,000 students at the degree level and 48,600 students at the diploma level.

In the Fourth Plan, Rs. 822.66 crores were provided in addition to an average annual non-plan expenditure of Rs. 550 crores. Of the play outlay, Rs. 551.66 crores (67 per cent) were in the state sector, Rs. 32.40 crores (4.0 per cent) in the centrally sponsored sector and Rs. 238.60 crores (29.0 per cent) in the Central sector. About Rs. 150 crores were available from non-Government sources.

Fifth Five Year Plan

In the Fifth Plan period 1974-79 elementary education was given a high priority. As regards expansion full time facilties were expected to be provided for 97 per cent of the children in the age-group 11-14 years by the end of the Fifth Plan. In addition, about 78 lakh children of the age-group 11-14 years were to be provided part-time education.

Although the expansion of educational facilities were to continue to receive emphasis and major share of the resources allocated for elementary education, the Fifth Plan proposed to lay much greater emphasis on improving the quality of instruction, particularly with a view to enhancing the efficiency and productivity of the schools.

In 1974-79, the enrolment was of the level of 120 lakh in classes I ov V and 105 lakh in classes VI to VIII and 45 lakh in part-time classes. The existing trend in the increase of enrolment had been kept in view. Against the additional enrolment of 15 lakh expected to be achieved in the first three years, an enrolment target of another 15 lakh in classes IX-XI/XII had been proposed for 1977-79. The percentage of children of the age-group 14-17/18, enrolled in classes IX-XI/XII was expected to increase from 20 lakh in 1973-74 to 25 lakh in 1978-79.

In higher education 88.2 per cent students were enrolled in affiliated colleges and 2,62,295 (11.8 per cent) in university teaching departments and institutions deemed to be universities. During this plan, the main emphasis in university education was on consilidation and improvement, Provision was, however, made to provide additional educational facilties to the weaker section of society and in the backward areas.

Sixth Five Year Plan

The Sixth Plan proposed that the importance of secondary education to prepare manpower for economic development should pay special attention to the quality of education at this stage. It is estimated that universalisation of the primary stage of education would imply additional enrolment of about 170 lakh children in an average annual rate of enrolment of 34 lakh. Planners felt that the achievement of total enrolment by 1985 was an uphill and challenging task.

During the Sixth Plan it was anticipated that the additional enrolment in secondary education will be about 30 lakhs. And as far as higher education is concerned it was proposed that in the Sixth Plan, no new universities should be set-up ; colleges should be established with great restraint and only after ensuring adequate resources in terms of teachers, finances and materials.

Seventh Five Year Plan

The Seventh Plan provides for reorientation of the education system so as to prepare the country to meet the challenges of the next century. The main thrust areas in the Seventh Plan would be : (i) achievement of universal elementatry education; (ii) eradication of illiteracy in the age-group 15-35 years; (iii) vocationalisation and skill-training programmes at different levels of education; (iv) upgradation of standards and modernisation at all stages of education with special emphasis on science and environment and on value orientation; (v) provision of facilties for education of high quality and excellence in every district of the country; and (vi) removal of absolescence in and modernisation of technical education.

The enrolment of the elementary stage is estimated to have reached nearly 112.10 million by the end of the Sixth Plan (1984-85). For achieving the goal of universalisation by the end of the Seventh Plan (1985-90), over 25.53 (11.46 & 14.07) million children will have to be additionally enrolled in full time schools. The total projected enrolment in full time schools (I-VIII) by the end of the Seventh Plan is estimated to reach 137.63 million including boys and girls (80.12 + 57.51). The number of children to be covered by the non-formal programme is estimated to reach 25 million.

Eradication of adult illiteracy and continuing education for adult literates is a major thrust area in the Seventh Plan. The national target is to make literate all the illiterates in the age-group 15-35. This is no doubt a formidable task. The number to be covered is 90 million.

Expansion of elementary education has added for their impetus to the growth of secondary education. Hence, more facilities have to be provided to cope with this growing demand. To link education with productivity, a major impetus has been given in the Senenth Plan to vocationalisation of the higher secondary stage. Facilities for vocational education have been diversified to cover a large number of fields in agriculture, industry, trade and commerce and services.

Expansion of general higher education was carefully planned. The weaker sections and backward areas were provided with more facilities for higher education through appropriate reservation for admission scholarships, provision of hostal facilties etc. Training of teachers in higher education is another area which needs special attention in the Seventh Plan. Besides, larger facilities for access to higher education of SC/ST students, positive programmes have been taken for those students in the forms of remedial teaching, preparatory training and special coaching. However, the implementation and achievement of the Seventh Five Year Plan proposals can only be evaluated at the end of the plan period after 1990.

5.9 Need for Vocationalization

The National Working Group Report on Vocationalization of Education (1985) has given many suggestions for further education in order to make vocational education more attractive. The institutions of higher level courses to provide for degree and professional growth and provision for bridge courses have also been incorporated into the Policy (NPE 1986). While steps in this direction are being taken which would no doubt help in increasing the popularity of vocational courses, the fulfilment of the real objectives of vocationalization will have to be sought primarily in the job market domain.

Conceptually, vocationalization for wage employment offers relatively less challenge than vocationalization for self-employment. However, some difficulties may be felt in both during the implementation. In most of the wage employment areas particularly in the organized sector such as health services, tourism, electronics, banking etc., the demand could be centrally forecast with reasonable accuracy and the educational profile for the same may also exist though it could be reviewed periodically.

What would be needed in this context is a system for indenting properly certified manpower which vocational schools can be expected to produce with the quality standards laid down. The enterprise and employing organizations would also be expected to contribute their resources—men, materials, machines and money for the training purposes as a participant in the process of human resource development. The challenge, however, would be mostly managerial which can be met by removing some of the mental barriers which have resulted due to the existing separation of education from industry. The employment of students into their areas of training would provide a great positively feed-back for the popularity of the courses.

If self-employment holds the key to the success of vocational education in India then various attributes in relation to self-employment must be clearly understood. It may be noted that those who like to go early into the world of work belong to a class where higher education has less premium for the reasons of opportunity cost, long gestation period, poor academic environment or aptitude and interest. Coincidently this is also the profile of the students who opt for vocational stream at present. Entrepreneurship and high academic achievement may casually go together but an early entrant to the job market is less likely to be a person with the desire and promise for higher levels of education. As such we may have nothing to compulsions. As a converse, however, it may be argued that self-employment as a career choice may be at a discount for some students even though while a vast majority may have to go for it. This justifies proper education and planning of self-employment as a large scale venture. These people would in the long-run create wealth for themselves and the nation a great deal more than the routine job seekers.

Some studies have brought out the fact and supported a common notion that previous experience of work with an enterprise before starting one's own venture is a great advantage to an entrepreneur. This has serious curricular implications for vocational education. Early years of schooling must provide a sound work experience programme to children since only a small fraction of the total population of school children would end up entering the portals of higher education. This will also lay down proper foundations for work ethics, eliminate inhibition for manual work, generate some competence in using one's own hands and confidence to take up a productive project. Further, as component of vocational education curriculum itself, there must be considerable chunk of time spent on work-site for on-the-job experience. All the theory and practice taught in the class room would still leave a serious gap in vocational preparation of the individual in absence of proper on-the-job experience.

While the students may have secured sufficient competence to start their own ventures by the time of their graduation from the higher secondary school a post-graduation apprenticeship training would go a long way in increasing his competence and confidence to enter the work on his own. Many entrepreneurs have found long association with others in a supportive capacity extremely rewarding when it comes to face the challenge on their own. It may be cautioned here that it is not intended to increase the training duration so as to be economically unattractive to the seekers of early employment. All such attachment should be 'earn while you learn' ventures through an information set up.

Our prevailing notion of apprenticeship would also require some modifications since attachment of an apprentice may often have to be ensured with small enterprises often limited less than 5 persons.

At the completion of education and necessary length of apprenticeship training, the individual must be in a position to march forward on a path he has envisaged for himself. Two types of input would help him to achieve his desired goal.

The first of these concern the development of entrepreneurship through which the acquired knowledge and skills could be put to effective use in self-employment venture and the second concerns the management of resources, more directly the finances needed for the entreprise. Both these inputs have implications for educational intervention more strongly the former. The development of entrepreneurial qualities amongst the prospective self-employed population would, in the long-run, widen the base of economic activities, reduce inter-regional disparities and ensure optimum utilization of available resources. These in turn would reduce the development of monopolies and concentration of economic power in the hands of a few.

It is widely believed now that entrepreneurs are not necessarily "born" but can be "made" through education and training. This is, of course, not to dispute that certain personal entrepreneurship characteristics may help some people in comprison to others. Yet, this belief coupled with reality that we have a large base of self-employment as growing sector has failed to touch the curriculum of the formal education system in schools and colleges and has been largely missed out even during the current policy pronouncements. Early cultivation of entrepreneurship among students must become an important area of school curriculum at an appropriate stage and should include : development of entrepreneurial quality, enterprise launching, enterprise management and entrepreneuring discipline as its basic component. The modern syllabus developed by National Institute of Entrepreneurship and Small Business Development (NIFSBUD), Ministry of Industries should serve as prototype for this purpose. While inclusion in the formal school may provide a wide base for a course in entrepreneurship for a vast majority of educated group, for the majority of vocational stream students who prepare themselves for self-employment, the need for an educational intervention in this area cannot be overemphasized. This would call for a mass approach to cover the student population in this category which even today is of the order of tens of thousands in the country as whole and is growing at a rapid rate. It should be ensured that the school time table provides for this component and that instructions are imparted in a manner befitting the need. The NIESBUD and other agencies working throughout the country would have to gear up themselves to meet this challenge if vocationalization is expected to make a significant impact on the economic front of the society.

5.10 Summing up

The role of education in the development of the traditional people has been very well stressed by educationists and sociologists. It no more viewed only in terms of developing an individual culturally, but its area has been widened considerably to cover socio-economic aspects leading to overall development of country. In democratic set-up, the transformed role of education is not only that of creating a balanced and socially integrated individual, but it is expected to ensure that the benefit of education goes to all the people irrespective of caste, sex, socially and locationally disadvantaged groups.

In the field of modern Indian Education patterm and content are the two most important components or ingredients of education. The new structural pattern as proposed by the Education Commission and as it exists in India has tremendously affected the entire field of education—secondary, higher secondary, collegiate and university education.

Since independence the number of recognized institutions and enrolment has increased substantially. As a result the national stock of educated manpower is estimated to have increased from less than 4 million to about 48 million. It is observed that growth over the period of 35 years in number of institutions is maximum at middle stage followed by professional institutions, whereas the minimum growth is witnessed in primary institutions. On the whole the general educational facilties have increased tremendously. But at the same time it is observed that quality-wise it has not able to serve the requisite purpose.

During different plan periods, in spite of massive quantitative expansion of education at all levels, much has to be achieved to reach the national goals. Only a little over 36 per cent of the population are literate and the remaining are illiterates. The national aim of universal elementary education is yet to be achieved as envisaged in the constitution. Fifty million children are yet to be enrolled and vocationalisation of secondary education has yet to make headway. The standard, or quality of higher education has to be raised or improved. The Seventh Plan has emphasised that one of the primary tasks is the harnessing of the country's abundant human resources and improving their capability for development with equity.

Despite tremendous growth in educational facilities, the country is facing acute problem of massive illiteracy and unemployment among educated as well as uneducated. There is, therefore, a need for human resource development strategy with less emphasis on formal education and would be more oriented towards productive work. The changing socio-economic conditions would demand a form of education and training which will enable the continuing development of the individual.

In the New Education Policy emphasis has been laid on the need of linking the educational planning with the manpower planning. Some of the priority areas identified for attention for implementation of new education policy are, as manpower planning and demand forecating and by strengthening the data base, monitoring and evaluation system. Even the Steering Groups on Education of the Planing Commission are giving stress on planning, monitoring evaluation and data base in connection with the formulation of the Eighth Five Year Plan.

For proper appraisal and an effective planning of the education system as a whole, it is imperative to have a strong and up-to-date information system. However, a number of sources and publications provide information on education even though they adopt varying concepts and reference periods and differ in coverage too thus making the data quite often uncomparable. The need for comprehensive and upto-date data is becoming increasingly imperative in the context of formulation of policies and programmes. While the collection of educational statistics has become a complex and time consuming process, the existing gaps listed in the text need to be filled for strengthening the data base requirement for educational planning.

During the past decade, there has been a growing interest in the economic aspects of education. The recent interest in educational planning follows as a result of the various developments in this sphere including huge public investment involved in it. With an increasing emphasis on the benefits of education, more materialistic view has been taken. In the foregoing discussions an evaluation has been made of several studies so far conducted in India. In spite of the differences in methodology, coverage and findings studies on India reveal certain general conclusions like—returns on college education vary between 4 per cent to 10 per cent, returns are high for matriculates and returns on education are found to be lower than those on physical capital etc.

Another important aspect which has been examined is the current status of relationship between education and employment in India. The figures of unemployment suggest that the education and employment matching is a dire necessity. This could be made possible by formulating the education and training programmes more closely related to available employment opportunities. The present education system is no longer capable of satisfying the increasingly diversified educational needs, which is seen through the mushroom growth of other institutions to compete or complement the existing system which by itself cannot meet the needs of individuals and that of society for their continuing development over a longer period of time. Therefore, there is a need for restructuring of the whole education system which would be geared to productive working life and may be called—'Active Education Policy'.

However, to get a more clear vision of the inherent potentialities of the New Education Policy, let us discuss certain aspects in more detail :

In the provision of delinking of degress from jobs, so far the only thing that has been made clear is that there would be a National Merit Examination conducted at + 2 level to select the candidates for government jobs. But what would be the contents and mode of such examination ? What would be the maximum and minimum age limits etc. have not been decided at all. Secondly, in the infrastructurally deprived areas, possibility of their competing with the students from elite families who are groomed for such type of competitive examinations is just remote. Thirdly, about 40 per cent of our population is below poverty line. Very few from this have reached the plus two stage. About 25 per cent population are marginal and small farmers who are just subsistence level and are dependent on family labour for agricultural activities. Their participation in higher education is almost nil.

Thus, in a country where the students from about 90 per cent of families either do not participate in higher education or some of them start thinking of competitive examinations for administrative and managerial jobs only at post-graduate level, how well the concept of equal opportunity for all in the aforesaid framework of the NEP will work can be imagined.

The second vital question that we confront is the conjectured role of the vocational approach in the absence of massive job opportunities (in both public and private sectors). Even the special developmental programmes including the self employment schemes have not made a significant dent in our country yet.

The issues emerging out of the foregoing discussion pertain to (i) education system, (ii) individual, (iii) society, and (iv) industry, commerce and administration.

(i) *Education System :*

— How the open university and model school will work is yet to be seen. The statistics explain that the large number of our primary schools do not have even buildings and black boards. Government's arguments have been that ours is a poor country running short of funds; contrary to this the government wants to establish 'Doon' type of model school in very district. How the gigantic amount of fund will be managed ? When these schools will be established ? Apart from that nothing has been said about the method of admission, and how the students from economically and socially weaker families will be selected ?

- Whether education should be narrow-based vocational education in secondary schools or be balanced between theoretical learning and practical experience in all branches of educational system.
- Whether the arbitrary separation between general and vocational education should continue or should be logically integrated.
- Whether access to higher education would be confined to those attending the formal education or should it be opened for those who have dropped out of education and wish to rejoin.
- How to achieve a feasible feedback system between the rapidly changing labour market demand and educational/ vocational and professional qualifications.
- Whether manpower and education and training policies be included in the labour market policy formulation for giving due recognition to the education, training and experience.
- Are the planners equipped with the knowledge of various forms, methods, objective, human and material resources and the utilisation of these resources and target clientel ?
- Are educational planners ready to accept a challenge of optional resource allocation for diversification.

(ii) *Individual*

- Is there possibility of readmission to sub-system after a period spent in another system, or in any economic, social or cultural activity ?
- Is there the need of gearing educational facilties to both young and adults ?
- For tackling the problem of unemployment and under-employment, is it necessary to allow alternation time for work and education ?
- Is there a necessity for career guidance for individuals in

respect of flexible and diversified structure (enabling them to adjust his qualification while producing in his/her career) ?

— Whether for social equity and economic development there is a need for more flexible educational system in which education and career preparation are properly interrelated and balanced ?

(iii) *Society*

— How to achieve attitudinal change for giving due recognition and status to professionals, para-professionals and vocationally trained personnel to support the rapid growth of service sectors and sophisticated industries which would offer advantages in terms of social structure and economic development.

— Whether there should be bridges, modulated activities etc. between the education and world of work ?

— Whether the industry, administration and commerce be involved in providing training opportunities in cooperation with educational authorities for combining theory and practice in an economically and socially acceptable way ?

— Whether the co-existence of young and adults in the universities is desirable for strengthening the links between education system and society ?

— Whether there should be a closer coordination between public authorities, responsible social groups, employers, trade unions, teachers, parents etc. in the process of policy formulation ?

(iv) *Industry, Commerce and Administration*

The central issues of diversification of educational activities however, may be be summed up as follows :

— To what extent does diversification contribute to a more effective utilisation of resources ?

— Does it contribute to economic development of society ?

— To what extent does it promote endogenous cultural development and respond to individual aspiration ?

The impact of different types and levels of training should, therefore, be analysed at both macro-social and individual levels.

Notes and References

1. Mrrovis Raza, Ahmad & S.C. Nuna (1984). *Social Education in India—The Regional Dimension*, Vol. I, NIEPA, N.D., p. 4.
2. A number of scholars have defined the terms, 'Formal education' and 'Non-formal education' and differentiated between the two. For instance :
   (i) George H. Axinn (1976). *'Non-formal Education and Rural Development,* East Lansing, Michigan State Univ. 1976.
   (ii) Beatrice Paolucci et al., *Women, Families and Non-formal Learning Programmes,* Michigan State Univ., East Langing, Michigan, 1976.
3. Ted W. Word and William. A. Herzog Jr., (1977). 'Effective Learning in non-formal education', Michigen State Univ., p. 76.
4. B.R. Purkait (1987). *New Education in India.* The Associated Publishers, Ambala, p. 457.
5. V.L. Ahuja, S. Kulkarni & H. Sharma (1988). *Active Education Policy for Skill Development.* Theme Paper of the Seminar, I.A.M.R., New Delhi, Unpublished, p. 7.
6. B.R. Purkait, *op. cit.*, p. 73.
7. *Ibid*, p. 73.
8. K.R. Sivaramakrishnan (1980). Problem of transition from technical and vocational education to work in India', Report presented in UNESCO Symposium at Berlin, German Democratic Republic, April 14-18.
9. B.R. Purkait *op. cit.* (1987), p. 458.
10. *Ibid*, p. 458.
11. *Ibid*, p. 70.
12. Literacy 1972-1976, *UNESCO* publication, 1980.
13. Chapter XXXIII—(Education) of the First Five Year Plan, Published by the Planning Commission, 1952.
14. *Ibid*, 1956.

6 Educational Planning

6.1 Introduction

There has been a growing interest in the economic aspects of educational planning during the past decade. Various reasons can be, and have been, advanced to account for this development. One is the considerable growth in the volume of educational activity to the point where today education is one of the largest industries in most countries and also one of the chief employers of highly skilled personnel. A second is the recognition that education may have a significant influence on the employment and income opportunities open to people and hence affect the distribution of income and wealth in society.

However, it is not necessary to continue with any careful cataloguing of such reasons in order to justify the contemporary economic interest in educational activities. But more interesting questions are : Why is educational planning necessary ? What is the mission of educational planning ? Whom does educational planning serve and benefit ? How does the educational planning process operate ? What types of tasks are suitable for the educational planning process ? What relationship exists between education, urban, transportation and economic planning, and other planning ?

The need for planning arose with the intensified complexities of modern technological society. Problems such as population, manpower needs, ecology, decreasing natural resources and haphazard application of scientific developments — all place demands on educational institutions for solution. If educational organizations are to meet the problems, then planning becomes a necessity and planning competence becomes mandatory. However, often the communities that these educational establishments serve are unwilling to recognize the need for planning. They, in effect, are demanding solutions while simultaneously rejecting a method by which these solutions could be found.

To rigidly maintain isolated process is to deprive the individual and society of optimal educational yields. To cope with social and physical problems and to overcome the inadeqacies of educational planning as it exists today, the following format of planning activities is proposed by Banghart and Trull[1] :

— Educational planning in general terms : research, development of theory and techniques; drawing-up state, regional and school district plans in broad quantitative terms.
— Educational planning in physical terms : middle-range and long-range plans (five, ten, fifteen and twenty-year intervals) of school buildings, layout of school buildings and their proper setting, establishing environmental criteria for learning activities, aesthetic questions, and technological research.
— Educational planning in social terms : surveys that reflect the people's wants, curriculum planning, instructional strategies, manpower and social, needs surveys, and physical designs that enhance personal and social interaction.
— Educational planning in administrative terms : developmental control, decision-making, management and operation, inventory-control, transportion planning and school plant surveys.

The purpose of comprehensive educational planning is to help ensure the accomplishment of the educational goals set by today's society for tomorrow's achievements. A systematic approach to the major phases of planning along with appropriate steps for solving a particular problem, should be most useful. This approach allows new methods to be fused with traditional ones into an effective framework for action.

However, the two major parts, i.e., economic aspects of educational planning and education employment linkages of the present section attempt to synthesize the building of unique model to necessitate and bring these interdisciplinary developments to the attention of the educational planner. This section does not presume to dictate all the steps. Additional steps may be added and variations on those listed may be found in certain basic phases of planning process. This is true regardless of the specific problems being considered, or the degree of depth and thoroughness being sought, or the level of quality desired.

6.2 Economic Aspects of Educational Planning

Educational planning has to be effectively integrated with the planning for the economy as a whole. While there are advantages from an increasing degree of privatisation of education, the recent trends in this direction have highlighted the difficulties in this context of educational planning *per se* and its integration with the national economic planning process.[2] Traditionally educational plan is conceived to be the plan for the educational development in the region as a whole (or a country as a whole); this macro approach is not the only approach to be used for the purpose of educational planning. The educational plan may also refer to the specification of the course of action to be undertaken by the various micro units within the sector of education.

6.2.1 Approaches to Educational Planning

As a part of a macro-educational plan, a number of attempts under the initiative of Jan Timbergen and H.C. Bos were initiated during the 1960s.[3] These attempts essentially considered education as a sub-sector of the economy and as a sector to supply the necessary skills for the growth of the economy. In view of the sophisticated econometric methodology involved in these attempts, the models thus developed could be applied in the context of a few selected countries though the essential idea behind these econometric models had a general appeal to the planning in all the countries. However, on a theoretical plan, three approaches to macro educational planning have been identified :

(*a*) Social Demand Approach
(*b*) Rate of Return Approach
(*c*) Manpower Requirement Approach

6.2.1.1 *Soical Demand Approach*

This approach is based upon the demographic trends. The estimates of the social demand are also based upon the transition probabilities of enrolment, the admission rates, the retention rates, drop out and wastage rates etc. at different levels of education.[4] Wtih regard to the demographic aspects of the existing population even though the policy-maker may be on a more firm basis it is doubtful whether the demographic trends in the future over a time period of 10 to 15 years, for which education needs to be planned, can be firmly predicted. In addition a good idea about the demographic aspects at disaggregated regional levels like blocks, villages etc. would be extremely helpful. But as it has been pointed out in

Chapter 4 that there are inconsistenciess in data between the two sources. The avaliable data on wastage, drop out rates, the stagnation rates, the intensity of utilisation of the various educational facilities are very weak. Hence, any attempt at developing any educational plan based upon the social demands would be obviously less dependable. However, this is a more general approach and does not explicitly recognise education as a crucial sector of the economy.

6.2.1.2 *Rate of Return Approach*

The rate of return approach looks upon education as a contributor to the productivity in the economy and helps in the prioritisation of education vis-a-vis. other sectors of economy.[5] In this approach education is treated as crucial component of the economy. However, by definition the rates of return for first level of education are larger than those for the subsequent levels of education. It is in this view, doubtful whether the rates of return can be used as a planning tool for allocations of resources to different levels of education.

At the same time key decisions as regards allocation of investment in education need to be taken to decide breakdowns between different types and levels of education, the impact of which, given the gestation lags, may take a long period to realise. What criteria should then be used to determine breakdowns between primary, secondary and higher education ? What factors, for example, should be taken into account in deciding investments within technical education between say engineering colleges and engineering universities ?

In answering these questions the rate of return method can provide a meaningful guide for the undertaking of educational planning both as regards investments in fields of education for the short and medium term where the projection approach is difficult to apply as well as for long term investments in skill formation where the gestation lag is long. Of course, there are some difficulties in calculting, as well as regidly applying, the rate of return criteria.

Although it is dengerous to generalise too mechanically, certain patterns can be easily detected from an internation comparison of rate of return estimates as given in Table 6.1.

Firstly, rates of return to investment in education is usually higher than the alternative rate for physical capital. Secondly, return to education is higher in countries at a lower stage of development, and with a narrow base of education. Thirdly, returns to primary education (whether social or private) are highest among all educational levels. Finally, the private returns are in excess of social returns, especially at the university level. This information can help us to decide the choice between Primary, Secondary and General Higher Education.

Table 6.1 : *Rates of Return to Education*

	Primary	Secondary	Higher	Number of countries
(1) All developing countries	24.2	13.4	12.3	30
(ii) Low income/adult literacy rate under 50 per cent	27.3	17.2	12.1	11
(iii) Middle income/ adult literacy rate over 50 per cent	22.2	14.3	12.4	19
(iv) Industrialised countries		10.0	9.1	1.4

Note : Studies refer to various years between 1957 and 1978, mainly in the latter half of the period.

Source : The World Bank, *Word Development Report, 1980,* Washington D.C., p. 49.

However, in the case of technical education, mainly two questions need to be answered. Firstly, as regards specific skills which need to be developed, and secondly the choice between different levels of technical education. A detailed exercise of cost estimates per enrolled student for different types and levels of technical education can prove exceedingly useful especially since it is generally known that technical education is costly, and if we compare it with general education it is much costlier at all levels.

Methods for Estimating the Rate of Return :

Calcultions of the rate of return should be made with great care and the pursuit of accuracy, within the limitations of the conceptual shortcomings of any result derived.[6] The methodology followed is to estimate the costs of education and the earning from education expressed in monetory terms over an individual's lifetime in the labour force. Once the stream of costs and benefits are estimated, the rate of return is the discount rate which equates the two streams at a given point of time. For example, consider the estimation of the private rate of return to investment in higher education in Figure 6.1. If Y stands for labour earnings and *h* and *s* for higher and secondary education, respectively, the rate of return (*r*) is found by solving the following equation for *r*[7] :

Discounted benefits to age 22 = Cumulated costs at age 22 :

(+ + + Area) = (- - - Area)

$$\sum_{t=1}^{n} \frac{(Y_h - Y_s)}{(1+r)^t} = \sum_{t=1}^{n} \frac{(Y_s)}{(1+r)^t} \qquad (6.1)$$

In the above private rate of return calculation, the only cost is the opportunity cost of staying in school beyond age of 18 instead of the labour market and is measured by the earnings of labour with secondary school qualifications. If one wishes to estimate the social rate of return one must add the cost of university education in the right hand side of the above equation.

However, the above method requires detailed data on age-earning profiles by educational level. This information is not only rarely available but even where it may be generated the problem of small number cells arises. Namely, the plotted age-earnings profiles exhibit a saw-tooth pattern that makes the rate of return estimation very sensitive, especially in the initial years after schooling, which carry a high weight in discounting. It is for this reason that smoothing out procedures are used and the rate of return being estimated in three stages.[8]

In first stage a regression of the type :

$$Y_i = a + b\ \text{age}_i = c\ \text{Age}_i^2 \qquad ...(6.2)$$

In the second stage an idealised age-earning profile is being constructed by predicting the value of Y for given ages and, educational level using the estimated function (6.2).

In the third stage the predicted values of earnings are inserted in formula (6.1) to compute the rate of return. While working out the stream of returns, adjustments also need to be made for the influence of non-educational factors such as location, occupation and also physical condition, drive and intelligence of the workers which directly determine the magnitude of wage earnings. It is customary in the rate of return analysis to multiply the earning differentials by a specific ratio also known as the alpha factor (0.66 in most cases) to allow for other factors which influence the earnings of workers and which are correlation with education.[9]

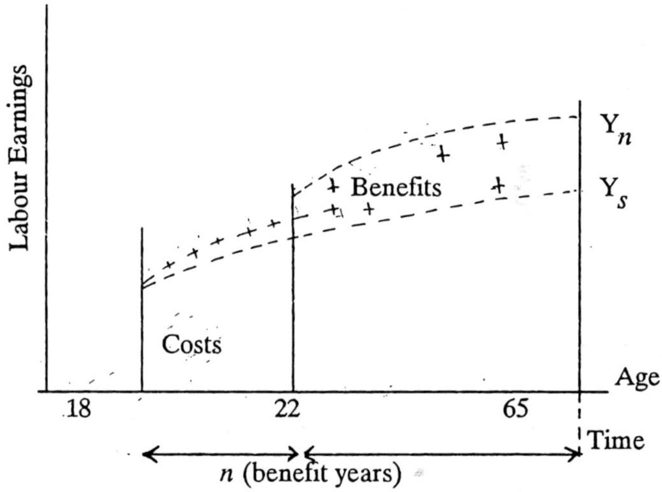

Source : ILO, (ARTEP), 1984

Fig. 6.1. Estimation of Rate of Return.

However, through educational process in the form of knowledge, skills, information and attitudes we transform raw material (uneducated students) or intermediate goods (continuing students) into capital goods. Everyone has become familiar in recent years that education is a type of investment and that economic development can be accelerated by spending more on education. But it is equally important to measure the expected returns of the investment to guide rational investment decision making in an educational project.

The *rate of returns* are the additional earnings after education is completed, and the costs are earnings forgone during education plus tuition costs, private or social. Whereas the *internal rate of return* is the rate of interest that equals discounted returns and discounted costs. When the earnings in the question are taken inclusive of income tax and when the costs of education are the total source costs to the economy as a whole one speaks of the *social rate* of return on investment in education. And when we take earnings exclusive of income tax and confine the costs of education to the costs borne by indivi-dual students or their parents, one speaks of the *private rate of return*.

In order to calculate rates of return on investment in education, we need to compare age-education-earnings profiles with the relevant cost of education at the level, either to the individual or to the society. Calculations of the full social opportunity cost of education at different levels should be an integral part of every government decision on investment in education, while the proportion of total costs borne by the individual, whether precisely calculated or not, is an important factor determining the private demand for education. However, we shall first look at the procedures/methodology for calculating *Private Rates of Return*.

The following variables and constants can be taken into account for calculating *Private* and *Social* Rates of Returns.

C = Social cost per student/year

$\bar{C}$ = Private cost per student/year

C_1 = Current cost per student/year

C_2 = Capital cost per student/year

C_3 = Income forgone per student/year

C_4 = Tutition cost per student/year

C_5 = Non-tution cost per student/year

W = Wastage Income per student/year

S = Stegnation period per student/year

Y = Average annual earnings of a given educated person

Y_o = Average annual earnings of an illiterate

U = Average annual unemployment period for a given educated person

P = Non-participation rate

e = Age specific mortality rate

K = Annual income tax rate

a = age of commencing a given level of education

a_o = age of completing a given level of education.

r = Rate chosen for discounting

t = age

C = $C_1 + C_2 + C_3 + C_5$

$\overline{C}$ = $C_3 + C_4 + C_5$

A = Adjustment for ability factor

Private Rates of Return :

A related application of the discounting technique has been to estimate private rate of return to investment in various amounts and types of education. These are the net returns the individual may expect to receive by investing on his own schooling. The calculation essentially involves determining that rate of discount which, when applied to the net stream of revenue expected from a particular level of education or occupation, will cause the present value of this stream to equal zero. The net stream of revenues is defined expected income less the cost of the schooling. The costs of schooling are normally incurred in the initial years of the time horizon and include tuition, foregone earning and incidental costs such as books and extra travel expenses. However, we generally use the following equations to measure private rate of return.

$$\overline{C}_1 = \sum_{a}^{a_0} \overline{C}_t \ (1 + r)^{a-t} \qquad ...(6.3)$$

$$\overline{C}_2 = \sum_{a}^{a_0} \overline{C}_t \ (1+S_t) \ (1+r)^{a-t} \qquad ...(6.4)$$

$$\overline{B}_1 = A \sum_{a_0+1}^{59} (yt\text{-}y_ot) \ (1+kt) \ (1+r\ )^{a-t} \qquad (6.5)$$

$$\overline{B}_2 = A \sum_{a_0+1}^{59} (y_t\text{-}y_ot) \ (1+kt) \ (1+ut)(1-et \ (1+r\ )^{a-t} \qquad ...(6.6)$$

where,

$\overline{C}_1$ = Present value of (crude) private costs of completing a given level of education

$\overline{C}_2$ = Present value of (adjusted) private costs of completing a given level of education

$\overline{B}_1$ = Present value of (Crude) private benefits of a given level of education

$\overline{B}_2$ = Present value of (adjusted) parivate benefits of education.

Age of retirement can be assumed to be equal to 59.

Social Rates of Return on Investment in Education :

Social returns to education, that is to say the returns which society as a whole might reap from investment in the education of its population, Social returns from investment in education might be compared with social returns from other public (or private) investments. Then, on the basis of the comparisons, the total quantity of resources to be devoted to education in the future and the types of educated people that should be produced could be determined. However, the computations for social rates of return are basically the same as for operation of physical plant and equipment (which include depreciation and implicit interest on the value of the physical assets) and counted as cost items in places of tuition. Second, on the revenue side, allowance must be made for the benefits to society of having a well educated population. These benefits may be classified into two types, those resulting from the advancement of knowledge, and non-pecuniary benefits. However, to obtain an estimate of the social returns following equations can be used:

$$C_1 = \sum_{a}^{a_o} C_t \, (1 + r)^{a-t} \qquad ...(6.7)$$

$$C_2 = \sum_{a}^{a_o} C_t \, (1 + W_t) \, (1 + r)^{a-t} \qquad ...(6.8)$$

$$B_1 = A \sum_{a_o+1}^{59} (y_t - y^o_t) \, (1 + r)^{a-t} \qquad ...(6.9)$$

$$B_2 = A \sum_{a_o+1}^{59} (y_t - y^o_t) \, (1 + ut) \, (1 + pt)(1 - et) \, (1 + r)^{a-t} \qquad ...(6.10)$$

where,

C_1 = Present value of (crude) social costs of completing a given level of education.

C_2 = Present value of (adjusted) social costs of completing a given level of education

B_1 = Present value of (crude) social benefits of a given level of education

B_2 = Present value of (adjusted) social benefits of a given level of education.

The calculation of rate of returns will be based on assumptions like earnings reflect productivity, the influence of ability and family background will be constant across all levels of education, future earnings can be estimated from cross-section data determined by current demand and supply relationships, current employment and non-participation rates reflect future trends, spill-over effects and externalities will be constant across all levels of education etc.

The Rate of Returns apporach is one of the very helpful devices for arriving at decisions regarding the amount of investments to be made in education on the basis of the returns that it can yield. According to this approach, investment in education should take place to such an extent that the returns from that investment are equal to the returns from other kinds of investment in physical capital. But these earnings are not dependent entirely on education. There are the family background and other considerations which are also relevant in determining the returns for educated individual. In addition, there are also intangible and qualitative returns accruing from education. Therefore, it is necessary to consider all the returns from investment in education—quantitative and qualitative, personal and social when the decision on investment in education is considered.

So many studies conducted to calculate the rates of return of education for different levels of education also provide some interesting insights. The World Bank indicates that the studies estimating the rates of return from primary education are fewest in number as compared to the studies in the subsequent levels of education making generalization difficult. This analysis would raise a fundamental question regarding the extent to which educational plans based upon the rate of return singals would really be advantageous from the point of view of the economy as a whole over a period of time. Since the earning differentials may not necessarily reflect the differentials with regard to the human capital endowments, the rate of return by the low earnings differentials may not necessarily give signals for allocation of resources for realising the productivity gains. That is why the debate in the field of economic of education as to whether education can be considered as an agent for human capital formation or simply as a screeming device, becomes extremely relevant in this context. If education is simply a screeming device and also if the filteration of the manpower classified according to the educational level is based more upon the illusory and controversial factors and also since there is no unainimity among the scholars, regarding effectiveness of even the filteration function of education, it is doubtful whether the rates of return can be used as useful signals for educational planning for the purpose of prioritisation within education and also of education vis-a-vis other sectors. It is therefore, in this approach that education is treated as a crucial component of the economy.

6.2.1.3. *Manpower Requirement Apporach*

The weakness of the rate-of-return approach, with its conceptual problems that prevent accurate measurement of the relevant variables, has encouraged support for other guides to educational planning. The most popular of these alternatives is the manpower requirement approach.[10] In this approach the linkage of education with the economy is more explicitly recognised by considering education as an agent in skill formation. The planner is expected to project the requirements of different categories of manpower classified according to the educational levels for different sectors of the economy over a specified period of time in the futrue. Based upon the projection the planners would indicate the directions of development of the educational sector over some specified period of time in the future.

As indicated by Panchmukhi (1988)[11] this approach would consist of the following components :

- Estimating sectoral requirements of manpower of different categories of skills and education as obtained at present.
- Projection of these manpower requirements over a period of 10, 15 and 20 years.

— Working out the educational equivalents of these categories of manpower.
— On the basis of realistic assumptions regarding the admission rates, transition probability wastage and stagnation rates, the prevailing educational facilities, etc. to estimate the changes in the educational institutions, existing as well as new ones, during the same time period.
— With certain norms about the unit cost to estimate the resource requirements of the educational sector if the manpower needs of the economy have to be met.

Between (a) and (b) a very significant and sophisticated exercise of estimating the technological change in the economy during the specified period of time will have to be attempted if manpower requirements of the future are to be realistic. It is said that invention and innovations are intrinsically unplanned phenomena. This seems to be true in the case of technological development also. It may be extremely trickly to project the technological change over the distant future in view of the significant technological strides in the diverse fields that are taking place in different parts of the world. To assume the existing manpower coefficients to hold true for even a short period of five years may be completely unrealistic leave alone the period of 15-20 years. Hence, the manpower planning approach suffers from a fundamental problem of lack of realism if it is static or is in danger of being incorrect if dynamic (adopting the changing manpower coefficients in accordance with the projection exercises relating to the technological change.)

Methods of Estimating Manpower Requirement Approach :

Now, let us have a look on the methodolgical aspects of this approach to have a clear understanding and limitations of this approach too. Let us take an example of demand for health personnel. The demand for the service of qualified manpower dealing with health exists within the public as well as private sectors of the economy. In the case of the former, the aggregate number of medical personnel can be projected on the basis of parameters such as the number of doctors or paramedical personnel, thousand of the population sought to be covered under health services scheme during the plan period. Given the targeted levels of population and also the policy based parameters, the incremental stock of skilled manpower required during the plan period can be estimated straight away.

However, in the case of the private sector the demand projections for medical personnel have to be linked to the potential increase in the demand for health services arising an account of increase in income of the population. In other words, we explicitly take into account two variables, namely : (a) the anticipated rate of growth of income per capita and (b) the income elasticity of demand for the specific category of the medical service. To take an example, the rate of increase in the private consumer demand for the services of the medical graduates may be estimated as follows[12] :

$$\frac{(1+e_i g)^t \left(\frac{N_p}{N_o}\right)}{(1+q)^t} = (1+e_i g)^t \left(\frac{N_p}{N_o}\right) (1+q)^t \qquad (6.11)$$

where,

e_i = Income elasticity of demand for medical graduate's service

g = Annual rate of growth of income per capita

N_p = Population in the terminal year of the plan

N_o = Population in the base year of the plan

q = Productivity increase per medical graduate

Subscript = Number of years in the plan period.

Similarly, the rate of increase in demand for other categories of health personnel can also be estimated if the corresponding values of the income elasticity of demand as well as the rates of increase in productivity are known. The rates of growth of demand thus derived when extrapolated on the base year stock of manpower in the health sector would provide the targeted levels of skilled personnel required at the end of the plan period within the private sector of health services.

Let us numerically illustrate the model [13] projecting demand for health personnel. Suppose in country X, where we need to project the demand for graduate doctors at the end of a plan period of five years, the following observations are made :

Base year population = N_o = 87.42 million

Projected population at the terminal year = N_p = 97.62 million

Estimated rate of growth of income per capita = g = 3.8 per cent

Income elasticity of demand for medical graduate's services = e_i = 1.25

Productivity increase per medical graduate = $\bar{q}$ = 1 per cent per annum.

Base year stock of graduate doctors = 3,668

$$\frac{N_p}{B_o} = \frac{97.62}{87.42} = 1.1167 \qquad ...(6.12)$$

The rate of increase in damand for graduate doctors over the Five Year Plan Period is :

$$\frac{[1+(1.25\times0.35)^5\,(1.1167)}{[1+.01]^5} = 34 \text{ per cent}...(6.13)$$

The stock of graduate doctors required at the end of the plan period = 4,915.

An important link in this discussion is the translation of the skill flow matrix of an economy into a corresponding matrix of educational requirements. The objective of such an exercise is to assess the educational composition of the future manpower required to achieve the plan targets. In most developing countries, the data that could be most handy and useful for an exercise like that are the prevailing pattern of educational qualifications of various skill categories in the labour force. The adoption of the current educational composition of occupations as a benchmark could provide the best foundation for making realistic assessment of educational requirements during the plan period and also serve to avoid a situation of deriving excessively ambitious plan targets for educated manpower. Such data being used as feedback the manpower planning agency can make projections of the estimated supply of educated manpower in a country during the plan period. Other essential components of information required for this projection exercise are : (i) The current capacity of the educational system in the country and the anticipated outflow of qualified manpower from different educational institutions; (ii) Existing stock of qualified manpower belonging to various skill categories, and (iii) Rate of attrition of the manpower stock on account of death and retirement during the plan.

A model which can be used for projecting the supply of manpower for an economy during a plan period has been spelled out in the ILO (ARTEP) (1984) study, which is briefly summarised here. The purpose of the model is to estimate the size of the labour force during or at the end of the plan period which is the sum of following: (a) the labour force newly entering from within or outside the educational system; and (b) the labour force already existing in the country net of attrition on account of health and retirement. The estimates of the educated entrants into the labour force by the level of education are based on assumptions about the number of school leavers during the plan period and their respective participation rates. First we take up the new entrants into the labour force.

The new entrants may be represented as follows:

$$ELF^{e}_{t} = p^{e}\ v^{ce}\ (1-qt^{c})\ ENR^{c}_{t} \qquad \text{...(6.14)}$$

where,

ELF^{e}_{t} = new entrants into the labour force by educational level e in year t.

V^{ce} = Conversion rate of school leavers by class c into educational level e.

P^{e} = participation rate of school leavers into the labour force by educational level e.

q^{c}_{t} = transition rate of students in class c in year t.

ENR^{c}_{t} = enorlment of students in class c in year t.

In the above equation, the school leavers by class $(1-q^{c})$ ENR^{c} are converted into school leavers by educational level V^{ce} $(1-qt^{c})$ ENR^{c} and multiplied by participaion rates (P^{c}) to give the number of new entrants into the labour force for each year by level of education. The next equation defines the labour force by educational level :

$$LF^{e}_{t} = (1-d)\ LE^{e}_{t-1} + ELF^{2}_{t} \qquad \text{...(6.15)}$$

where,

LF^{e}_{t} = labour force by educational level e in year t

d = rate of deaths and retirements.

The labour force by educational level in this year is the level of the previous year minus death and retirements plus the new entrants in the labour force. Finally, the model also specifies an equation to estimate the uneducated labour force e = 1 (less than primary).

$$LF^{1} = (1+r)^{t} . LF_{t-1} - \sum_{e=2}^{5} LF^{e} \qquad (6.16)$$

where,

LF^1 = number of illiterates plus less than primary in the labour force in year *t*

LF = total labour force

r = growth rate of the labour force.

To find out the uneducated labour force (illiterates plus less than primary) one deducts the sum of the educated labour force from the total labour force which is projected to grow at a constant rate *r*. The number of persons likely to retire each year can be estimated from the age distribution of the labour froce. The mortality rate of the labour force can be calculated taking into account the age and sex distribution of the labour force and applying this distribution to the age and sex specific mortality rates for the whole population. The total annual rate of attritions from the labour force will be the sum of retirement and mortality rates in each year.

Some of the recent studies conducted in this field have shown that the approach of developing the global estimates simply as a summation of the firm level manpower estimates is basically defective as a tool for manpower planning and hence educational planning because education does not enter significantly into the production function of the firms. But when education enters as a significant variable into the production function of the firm, it would be possible to consider education as an agent for skill formation. It is for this reason, it appears that the Burges, Layard, Pant technical study which was the basic for estimating the sectoral education manpower reqirements over the 20 years period (of 1965-85) and which provided the necessary technical inputs for the quantitative recommendation of the Kothari Commission for the purpose of educational planning has ultimately turned out to be less useful in actual practice than expected. In addition to this, an unrealistic estimate of the overall growth rate of the economy at around 5 per cent distorted the estimates of the manpower requirements and hence the educational plan.

Comments of different approaches :

In the social demands approach the demands on education are from the population as a whole; in the latter two approaches, the demands on education are from the economy as a whole with further break up of the economy into different sectors. The social demand approach is a more general approach and does not explicitly recognise education as a crucial sector of the economy. The rate of return approach, on the other hand, looks upon education as a contributor to the productivity in the economy and treated as a crucial component of the economy. In the manpower requirement approach, the linkage of education with the economy is more explicitly recognised by considering education as an agent in skill formation.

However, these theoretical approaches are hardly made use of except for developing some justification for some or the other argument. For instance, in order to highlight the importance of elementary education its rate of return which is higher than the rate of return for the subsequent levels of education, is used as a strong argument for supporting the policy of preferential treatment of elementary education. But before these approaches are used even as the basis for some such argument, their limitations even on theoretical level need to be fully recognised.

6.2.2 Informations Requirement for the Educational Planning

Modern goals raises a multiplicity of problems for the educational planning, development and policy making and leads to demands for particular pieces of information. The major problem areas where information is vital and required are :

— For the objective of literacy, one needs to know not only the age and educational attainment by regional distribution of the population but also the cost-effectiveness of different available technologies for improving literacy.

— For the objective of economic growth and manpower needs one must have good knowledge of the links between education and the economic system, plus a host of other parameters depending on the particular methodoly one wishes to follow (e.g. manpower-forecasting or rate of return).
— For the objective of employment, one must know the labour force participation and unemployment rates of the educated.
— Social demand statistaction necessitates through knowledge of population dynamics and people's responses to economic and other incentives (e.g. fellowships, grants, tuition fees and educational loans).
— Regional concerns require disaggregation of many national statistics by geographic area.
— The objective of democratization and equality of opportunity presupposes disaggregation of national statistics by sex, by socio-economic categories and by population (e.g. tribal or ethnic) groups.

Most of the statistical informations in terms of the modern goals of educational planning and policy making are not readily available in our country, as it has been discussed in Chapter 4.

The kind of information required is one thing and the way to obtain, disseminate and use this information of the local/state and national level is another. However, keeping in view the relevance and importance of statistical information an attempt has been made here to evaluate methodology to obtain, disseminate and use the information for educational planning, development and policy purposes.

Educational Planning Methodologies :

What are the specific bits of information (statistical or other) the decision maker would (or should) have at his disposal in order to be helped in his task ? The sequential list of such information can be derived by following a natural (although not unique) time path of equational-planning activities. The natural steps in the educational planning are[14] :

— The planner assesses the social demand for places in different educational institutions (supply side).
— The planner assesses the demand for qualified manpower for serving production targets (demand side)

- The planner attempts to reconcile probable imbalances between supply and demand,
- The planner might wish to incorporate neo-classical (in educational planning terms) criteria for arriving at his preferred solution, such as income distribution and employment.
- The planner might wish to 'correct' the various 'solutions' in order to take into account peripheral goals such as self-reliance, participation and sectoral integration.

Each possible procedure followed within a given step will give rise to different kinds in information as has been explained in the subsequent paragraphs.

A. *Measuring social demand*

It amounts to predicting for some years in the future the number of school and university places likely to be demanded by students and their families. Analytically, the projection model in, 'grasso modo'[15].

$$S_t + P\,S_{t\text{-}I} = M_t$$

where : S_t is a vector of student enrolments by educational level in year *t*; $S_{t\text{-}I}$ is a similar vector referring to one year in the past; P is the so-called transition probability Matrix ; M_t are 'migrations' i.e. inflow (+) or outflows (–) between the educational system and the outside world in year *t*.

In order to apply the social-demand model in its base elements, as has been rightly pointed out by P Sacharopoulos (1980)[16] the planner would like to have the following pieces of information :

(i) *Past demographic trends and projection of the number of births for some years into the future* : This information is necessary because the starting point of any social-demand model is the number of school-age children who will enter the educational system at a given point in time.

(ii) *Enrolment by individual grade (or class) and age for some years in the past* : This information is necessary for the establishment of the transition probability matrix i.e. the link between enrolments in grade 1 in year 1 to enrolments in grade 2 in year 2.

(iii) *Migration of school-age population in and out of the country or region where the projection takes place* : This is essential because no matter what the number of births is, the demand for school places can be affected by migration. This information is vital in India and other developing countries where rural-urban migration affects the demand for education at the regional level.

However, people's behaviour also matters, and recent attempt have been made to understand what factors (other than demographic) affect the demand for higher levels of education. The projection model should try to explain students' plans or actual enrolment by a set of socio-economic characteristics like the following[17] :

D_h = (household characteristics, price of education, expected monetory rewards)

where : D_h, a dependent variable, stands for the demand for, say, higher education as expressed by the students' aspirations to enrol or not in higher education; household characteristics include such variables as father's occupation and the number of siblings; price of education is measured by what the student is expected to contribute out of his pocket towards higher education. The results could be used by the planner to affect behaviour via certain policies and/or compensate for certain adverse factors affecting particular disadvantaged groups of the population and thus equalize educational opportunities. The following additional informations are required to apply this version of the social-demand model.

(iv) *Student aspirations by region, socio-economic group and household composition* : Some specific variables to be measured under each sub-group are family income, father's occupation, parents' educational level, house ownership, number of siblings, birth order and opportunity cost of studying i.e. the student's forgone earnings in the occupation he could enter given his present qualification.

B — (i) *The target sectoral growth of output* : This information is essential for establishing the vector X and is usually taken from the development plan.

(ii) *Future movement of productivity for each occupation and economic sector* : This information is necessary for correcting the base-year matrix for future productivity growth, since increases in productivity reduce the demand for certain kinds of skills.

(iii) *The formal educational content of each occupation* : This information is necessary for the translation step Locc Led. It amounts to recording the educational distribution equivalent of each occupation forming every single dimension of the Locc vector.

For the crude manpower forecasting the above mentioned informations are sufficient.

C. *Cost-Benefit analysis*

The cost-benefit analysis consists of assessing the marginal social costs and benefits associated with given incremental levels of education. When the earnings in question are taken inclusive of income tax and when the costs of education are the total resource costs to the economy as a whole, one speaks of the social rate of return on investment in education. At the crudest level, it consists of finding the social rate of return (r_s) to educational levels, i.e., by evaluating the expression :[18]

$$r_s = \frac{W_s - W_s - 1}{N(W_s - 1 + C_s)}$$

where, W stands for the average wages of those with educational level *s* or *s*–1; C_s is the annual direct social cost of school level *s*; and N is the number of years of study between school level *s* and *s*–1.

In the above formula the numerator shows the annual increment in earnings that is assumed for expository simplicity to be constant throughout the individual's lifetime, whereas the demoninator shows the lump-sum cost of acquiring that level of education. A substantial part of the cost is the foregone earnings of the individual while studying. However, informations required in this respect are :

(i) *Age/earnings profiles by educational level* : The information is necessary for correcting the previous expression for discrepancies in the lifetime shape of the earnings differential between the various educational groups.

(ii) *Pre-tax wages and salaries of employed persons* by educational levels are also required for estimating the social rate of return.

When we take earnings exclusive of income tax and confine the costs of education to the costs borne by individual students or their parents, one speaks of the private rate of return. The reasons for studying the private rates of return is to assess the private signal to which individuals respond in seeking different levels of education. It is closely linked to social demand-aspect of educational planning. The estimating formula[19] differs from (4) above :

$$r^1_s = \frac{W^1_s - W^1_{s-1}}{N(W^i_{s-1} + C^1_s)}$$

where ; W^1 stands for after tax earnings; and C^1 for the private direct cost of education. Here, the after-tax earnings of the previous level of education is only what the individual pays out of his pocket in order to study at the given level of education. The above formula require following informations :

(iii) *After-tax earnings by educational level* : The direct private cost of education is usually assumed to be equal to zero or to be simply cancelled out by part-time earnings while studying. For the private estimation, earnings data must include public sector.

D. *Achieving equality and employment objectives*

The above listed information may enable the planner to achieve economic growth targets or to allocate the educational budget. However, the planner may wish to observe in addition to this an equality objective. Equality means (a) equality of educational opportunity; and (b) equality of income distribution. For the eductional opportunity planner may wish to know :

(i) The distribution of educational attainment of the population by socio-economic background and region : Attention is drawn here to the fact that the information on 'group disparities' pertains to the population as a whole, not only to the labour force as was the case with the traditional objective of efficiency.

Information also becomes vital when the planner wants to assess the relationship between education and income-distribution in order to affect outcome disparities. The standard procedure is to relate the variance in earnings to the distribution of education.[20]

Vay (Log Y) = Vay (S and related parameters)

where S is the number of years of schooling of the individual.

When the income distribution question is investigated in the context of a developing country like India where some people work for paid employment, one would like to concentrate on the poverty conditions of just a target group of the population. This amounts to approximating[21] :

(ii) Real-income measures of the lower part of income distribution : This information ties in with the recent focus on basic needs and informal sector employment conditions.

(iii) Labour-force participation and unemployment rate by level of education: A given educational policy will have a differential impact on the overall employment level if graduates of the various schools face different opportunities. This is something the planner wishes to know.

However, a final remark has to do with possible (if not certain) trade-offs between different objectives. For example, one can pursue the equality objective at the expense of some efficiency or vice versa.[22]

E. *Some additional information*

It has been recently recognized that the determinants of performance at school (as measured by grades or marks) do not depend only on school inputs : family and other environmental characteristics play an important role.[23] For an educational production function one needs :

(i) Data on school and family inputs in relation to the scholastic achievement of school children : The analysis of such data can be used for policy purpose to compensate for the poor performance in school of children of a particular socio-economic group.

(iii) Educational disparities between parents and teachers (formal subsystem) and between trainees and trainers (informal sub-system): This measure is particularly important given the fact, known from research in educational production functions, that the parent contributes significantly to the absorption of the school curriculum by the child.

A list of specific informational bits the educational decision-maker should have at his disposal which can be summarized as follows :

Information-1. Last demographic trends and projection of the number of births for some years into the future.

Information-2. Enrolments by individuals grade (or class) and age for some years in the past.

Information-3. Migrations of school-age population in and out of the country or region where the projection takes place.

Information-4.	Student aspirations by region, socio-economic group and household composition.
Information-5.	The three-dimensional cross-classification of the labour force by sector of economic activity, occupation and education.
Information-6.	The most likely or the target sectoral growth to output.
Information-7.	The likely future movement of productivity for each occupation.
Information-8.	The formal educational content of each occupation.
Information-9.	Data on the OCC-SEC-ED distribution of the labour force in other countries.
Information-10.	Pairs of relative wages and relative skill utilization in a number of firms.
Information-11.	Pre-tax wages and salaries of employed persons by educational level.
Information-12.	The direct social cost structure of each level of education.
Information-13.	Age/earnings profiles by educational level.
Information-14.	Shadow pricing of the different kinds of labour.
Information-15.	Micro-data on the personal and family characteristics of a representative sample of employed persons in the economy.
Information-16.	A tractor study on the employment conditions and socio-economic background of recent graduates.
Information-17.	After-tax earning by educational level.
Information-18.	The distribution of the educational attainment of the population by socio-economic background and region.
Information-19.	The entrance ratios of selected population groups to different levels of education.
Information-20.	Real-income measures of the lower part of income distribution.
Information-21.	Data on school and family inputs in relation to the scholastic achievement of school children.
Information-22.	Labour-force participation and unemployment rate by level of education.
Information-23.	Adult participation rates in formal educational activities.

Information-24. Distribution of informal and non-formal education by population groups.

Information-25. Educational disparities between parents and teachers (formal subsystem) and between trainees and trainers (informal subsystem)

Information-26. The actual degree of transferability between different curriculum streams of the educational system.

Information-27. Information feedback from the labour market to the student and his family.

The identified gaps in the process of information generation and transmission are summarized in the following list :

Gap-1. The educational decision-maker is not aware of existing information that might help him in his decision.

Gap-2. The technocraft who advised the education decision-maker might not himself be informed of existing research results that might affect his recommendation.

Gap-3. There still exist a great distance between the producers of educational information and the users.

Gap-4. The user's incentive for assembling up-to-date information is sometimes lacking.

Gap-5. There are important lacunae in existing information net working facilities.

Gap-6. Existing information for educational decision-making is extremely unbalanced.

Gap-7. The content of the international exchange of information related to educational decision-making leaves much to be desired.

Source: George P Sacharopoulos (1980), 'Some proposals for the future' (in Ed.) 'Information : an essential factor in educational planning and policy', *UNESCO*, pp. 49-50.

Educational activity had been, for a long time, held as an unproductive sector in an economy and the concept of gain or loss was hardly ever associated with it. Until recently study on efficiency of educational expenditure had not drawn much attention of the economists. But gradually more and more studies on this branch of economics are being undertaken. The concept of no-gain no-loss is changing and as in any other branch of economics, efforts are being increasingly made to compare cost of education with efficiency and productivity. The practice of measuring this branch of activity together with consumption of input and employment of capital and labour is gradually developing. Even the introduction of input-output analysis in the field of education is not far-off.

Thus, economics of education—more particularly investments in education is now included in the mainstream of economic analysis. The principal approach in this regard is determination of the relationship between expenditure on education and growth in income.

6.3 **Education Employment Linkages**

6.3.1 BACKGROUND

The Indian education system, copied from the western model and introduced by the Colonial government, was geared to the administrative needs for a body of Indians who could help run the modern administration (Naik 1965). Our reliance on inculcation of generic knowledge has been rather excessive. Education in India has been almost oblivious of the heterogeneity of job situations and accelerating pace of technology. It was alright to do so upto a certain period under Colonial domination where the prime job of educational sector was to produce functionaries for the State which was committed to only a few law and order problems. But with the new developmental role of State, which has been the hallmark of post-independence era, the praparation of the workers required for different jobs is more varied. And education has not addressed itself to their new role and has been rather slow in responding to these pressures. It is, therefore, not withstanding the fact that the Kothari Commission which titled its Report as Education and National Development tried to put this role of education in focus. Even then the further implications of this role vis-a-vis job specific training could not be pursued in detail.

The relationship between education and employment has always been one of the major preoccupations of educational planning. In fact, one of the main reasons why some form of educational planning was adopted in many countries was the desire to achieve a better match between the graduates of the different levels and sectors of the educational system and the needs and capacities of the labour market (Marin 1977, UNESCO). In India, it is observed that the demand for education is growing within the country. Looking at in a narrow framework, this apparently is a paradoxical situation. However, there have been several factors which have jointly contributed to the deteriorating education employment linkages such as (i) Changing requirements of job positions ; (ii) the de-skilling process of those already educated ; and (iii) the slow response of educational system to changes in the job market. The magnitude of such a mis-match between the output of the education sector and the needed inputs of the labour market increases due to the excess supply of educated manpower.

In view of the above state of affairs there is an urgent need to intervene in the process so that the vitality of education could be restored and the yield from manpower skills could be obtained. The role of education vis-a-vis India's socio-economic development can hardly be over-stated. But it needs to be structured and aligned with other development sectors in a manner in which it can yield useful results. Mere expansion of educational opportunities cannot solve the problem which is deeply rooted in the socio-economic development of the country, its past legacy and the prevalent institutional arrangements.

However, what is more important are the micro aspects of the relationship. In the analysis of the relationship between education and employment, we are concerned with individual human beings and individual enterprises. Their background, attitudes and expectations play an important role in this relationship (Sanyal 1987). What goes on in the labour market is a reflection of the social set-up, including the educational system. We believe that the economy and the society, the human resource potential of the country and the education system as it is, influence the behaviour, attitudes and expectations of the individuals, their families, their community and their educational history. These factors again influence directly the expectations of each individual in respect of his or her social role, as does the operation of the labour market through its selection criterion, recruitment practices, labour market information system etc. But the occupational expectations are also indirectly influenced by resource potential, economy and the society and the educational system through the individual characteristics.

6.3.2 Programmes for Educated Unemployed

To deal with the educated unemployment a number of employment generating schemes have been launched by the Central and State Government. However, these programmes or schemes vary in details and objectives, as also coverage, but one common thread running through all of them is the emphasis on expansion of employment opportunities. During 1970s, the Central Government initiated some special schemes to create additional employment opportunities for the educated unemployed. These schemes were to be implemented by various Ministries of the Central Government in collaboration with the State Government.[26] Another massive programme called half-a-million jobs programme was launched by the Central Government for the benefit of the five lakh educated unemployed during the year 1973-74 and asked the State Governments to formultte feasible proposals after taking into consideration the suggestions contained in the guidelines and the special socio-economic conditions in the State.[27] The programmes were to cover all economic sectors, e.g., agriculture, animal husbandry, mines, industry and education.

Keeping in view the fact that the various sectoral programmes will focus attention of self-generating employment schemes through the employment promotion programme an employment promotion programme was started during Fourth Five Year Plan (1974-75). The main objective of the programme that the educated unemployed should be given such in plant training as would make it possible for them to stand on their own legs and that they may be assisted through stipends or subsistence allowance during this period and thereafter enable to obtain bank-institutional finance for taking up self-generating employment.[28]

However, different programmes for educated unemployed have been organised by the Central and State Governments but broadly speaking following were the main components :

— Self-Employment ;
— Training and Surveys ;
— Social and Local Government Services ;
— Construction Trades ;
— Research and Development ;
— Employment Incentive Schemes ;
— Strengthening Administrative Services ; and
— Public Distribution System.

The problem of unemployment among the educated should be viewed as a part of the total problem of unemployment and under-employment and the policy measures initiated should not result in merely reducing the unemployment of high level educated manpower at the cost of those who are less educated. Further, as the dimension and gravity of educated unemployment vary from state to state, a decentralised approach would be adopted based on the district employment plan.

Since it is not possible to have separated employment programmes exclusively for the educated manpower, those programmes which are likely to generate substantial employment opportunities for the educated have been analysed. In particular, various programmes in the primary sector are formed to considerable potential for the educated.

The expansion of rural infrastructure and social services under the revised needs programmes will also absorb a sizeable number of educated persons on a part-time or full-time basis. Work opportunities for the educated people are, however, not confined to the above mentioned schemes with largely wage paid/regular employment. For instance, even within agriculture and allied activities, a large number of matriculates and degree holders would be utilised in the farming operations, dairies, fisheries and other projects. Avenues for self-employment[29] are broadly classified under three heads, viz., (a) land and water based occupations, (b) small, medium and large industries and (c) the services sector, which are sound from the point of view of their cost, return and risk structure.[30]

The following schemes are being implemented at the national level for the educated unemployed :

(i) *Training of Rural Youth for Self-Employment (TRYSEM)*

The scheme of Training of Rural Youth for Self-Employment was started on 15th August, 1979 with the objective of providing technical skills to rural youths to enable them to take up self-employment in the broad fields of agriculture and allied activities, industries, services and business activities. The target group comprised rural youths between the ages 18 and 35 from families living below the poverty line. It was also indicated that a minimum of 30 per cent of the trained youths should belong to scheduled castes and scheduled tribes and a minimum of $33^1/_2$ per cent of the rural youths trained should be women.[31]

Against the target of 10.05 lakh youths to be trained during the Sixth Plan, 9.4 lakh youths were actually trained which accounts for

93.3 per cent at the target. Of the 9.4 lakh trained 4.64 lakh youths (49.4 per cent) were self-employed. Members of SC and ST accounted for 31.5 per cent of the persons trained, while women accounted for 34.8 per cent of the total number of persons trained.[32]

The Sixth Plan outlay for the scheme was Rs. 15.60 crores which was to be shared equally by the Centre and States. In addition, UNICEF assistance was to be made available to the extent of Rs. 5.40 crores.[33] The programmes will continue to aim at the poorest among the poor who will be identified by an annual household income of Rs. 4800 which is substantially lower than the out-off income of around Rs. 6400 at the poverty line level. A trainee selected under the scheme gets Rs. 100 (Rs. 50 for local trainee) as stipend per month during the training period. The training period is between 3-6 months. If any trainee leaves the training in between, he has to pay the full amount incurred on his training.

(ii) *Self Employment to Educated Unemployed Youths (SEEUY) Scheme* :

The scheme of Self-Employment to Educated Unemployed Youths (SEEUY) has been introduced in the country during 1983-84, with the aims at providing employment to the educated unemployed youths through industries, services or business. In view of the acute unemployment problem with limited scope for gainful employment in the Central, State, Public as well as in the Private Sector Establishments and Industries, the SEEUY scheme seems to be timely and effective towards easing the problem of educated unemployment in the country.

The scheme provided financial assistance to the prospective entrepreneurs for setting up industries as well as for servicing and running various trades for which the maximum financial assistance to the tune of Rs. 25,000 is stipulated in the scheme and released through various commercial banks. The system has slightly been changed from the year 1986-87 raising the limit of financial assistance from Rs. 25,000 to Rs. 35,000 in case of industrial ventures whereas in case of service ventures the limit remains at Rs. 25,000 and in case of business ventures the loan limit is reduced to Rs. 15,000 for each unit.[34]

The scheme covers all educated unemployed youth who are matriculates (class X passed) and one within the age group of 18-35 years. Women and technically trained persons are being given due consideration/weightage. From 1986-87, a minimum of 30 per cent of the total sanctions has been reserved for Scheduled Castes/Scheduled Tribes persons. ITI passed youths are also now eligible to set up industry service ventures.

The scheme provides for the grants of loan to educated youth residing in areas other than cities with a population of 10 lakh or more and having no other source of finance for setting down in self-employment. The scheme aims at providing self-employment to 2,50,000 educated unemployed youth through industry, service and business routes in each year. The implementation of the scheme was entrusted to the District Industries Centres under the guidance of the Development Commissioner for Small Scale Industries. An allocation of Rs. 25 crores was made for the programmes during 1984-85 in the central budget to cover Government assistance in the shape of an outright capital subsidy to the extent of 25 per cent of the loans taken by the entrepreneurs from the bank.[35] According to available data, 1.01 lakh beneficiaries have been assisted with aggregate credit of Rs. 207.93 crores during the year 1987-88 against the target of 1.25 lakh beneficiaries.

Many of the educated unemployed may have some basic knowledge about financial management, accounting, inventory management, etc. and training courses will not be generally necessary except in industry sector. However, for those who require some basic training and advice about selection and use of equipment the State Government will utilise the services of ITIs, Polytechnics etc. (from own budgets) to provide training to them.

The scheme will extend to all areas of the country except cities with more than one million population as per 1981 census. It will continue till the end of 7th Plan and highest priority should be given by DIC's, banks and all concerned for successful implementation of the scheme.[36]

District Industries Centres are assigned operational responsibility of the scheme at the district-level, over and above their present normal activities. DICs in consultation with the lead Banks of the respective areas would function as the Nodal Agency for formulation of self-employment plans, their implementation and monitoring under the overall guidance of the State Governments. The overall supervision will be provided by Development Commissioner, Small Scale Industries with the assistance of the

Banking Division of the Department of Economic Affairs and the Industry Departments of the State/Union Territory Governments.

(iii) *Self-Employment Programme for Urban Poor* :

The Government of India in consultation with the Reserve Bank of India launched the programme from 1st September, 1986 for providing self-employment to urban poor with the objective to identify families living below the subsistence level in cities/towns with population exceeding 10,000 as per 1981 census.[37] The applicant should be a permanent resident of the city/town and income of the beneficiaries should not be more than Rs. 600 per month. The applicant should have previous experience and aptitude for undertaking the activity for which assistance is applied for.

The scheme extends to all centres/cities/towns with population exceeding 10,000 as per census in whole of the country, which are not covered under IRDP. From each city/town one beneficiary for every 300 population (1981 census) was to be assisted.[38]

Assistance upto Rs. 5000 depending on unit cost is sanctioned to a beneficiary for undertaking any of the prescribed activities. Subsidy equivalent to 25 per cent of the total assistance is provided by the Government of India through Reserve Bank of India.[39]

(iv) *Other Programmes* :

Since the entrepreneur is the pivot of industrial development considerable thought was devoted to finding out whether qualities of entrepreneurship can be inculcated in a person who does have the family background of business or industry. Social research came to the conclusion that the qualities of entrepreneurship can be developed in some persons by suitable training. The assumption underlying various entrepreneurial development training programmes is that entrepreneurs are not born with a feather cap but can be developed[40] Entrepreneurial development programmes have thus been initiated by various banks, financial institutions, state directorates of industries, small industries development organisations and management institutes. Generally, state level EDP campaigns are organised for modern type sophisticated small and medium industires. For such programmes entrepreneurs from amongst the graduate engineers, technologists and commerce, science and business management trained persons are identified.

Apart from EDTPs there are a number of industrial activities such as skill development, use of improved technology, modernisation and productivity which require suitable training. Such training programmes are conducted by specalised agencies. Recently (in March, 1989) on the eve of the birth centenary of Pandit Jawaharlal Nehru, the architect of modern India a new programme called Jawaharlal Nehru Employment Programme was announced. It is proposed to merge NREP/RLEGP into a single programme, and to decentralise its implementation. This merged programme will operate throughout the country and will be funded 75 per cent by the Centre. The funds for this scheme will be in addition to the provision available to the distinct under the NREP and RLEGP programmes. These funds will be merged and locally useful schemes will be taken up to maximise employment opportunities and the creation of production assets. In 1989-90, the provision for this programme will be Rs. 1,711 crore. This new programme will allow fuller employment opportunities to at least one member of each family living below poverty line.[41] The details of the programme will be announced later.

(v) *Employment Oriented Schemes of State Government in Operation*

In addition to these national schemes to promote the cause of self-employment among the youths, there are also many more schemes launched and implemented by the State Governments. The State Governments which have introduced their own special employment programmes are Andhra Pradesh, Gujarat, Jammu and Kashmir, Karnataka, Madhya Pradesh, Maharashtra, Nagaland, Tamil Nadu and West Bengal. The Seventh Plan outlay for these schemes is Rs. 509.24 crores.

Among the different schemes in operation employment oriented and self-employment and training programmes for the educated unemployed are the major on going schemes. However, State and Union Territories have taken up the following types of schemes for implementation.

(a) Schemes for engineers and highly qualified technologists whose names are contained in live registers;
(b) Training for self-employment;
(c) Promotion of individual/cooperative, self-employment ventures with seed capital/margin share capital assistance; and
(d) Establishment of industrial/commercial estates.

Mainly funds for the programmes can be provided to the prospective entrepreneurs in the form of margin money to enable them to raise additional resources from financial institutions/banks. The nationalised banks have formulated a number of credit schemes to provide self-employment.

However, it seems clear that even if these programmes generate employment as per expectations, unemployment would not be eliminated within the Seventh Plan unless efforts are immediately made to make the current unemployed more employable through short-term training/vocational programmes and special employment programmes directed towards their absorption. Efforts would be made, in particular, to direct matriculates, who form the bulk of the educated unemployed, to non-clerical occupations and self-employment. Concurrently, steps will be taken to link education and employment in a virtually supportive manner.

6.3.3 Educated Unemployment in India

There are three main sources which provide data on educated unemployment. These are NSS, DGET and Census. In the census, the population census and special cards for technical and educated persons provide data on unemployment. Since the coverage of the former is unknown and the latter lacks in required classification characteristics the reserachers/planners do not pay much attention to the unemployment estimates of census. It will not be discussed in the present paper also.

The DGET data on live register also have known limitations, such as, registration is voluntary and all unemployed persons might have not registered themselves; on the other hand, all registered persons are not unemployed (some students and employed persons also get registered) and one person may get registered at more than one employment exchanges. Though due to these limitations, the DEGT data do not consider an appropriate estimate of unemployment but the researchers and planners have been using them when reliable data are not available. Exponentially rising trends in these data relating to the educated registrants are found. It is seen that educated job seekers was 2.3 million in 1971 and rose to 16.5 million in 1986 exhibiting a growth rate of about 48% during the entire period. These growth rates during 1971-76, 1976-81 and 36.5% respectively. Technical and professional persons having graduate as well as post-graduate degree have shown least growth than that of other educational categories.

Looking at the annual registration and placement figures one sees that placement has decreased even in absolute number from 208 thousand to 143 thousand during 1971 and 1986 and this has happend to all categories of persons excepting commerce and technical and professional graduates and post-graduates where it has shown a slight increase in absolute numbers, though in terms of proportion of placement the total annual registration was 9.0% in 1971 which has decreased to 4.6% in 1986.

The data on unemployment thrown out by the National Sample Survey Organisation (NSSO) have been extensively used by the researchers and planners. In fact, the NSS estimates on unemployment, whether general or educated, and utilized by the Government for planning purposes and referred to in Plan documents are based on these surveys.

Before coming to uneployment situation in Sixth, Seventh and Eighth Plan periods, it is essential to keep two points in mind. These are about the changes occurred in LEPRs and unemployment rates during 1977-78 and 1983 and difference in stock estimates for 1980, 1985, 1990 and 1995 prepared by Planning Commission and IAMR. The labour force participation rates and unemployment rates according to different educational categories for 1977-78 (32nd Round) and 1983 (38th Round) have decreased during 1977-78 and 1983 for all educational catego-ries excepting engineering where they remained more or less constant.

On comparing the stock estimates prepared by IAMR and Planning Commission, it is found that estimates prepared by IAMR are on higher side in comparison to those of Planning Commission. The total stock estimates of all educated categories is compared below for 1980, 1985 and 1990.

(in Thousands)

	1980	1985	1990
Planning Commission	34382.2	47159.5	63654.4
IAMR	36713.0	51874.0	70497.0

The estimates of stock prepared by IAMR are used to get estimates of labour force and unemployment by applying rates of 1977-78 in 1980 and of 1983 in 1985, 1990 and 1995.

Sixth Plan : The stock of educated person has increased from 36.7 million in 1980 to 51.8 million in 1985. The corresponding increase in labour force is from 23.9 million in 1980 to 32.5 million in 1985 giving net addition to labour as 9.4 million during the period. Similarly, the net addition to educated unemployment is of the order of 1.19 million during the Sixth Plan.

Seventh Plan : The estimates of educated persons at the beginning and end of Seventn Plan are 3.4 million and 4.6 million respectively giving net addition of educated unemployment as 1.3 million during the period. On the other hand, net additions to labour force are expected to be of the order of 11.6 million.

Eighth Plan : The estimates of net additions to educated labour force and unemployment are expected to the order of 13.6 million and 1.4 million during the Seventh Plan period. The volume of educated unemployment at the end of Eighth Plan (beginning of 1955) is expected to reach the level of about 6 million on the basis of 1983 unemployment rates.

6.3.4 EDUCATION AND EMPLOYMENT LINKAGES

The relevance and relation of education to employment assumed added significance ever since pervasive unemployment among the educated became a reality. Some have squarely put the blame on the non-performance of the educational system while others have attempted to highlight the dichotomy between education and development in changing technological context. It is because technology is perceived as important intervening factor in deciding the skill-job linkages and this technological progress is seen to have direct implications for the quantity and quality of labour demanded.

Technological development in India had been on a narrow base mostly confining to the organised sectors. Organised sector formed only a small segment in terms of employment. But the educational sector was more broad-based. Secondly, technological developments were at a fast rate and our educational system failed to respond satisfactorily to these changes; consequently, the expansion witnessed in the educational sector was more of quantitative than qualitative nature. In other words we were caught in a peculiar position characterised by two sets of factors :

(a) more graduates are produced than demanded by the technological development; and

(v) even those who could be absorbed could not be absorbed because their skill levels were not suited to the changed situation.

The dilema in education-employment relations in India is the excessive orientation of education towards employment, especially of organised sectors, and the remote relation between the educational process and skills requirement of the very same sector.

However, organised employment is classified under two sectors: Public and Private. The Public Sector comprises of 5 areas: Central Government, Central Government Quasi, State Government, State Government Quasi and the Local Bodies. About 48 per cent of the total public sector employment is provided by the State Government out of which 36 per cent is by the State Government itself and another 12 per cent by the State Government Quasi organisation. The Central Government accounts for 20 per cent and the Central Government Quasi establishments account for another 10 per cent of the employment. The local bodies make up for the remaining 13 per cent employment.

Over the last two decades (between 1961-81) employment in the organised sector has grown from 120.9 lakhs to 225.78 lakhs, i.e., at an annual compound rate of 3.24 per cent. Among the industrial sectors electricity, gas and water witnessed maximum growth rates (5.1) followed by services (4.4) and manufacturing (2.9). But the share of electricity, gas and water is very small in the total employment. The industrial divisions, i.e., services, manufacturing and transport and communications account for nearly three-fourth of the total employment in the organised sectors.

Over the period of two decades the relative share of service sector in employment has gone up whereas share of other two (manufacturing and transport and communications) declined marginally. In fact, services sector increased its share from 33 per cent in 1961 to 41 per cent in 1981. Services sector alone accounted for more than half of the total increase in employment during the corresponding period (Table 6.2).

The detailed educational break-up is available for employees in occupational divisions 0 & 1 and 2; for the category of craftsmen and production process workers (7, 8, and 9) similar educational break-up is not available. Occupational division 0 and 1 is dominated by professional qualified people in the public sector. About 69 per cent possesses professional degree or diploma and the remaining

32 per cent possesses degree in general education. The major shifts in this occupational division are : (i) a decline in the proportion of degree holders (professional and general), (ii) increase in the proportion of diploma holders (professional), and (iii) other general educated categories more or less maintained their share.

The educational profiles of the employees in occupational division (0 and 1, 2) in the private sector are different from that of public sector. In the administrative, executive and managerial (division 2), most of the employees have general education. However, over the years a tendency of this category to attract professionally qualified workers, especially graduates, is evident. The major shift is that the proportion of non-matriculates and diploma holders has come down and correspondingly there is a shift towards graduates.

Table 6.2 : *Total Employment by Industry Division*

(in Lakhs)

	1961	1971	1981	Growth Rates (1961-81)
Agriculture and Hunting etc.	8.5 (7.03)	10.74 (6.15)	13.21 (5.77)	2.22
Mining and Quarrying	66.79 (5.62)	5.86 (3.35)	9.48 (4.14)	1.68
Manufacturing	33.89 (28.03)	47.61 (27.24)	60.47 (27.43)	2.94
Electricity, Gas & Water	2.64 (2.18)	4.81 (2.75)	2.18 (3.18)	5.13
Construction	8.43 (6.97)	10.19 (5.83)	11.61 (5.07)	1.61
Wholesale & Retail Trade	2.54 (2.11)	6.32 (3.62)	3.94 (1.72)	2.22
Transport & Communication etc.	18.04 (14.92)	23.13 (13.24)	27.69 (12.10)	2.16
Services	40.07 (33.12)	66.07 (37.81)	95.21 (41.61)	4.42

Note : Figures in brackets are percentages to the total.
Source: Statistical Outline of India, 1984, Tata Services Ltd., Deptt. of Economics and Statistics, Bombay, 1984.

Indian experience shows a conflicting trend of declining job opportunities and continuing expansion of the educational system. The recruitment policy of showing preference to higher educated personnel is atleast partially responsible of this. The process in operation is an increased demand for higher levels of education as a result of the preference shown to higher educated in the employment market. Organised sectors being small segment in the total employment in the economy, it becomes difficult to absorb all the educated persons in this sector. In addition to this is the question of irrelevance of the educational system to provide required type of skills for the job market.

In view of the above discussions, for matching of education and employment, the following suggestions are listed.[28] :

— Assessment of employment potential in future, through growth targets or investment targets.
— Approach should be practical rather than machanical and theoretical.
— The private sector should be pressurised through industries department to cooperate with education department. (Ministry of HRD).
— Technical, vocational and professional education should be subsidised with proper balances between social costs and private costs.
— Decentralisation of organisational and management structure of education (need based power allocation on regional local basis)
— Involvement of users of outputs of education system in planning the course, designing the curricula, identification of methods and equipment for skill formation, evaluation of procedures is necessary.
— Users should come forward with scholarships for successful candidates at national entrance level.
— The tax be imposed on industry by the education system for producing skilled manpower (because industry will use them). This revenue should recycle in education system.
— Separate department of non-formal education (for all the population) should be set up and bring all forms of adult and other non-formal education under one umbrella, the main objective of which should be boosting productive skills.
— A monitoring cell should be started to look seriously into the current status of limited participation of target population—women, SC/STs and other weaker sections, for corrections in future.

In brief, "a rich and meaningful interaction between education and employment requires metamorphic, wholesale unweaving of the current fabric of our economy and the reweaving of the same with new educational threads. Proper educational planning meets the task only half-the way".

6.4. **Summing up**

In the light of foregoing discussions this final section of the paper concludes the study. However, as we have noted in the earlier sections, independent India inherited a higher education system as an integral element of its colonial under-development. The system was both quantitatively microscopic as well as highly inadequate and qualitatively anaemic as well as dysfunctional. The constraints of such a situation did not permit an option between quantity and quality.

But since independence the number of recognised institutions and enrolment has increased substantially. As a result the national stock of educated manpower is estimated to have increased from less than 4 million to about 48 million. It is observed that growth over the period of 35 years in number of institutions is tremendous. But at the same time it is also observed that qualitywise it has been able to serve the requisite purpose on the one hand whereas on the other the country is facing acute problem of massive unemployment among educated.

The problem of educated unemployment is becoming increasingly serious in the country in view of rapid expansion of education and the slackening rate of economic development. It is serious from the point of view of utilising fully labour as also the capital that is required in the process of education. Great concern is raised at the under-utilisation of industrial capacity because the capital invested remains under-utilised. In the case of educated unemployment also there remains non-utilisation of capital that is earmarked for being spent in the process of education. The problem has naturally become most serious for India where the pace of economic development has been very low.

Looking at the annual registration and placement figures one can say the placement has decreased from 208 thousand to 143 thousand during 1971 and 1986 and this has happened to all categories of persons excepting commerce and technical and professional graduates and post-graduates where it has shown a slight increase in absolute numbers though in terms of proportion it has decreased in all categories. However, the education specific work force participation rates and unemployment rates exhibited that participation rates are lower for middle and secondary education and below middle education as compared to that of higher education. Contrary to this, the unemployment rates are increasing as education levels increase and thus, they are highest in graduates and above.

A number of sources and publications provide information on educated unemployment even though they adopt varying concepts and reference periods and differ in coverage too, thus, making the data quite often uncomparable. Among the different sources, census, DGF&T and NSS are three main sources which provide data on educated unemployed. Researchers and planners do not pay much attention to the unemployment estimates of census because of the unknown coverage and lacking in required classification. Second source, i.e., DGF&T have also some limitations, such as, registration in live register is voluntary and all unemployed persons might have not registered themselves; secondly, all registered persons are not unemployed and one person may get registered at more than one employment exchange. Despite these limitations, the researchers and planners have been using the estimates of unemployment when other reliable data are not available. However, the unemployment data thrown out by the NSS have been extensively used by the researchers and planners. The unemployment estimates, both general and educated, are used by the Government for planning purposes and referred to in plan documents.

There are general schemes launched by the Central and State Governments from time to time. But even if these programmes generate employment as per expectations, unemployment would not be eliminated within the Seventh Plan unless efforts are immediately made to make the current unemployed more employable through short-term training/vocational programmes and special employment programmes directed towards their absorption. In particular, efforts should be made to divert matriculates, who form the bulk of the educated unemployed, to non-clerical jobs and self employment.

Notes & References

1. Frank W. Banghart & Albert Trull, Jr. (1973), *Educational Planning,* The Macmillan Company, N.Y. pp. 6-7.

2. P.R. Panchamukhi (1988), 'Economics of Educational Planning—The Myth and the reality of the theory and practice', *Journal of Edl. Planning & Adm.*, NIEPA, ND, p. 1
3. *Ibid*, p. 2.
4. *Ibid*, p. 2.
5. *Ibid*, p. 2.
6. Richard Perlman (1973), 'The Economics of Education : conceptual problems and policy issues', McGraw-Hill Book Company, New York, p. 62.
7. For more detailed discussion, see G. Psacharopoulos, 'Returns to Education : An Updated International Comparison', in T. King (ed.), *Education and Income,* Work Bank, Staff working paper, No 402, Washington D.C., 1980.
8. For detailed, see 'Employment and Manpower Planning — A manual for training in basic techniques', ILO (ARTEP), Bangkok, 1984.
9. For a discussion of the alpha factor (originally discussed in Dension, F.F., 'Measuring the Contribution of Education to Economic Growth', in *The Residual Factor in Economic Growth,* OFCD, Paris, 1984) see K. Inone and A. Izawa 'Cost-Benefit Analysis — Its Application in Manpower Planning' in *Manpower Assessment and Planning Project in Asia,* ILO, Geneva.
10. Richard S. Fckaus, 'Economic Criteria for Education and Training', *Review of Economics and Statistics,* Vol. 46, May 1964, presents a detailed application of the manpower-forecasting approach to educational planning.
11. Panchmukhi (1988), *op. cit.*, p. 8.
12. ILO (ARTEP) Study, *op. cit.*, p. v-21.
13. *Ibid*, p. v-22.
14. G. Psachoropoulos (1980) (Ed.) : 'Information : an essential factor on educational planning and policy, UNESCO, pp. 22-23.
15. For expository purpose only the most crucial variables of a model will be presented and a couple of key references given, On the analytical side of projecting social demand, see R. Stone, 'A Model of the Educational System', *Minerva*, Winter 1965.
16. See, Psacharopoulos (1980), p. 23.
17. On the issue of exploring actual enrolments see J. Bishap. 'The effect of Public Policies on the Demand for Higher Education'. *Journal of Human Resources, Summer,* 1977. For a case-study of exploring student plans, see G. Psacharopoulos and C. Sonwelies, 'A Socio-economic Analysis of the Demand for Higher Education'. London, (ISF), 1978 (Mimea).
18. *Ibid*, p. 29.
19. *Ibid*, p. 31.
20. *Ibid*, p. 32.
21. G. Psacharopoulos (1977), 'Socio-economic Background, Education and Achievement', *British Journal of Sociology,* September, 1977.
22. For some actual estimate of this trade-off, sea G. Psacharopoulos, 'Estimating the Welfare Effects of Educational Policies', In V. Halberstaot And a. Cuyler, *Public Economics and Human Resources*, Cujas, 1977.
23. J. Coleman *et al.* (1966), *Equality of Educational Opportunity*, U.S. office of Education, for a review of findings in developing countries, see. J. Simons, 'The Determinants of School Achievement in Development Countries : The Educational Production Function, International Bank for Reconstruction and Development (Bank Staff Working Paper No. 201), March, 1975.

24. F. Harbison and C.A. Myers, *Education, Manpower and Economic Growth,* p. 5.
25. Gautam Mathur, *The Economic Principles of Long-term Educational Planning* (Mineographed).
26. B.L. Agarwal (1977), 'Educated Unemployment in India', *Commence,* Pamphlet - 109, p. 14.
27. *Ibid*, p. 15.
28. *Ibid*, p. 15.
29. Self-employment implies 'Creation' of a 'Job' for ourself, by engaging in a gainful econonric activity and earning one's livelihood.
30. Y.L. Ahuja, Trilok Singh and Y. Gunasekar (1988) 'Educated Unemployed in the North Eastern, IAMR Status Paper (Unpublished), Aug. 1988, p. 22.
31. Govt. of India, Planning Commission (1985). The Seventh Five Year Plan — 1985-90, Vol. II, p. 54.
32. *Op. cit* (Seventh Plan), p. 54.
33. *Ibid*, pp. 54-55.
34. *Op. cit* (Ahuja, Singh & Sekar), p. 115.
35. Central Institute for Research & Training in Employment Service (CIRTES) — *Hand-book on Promotion of Self-Employment for the Use of Employment Offices* (Revised), DGF&T, Ministry of Labour, Govt. of India (1987), pp. 29-30.
36. *Ibid*, p. 31.
37. CIRTES (1987), *op. cit.*, p. 31.
38. *Ibid.*
39. *Ibid*, p. 32.
40. B. Kumar (1980). *Self Employment Opportunities for Educated Unemployed,* Anuj Publications, Lucknow, p. 29.
41. Hindustan Times dated 1st March, 1989.

7. Conclusions, Suggestions and Recommendations

In the preceding chapters, an attempt was made to assess the extent of education development made in India. What emerges from the foregoing discussion is the fact that since the level of educated unemployment is serious, the public funds may be allocated rationally in order to create more productive and labour intensive activities. For utilizing the available manpower resources in a more efficient way, it is imperative to explore the possibilities of widening the prospects of self-employment in unorganized sector. To conclude, since education, employment and economy are inextricably interlinked, the success of planners and policy-makers in alleviating poverty and eradicating illiteracy would depend largely upon the extent to which education and manpower planning strategies are interlinked and properly co-ordinated with an overall approach to socio-economic development.

However, in subsequent paragraphs this chapter summarizes the different aspects of education relating to its system, policy, strategies, processes, programmes, schemes and approaches for implementation of education decisions and suggest some alternative strategies for the improvement.

In spite of various commissions, committees and panels appointed by the Central and State Governments from time to time Indian education is still at the cross-roads. Education has failed to evolve a national pattern so far. However, the new pattern of education popularly known as 10+2+3 had raised fresh hopes. It is destined to be the national system of education in due course of time. It has been accepted in principle by almost all the States of India.

The report of Kothari Commission is a synoptic survey of the entire educational situation in all its complexities (Annexure). The Education Commission, for instance, is not clear and definite enough on the content and courses for elementary stages. A redefinition of basic education and an examination of the merits of the earlier eight year composite basis school would have been worthwhile. The division of the primary stage into lower and higher, the nature of work experience, the qualities, aspects of the elementary stage are issues which need explanation.

The new pattern (10+2+3) introduced science and mathematics, work experience and vocational courses. A glance at the implementation on the pattern reveals that we have failed to provide the facilities needed for its successful implementation. It would be worthwhile if students are asked to express their views openly about their experiences of the new system.

In the New Educational Policy emphasis has been laid on the need of linking the educational planning with the manpower planning. Some of the priority areas identified for attention for implementation of new education policy are, as manpower planning and demand forecasting and by strengthening the data base, monitoring and evaluation system. Even the Steering Groups on Education of the Planning Commission are giving stress on planning, monitoring, evaluation and data base in connection with the formulation of the Eighth Five Year Plan.

During colonial period education served to the advantage of the upper and middle strata of the society. But emphasis was laid on the importance of mass education based on the tradition of the nation and its needs and aspirations. The National Council of Education (1906) was broad-based and comprehensive. Its scheme of studies was to be imparted in three stages, viz., (a) primary — 3 years course (6-9), (b) Secondary—7 years course (9-15) and collegiate—4 years course (16-19). On the whole this system of education was condemned as academic and too literacy.

After independance it was felt that in the field of education a change in pattern and content of education set-up is must. The present experiment has not been introduced all of a sudden but it is the product of historical developments. Rather it is the results of successive experiments before and after independence. However, the entire period of formal education has been divided into two main stages, viz., school education and higher education. Education is further classified into two major categories, viz., (a) General Education and (b) Vocational/Technical/Professional Education. The C.A.B.F. strongly recommended the introduction of the 10+2+3 pattern of education all over the country during the Fifth Plan period. The National Education Policy has suggested 12 years of school education and three year undergraduate course. Where a university desires, it could have a two-year pass course and three-year honours course. By 1980 this pattern had been introduced in almost all States and Union Territories of India. This structural pattern of education has tremendously affected the entire field of education—secondary, higher secondary, collegiate and university education.

At the end of formal education social education can make an individual a true, dutiful and responsible citizen. For fullest development of an individual social education is essential; however, the Union Ministry of HRD (Department of Education) initiates social education schemes in co-operation with the Planning Commission. The different Central Ministries like Labour, Industry, Defence, Railway have their own social education programmes.

A little less than two-third or 64 per cent people in India are illiterates. Therefore, the Government of India has given a very high priority to to adult education. About 65 million (650 lakhs) illiterate persons in the age-group 15-35 have been covered through National Adult Education Programmes, and 7 lakhs adult education centres have been set up throughout the country.

To ensure life oriented basic literacy and skill for the children of the age group 6-14 and to supplement and reinforce formal education, non-formal education initiated in the nine educationally backward states since the Sixth Plan. In this scheme, assistance has been given to state governments and voluntary agencies for setting up about 1.50 lakhs centers. Later on, it is proposed to extend this scheme in ten more educationally backward states.

However, the success of both, non-formal and social education programmes, depends to a great extent on the degree of motivation on the part of the learners.

The role of education in the development of the traditional people has been very well stressed by educationists and sociologists. It is no more viewed only in terms of developing an individual culturally, but its area has been widened considerably to cover socio-economic aspects leading to over all development of country. In democratic set-up, the transformed role of education is not only that of creating a balanced and socially integrated individual, but it is expected to ensure that the benefit of education goes to all the people irrespective of caste, sex, socially and locationally disadvantaged groups.

In the field of modern Indian Education pattern and content are the two most important components or ingredients of education. The new structural pattern as proposed by the Education Commission and as it exists in India has tremendously affected the entire field of education—secondary, higher secondary, collegiate and university education.

Since independence the number of recognised institutions and enrolment has increased substantially. As a result the national stock of educated manpower is estimated to have increased from less than 4 million to about 48 million. It is observed that growth over the period of 35 years in number of institutions is maximum at middle stage followed by professional institutions, whereas the minimum growth is witnessed in primary institutions. On the whole, the general educational facilities have increased tremendously. But at the same time it is observed that quality-wise it has not been able to serve the requisite purpose.

During different plan periods, in spite of massive quantitative expansion of education at all levels, yet much has to be achieved to reach the national goals. Only a little over 36 per cent of the population are literate and the remaining are illiterate .The national aim of universal elementary education is yet to be achieved as envisaged in the constitution. Fifty million children are yet to be enrolled and vocationalisation of secondary education has yet to make headway. The standard, or quality of higher education has to be raised or improved. The Seventh Plan has emphasised that one of the primary tasks is the harnessing of the country's abundant human resources and improving their capability for development with equity.

Despite tremendous growth, in educational facilities, the country is facing acute problems of massive illiteracy and unemployment among educated as well as uneducated. There is, therefore, a need for human resource development strategy with less emphasis on formal education and would be more oriented towards productive work. The changing socio-economic conditions would demand a form of education and training which will enable the continuing development of the individual.

In the New Education Policy emphasis has been laid on the need of linking the educational planning with the manpower planning. Some of the priority areas identified for attention for implementation of new education policy are, as manpower planning and demand forecasting and by strengthening the data base, monitoring and evaluation system. Even the Steering Groups on Education of the Planning Commission are giving stresss on planning, monitoring, evaluation and data base in connection with the formulation of the Eighth Five Year Plan.

For proper appraisal and an effective planning of the education system as a whole, it is imperative to have a strong and up-to-date information system. However, a number of sources and publications provide information on education even though they adopt varying concepts and reference periods and differ in coverage too thus making the data quite often uncomparable. The need for comprehensive and up-to-date data is becoming increasingly imperative in the context of formulation of policies and programmes. While the collection of educational statistics has become a complex and time consuming process, the existing gaps listed in the text need to be filled for strengthening the data base requirement for educational planning.

During the past decade, there has been a growing interest in the economic aspects of education. The recent interest in educational planning follows as a result of the various developments in this sphere including huge public investment involved in it. With an increasing emphasis on benefits of education, more materialistic view has been taken. In the foregoing discussions an evaluation has been made of several studies so far conducted in India. In spite of the differences in methodology, coverage and findings studies on India reveal certain general conclusions like: returns on college education very between 4 per cent to 10 per cent, returns are high for matriculates and returns on education are found to be lower than those on physical capital etc.

Another important aspect which has been examined is the current status of relationship between education and employment in India. The fixtures of unemployment suggest that the education and employment matching is a dire necessity. This could be made possible by formulating the education and training programmes more closely related to available employment opportunities. The present education system is no longer capable of satisfying the increasingly diversified educational needs, which is seen through the mushroom growth of other institutions to compete or complement the existing system which by itself cannot meet the needs of individuals and that of society for their continuing development over a longer period of time. Therefore, there is a need for restructuring of the whole education system which would be geared to productive working life and may be called — 'Active Education Policy'.

However, to get a more clear vision of the inherent potentialities of the New Education Policy, let us discuss certain aspects in more detail.

In the provision of delinking of degrees from jobs, so far the only thing that has been made clear is that there would be a National Merit Examination conducted at +2 level to select the candidates for government jobs. But what would be the contents and mode of such examination? What would be the maximum and minimum age limits etc. have not been decided at all. Secondly, in the infrastructurally deprived areas, possibility of their competing with the students from elite families who are groomed for such type of competitive examination is just remote. Thirdly, about 40 per cent of our population is below poverty line. Very few from this have reached the plus two stage. About 25 per cent population are marginal and small farmers who are just at subsistence level and are dependent on family labour for agricultural activities. Their participation in higher education is almost nil.

Thus, in a country where the students from about 90 per cent of the families either do not participate in higher education or some of them start thinking of competitive examinations for administrative and managerial jobs only at the postgraduate level, how well the concept of equal opportunity for all in the aforesaid framework of the NGP will work can be imagined.

The second vital question that we confront is the conjectured role of the vocational approach in the absence of massive job opportunities (in both public and private sectors). Even the special developmental programmes including the self employment schemes have not made a significant dent in our country yet.

In the light of foregoing discussions this final section of the paper concludes the study. However, as we have noted in the earlier sections, independent India inherited a higher education system as an integral element of its colonial under-development. The system was both quantitatively microscopic as well as highly inadequate and qualitatively anaemic as well as dysfunctional. The constraints of such a situation did not permit an option between quantity and quality.

But since independence the number of recognised institutions and enrolment has increased substantially. As a result the national stock of educated manpower is estimated to have increased from less than 4 million to about 48 million. It is observed that growth over the period of 35 years in number of institutions is tremendous. But at the same time it is also observed that quality-wise it has not been able to serve the requisite purpose on the one hand whereas on the other the country is facing acute problem of massive unemployment among educated.

The problem of educated unemployment is becoming increasingly serious in the country in view of rapid expansion of education and the slackening rate of economic development. It is serious from the point of view of utilising fully labour as also the capital that is required in the process of education. Great concern is raised at the under-utilisation of industrial capacity because the capital invested remains under-utilised. In the case of educated unemployment also there remains non-utilisation of capital that is earmarked for being spent in the process of education. The problem has naturally become most serious for India where the pace of economic development has been very low.

Looking at the annual registration and placement figures one can say that placement has decreased from 208 thousand to 143 thousand during 1971 and 1986 and this has happened to all categories of persons excepting commerce and technical and professional graduates and post-graduates where it has shown a slight increase in absolute numbers though in terms of proportion it has decreased in all categories. However, the education specific work force participation rates and unemployment rates exhibited that participation rates are lower for middle and secondary education and below middle education. Contrary to this, the unemployment rates are increasing as education levels increase and thus, they are highest in graduates and above.

A number of sources and publications provide information on educated unemployment even though they abopt varying concepts and reference periods and differ in coverage too, thus, making the data quite often uncomparable. Among the different sources, census, DGF&T and NSS are three main sources which provide data on educated unemployment. Researchers and planners do not pay much attention to the unemployment estimates of census because of the unknown covergage and lacking in required classification. Second source, i.e., DGF&T have also some limitations, such as, registration in live register is voluntary and all unemployed persons might have not registered themselves; secondly, all registered persons are not unemployed and one person may get registered at more than one employment exchange. Despite these limitations, the researchers and planners have been using the estimates of unemployment when other reliable data are not available. However, the unemployment data thrown out by the NSS have been extensively used by the reserchers and planners. The unemployment estimates, both general and educated, are used by the Government for planning purposes and referred to in plan documents.

There are general schemes launched by the Central and State governments from time to time. But even if these programmes generate employment as per expectations, unemployment would not be eliminated within the Seventh Plan unless efforts are immediately made to make the current unemployment more employable through short-term training/vocational programmes and special employment programmes directed towards their absorption. In particular, efforts should be made to divert matriculates, who form the bulk of the educated unemployed, to non-clerical jobs and self employment.

Suggestions & Recommendations

— The pattern of education which India inherited at the time of its independence will not suit its need. Each stage in education is linked to the next one without any terminal stage. As a consequence there has been an ever increasing pressure for the provision of university education. A developing country like India can ill efford expansion of expensive university education when it has not been able to provide universal primary education to its children in fulfilment of the constitutional provisions.

— The products turned out by the educational system are not in tune with needs of the country. The educated persons have looked down upon manual work and held white collar jobs and greater esteem; they have preferred wage-employment to self-employment. Consequently expansion of education facilities has been accompanied by an increase in educated unemployment which the government is finding it difficult to solve by creating more white collar jobs and wage-employment opportunities.

— Therefore, instead of solving unemployment problem the educational system is accentuating it. The change in attitude of the students towards the dignity of manual work and a preference for self-employment can be brought about through introduction of vocational bias in education.

— Another question is whether education should be narrow based vocational education in secondary schools or be balanced between theoretical learning and practical experience in all branches of educational system.

— In order to provide education and training and developing and skills, provision of vocational education is essential. Besides the development planning envisages an increase in productivity of labour engaged in different sectors of the economy. This can come about only by providing vocational education to the people engaged in work or who are to join the work.

A number of sources and publications provide information on education even though they adopt varying concepts and reference periods and differ in coverage too thus making the data quite often uncomparable. The need for comprehensive up-to-date data is becoming increasingly imperative in the context of formulation of policies and developmental programmes. While the collection of educational statistics has become a complex and time consuming process. The following suggestions/recommendations may be given under different heads for the improvement of the data.

(i) *Institutions*: Separate data for teaching institutions which prepare students and conduct examinations leading to award of degree, diploma, certificate and non-teaching institutions which simply conduct examination should be given.

(ii) *Intake/Enrolment*: Enorlment data for professional and technical courses should be published individual course-wise and subject-wise each year. Secondly, intake data should be given for each class for course/subject with further break-up as freshers and repeaters. Thirdly, intake capacity as well as actual intake may be made available for each course and subject of each discipline/faculty at various stages/levels for different types of institutions whether recognized/not recognised or formal/non-formal sector. Further details such as rural/urban sex, SC/ST etc. may also be given.

(iii) *Outturn:* (a) There are certain examining bodies, whose outturn is not recorded by the Ministry of HRD, Department. of Education or any other agency, for instance, Institution of Engineers, Institute of Chartered Accountants of India etc. The same should be made available, (b) Age-wise outturn data should be made available for different stages and levels of education and (c) separate information about number of students appearing privately and causally in High/H.S./Degree/Diploma examinations and passing out should be available by course, sex, type of education and State/Union Territory.

(iv) *Teachers*: Data on teachers should be available by educational qualification, subject of specialisation and experience for each State/Union Territory.

(vi) *Cost of Education*: Data on cost of education (both recurring and non-recurring) by item and type of institutions for informal sector should be made available.

(vii) *General*: (a) The NCERT should concentrate on the collection of data for the informal and non-formal system of education. It should collect details of enrolment and outturn by type and levels of education. (b) Since the information on enrolment and examination results or University teaching departments, colleges and institutions deemed to be universities is collected by the UGC, so the same should not be collected by the Ministry. This will remove duplication of effort and reduce the delay in the publications of data. (c) Data on non-formal education imparted by unrecognised institutions in trades, viz., typing, stenography, book-keeping etc. should be collected and published by the Ministry. (d) There should be a Data Bank for collection, storage and restrieval of the entire educational statistics covering both the general and vocational/professional/technical education whether imparted under the formal or the non-formal system. The Data Bank can be a part of the Ministry of HRD, Department of Education, which as a centralised Agency will also take care of the statistics maintained by various technical/vocational/professional councils/bodies.

It may also be added here that while trying to increase the flow of additional data to fill up the data gaps, it must be ensured that the comparability and consistency in data is maintained.

Glossary

Adult Education

Education for illiterate adults*

Applied Manpower Research

Research undertaken in the field of manpower with specific applications in view.

Apprenticeship

A system under which an employer undertakes by contract to engage a person, train him for a trade or occupation for a period the duration of which has been fixed in advance.

Aspirations

Strong desires or goals

Attrition

Diminution in the stock of manpower as a result of death, retirement and net out migration. However, attrition relating to an occupational category must also take into account their mobility to other occupations.

Census

The term 'census' means to take a total count of something, usually a country's population, on a given day of the year or over a period of weeks.

Cohort

A batch of persons belonging to the same time period representing common features, e.g., students admitted to an educational course in a year, or persons employed in a firm in a year etc.

Cost of Education

The total cost of schooling including institutional cost, private cost and opportunity cost.

Course of Study

Theoretical and practical lessons in a discipline or a combination of disciplines for the acquisition of knowledge and skill during a specified term of study, generally leading to the award of certificates/diplomas/degrees.

Critical Skill

That type of skill which is scarce and involves a high level of brain power. The generation or development of such skill usually requires a long period of formal education and training.

Curriculum

The planned composite effort of any school to guide pupils towards a predetermined level of learning. It may indicate the time to be devoted to each part of education and/or training and the order in which the items are to be learnt. The term is sometimes used as synonymous with 'syllabus'.

Cyclical Unemployment

Unemployment associated with the downswing of the business cycle.

Drop outs

See, Educational wastage.

Economics of Education

A study of those functions of education, which deal with investment in man and of returns thereon, and the impact of education on occupational structure, migration of labour etc.

Educated Manpower

In the Indian context, 'educated manpower' refers to all educated persons with Matriculation or equivalent and above qualifications excluding those enrolled as students.

Educated Unemployed

In the Indian context, the term refers to persons with matriculation or more during the reference period. This group of persons excludes housewives, students and those 60 years of age.

Educational Expenditure:

In India, the national educational expenditure includes all

expenditure incurred by educational institutions throughout the country as well as expenditure incurred on educational purposes (other than through educational institutions) by Government. It also includes private educational expenditure in the form of fees paid by parents of pupils or regular contributions made by managements of private educational institutions, ad hoc contributions, donations and subscriptions made for particular educational projects.

Educational Planning

The overall planing of education in a continuous and systematic manner, involving the application and coordination of social research methods and of principles and techniques of Administration, economics and finance with definite aims such as providing everyone with an opportunity of developing his potentialities and making the most effective contribution to the social, cultural and economic development of the country. (The World Yearbook of Education, 1967).

Educational Stages

The educational ladder beginning (as in India) from pre-primary, primary (I to IV/V) and continuing through middle school (V/VI to VII/VIII), high/higher secondary (VIII/IX to X/XI/XII) and higher education (Graduate and above).

Educational Wastage

It covers the phenomena of *Stagnation* and *drop-out*. *Drop-out* refers to withdrawal of pupils from a course without completing it. *Stagnation* means the stayg of pupils in a class for more than the prescribed period.

Education as Investment

Education when thought of as investment refers to expenditures on human capital formation through education which brings in larger returns in the form of higher earnings. Education as consumption represents a durable good that yields a stream of satisfaction and pleasure to its owner over a period of years.

Education Explosion

Abnormal increase in enrolments and outturns for an excess of what the economy can absorb.

Education-Occupation Matrix

Distribution of occupation for given educational qualifications depicted in rows and columns.

Efficiency

The ability to achieve desired results with economy of time and effort in relation to the work accomplished.

Enrolment

It refers to the total student body in all the classes of a course of study (Also see, intake).

Flow Chart

A diagrammatic representation of a system, in which inter-relationships between its component parts are shown by various symbols and inter-connecting arrows. For instance, the promotion rate, repetition rate and drop out rate are plotted to indicate the student wastage rate for each year in a course of study.

Functional Literacy

Minimum education that is necessary for a worker to be effective in his job.

Further Education

Voluntary continuation of education beyond the level reached through compulsory schooling and preparation for employment. Further education is, in some cases, acquired through special systems of part-time or full-time courses devised to prepare for access to universities, or similar institutes, persons who have not followed the normal course of education leading to that level.

General Education

The streams of education which, is their choice of subject matter, etc., envisage any kinds of specialisation with a view to preparing the students for work in a particular sector of economic activity.

Higher Education

Education at post-secondary level given in educational institutions which are open to students who have successfully completed secondary education or reached an equivalent level, e.g., universities, institutes of technology and higher commercial colleges and other institutions which confer degrees or diplomas of a level substantially equivalent to university degrees. This education is usually very specialised in nature; the various programmes are directed to particular disciplines and related areas.

Indicators in Education (some selected indicators)

The Indicas used to measure the impact of educational system in India are:

(i) *Index of Enrolment Growth at Stage I*

$$= \frac{\text{Enrolment at stage } i \text{ for a year}}{\text{Enrolment at stage } i \text{ for base year}} \times 100$$

(ii) *Gross Enrolment Ratio:* This is a very important index for measuring the efficiency of the Educational system. It measures about what percentage of the total population in the relevant age-group is being covered by the various educational programmes being run in the country.

$$\text{Gross Enrolment Ratio at Stage i} = \frac{\text{Enrolment in stage } i}{\text{Population in the age group corresponding to the } i \text{ th stage}} \times 100$$

(iii) *Students Flow Statistics:* It gives information about the movement of students enrolled in class I to higher classes (upto class VIII) and give the retention ratios in different classes as measured from the cohort year. These statistics are useful for Educational Planning as these measure the extent of drop-outs and stagnation for different classes (I-VIII) during the period.

(iv) *Teacher-Pupil Ratios:* It is defined as the average number of students per teacher for a particular type of school, e.g.,

$$\text{Teacher Pupil Ratio for Primary} \quad \frac{\text{Total Enrolment in Primary Schools}}{\text{Total number of Teachers in Primary Schools}}$$

(v) *Average annual Cost per Student* : This index gives an idea about the average expenditure incurred for one student for a particular type of institution. While calculating this index only direct expenditure on institutions has been taken into account. Indirect expenditure which consists of expenditure incurred on direction, inspection, buildings, furniture, scholarships, hotels and other miscellaneous items has not been taken into account as these items cannot be apportioned to each type of institution. For example, average annual cost for Primary schools will be defined as:-

$$\text{Average Annual Cost per Student for Primary Schools} = \frac{\text{Total Direct (Recurring) Expenditure on Primary Schools}}{\text{Total Enrolment in Primary Schools}}$$

(vi) *Extent of Coverage* or *Co-efficient of Elitya for SC/ST*: This index quantifies the share of SC/STs population enrolled at different stages. For example:

$$\text{Extent of Coverage for SC/ST at Primary Stage} = \frac{\text{Percentage Enrolment of SC/STs to Total Enrolment}}{\text{Percentage of SC/ST Population to Total Population}} \times 100$$

Intake

In the field of educational and manpower planning, this term refers to only that part of the total student body who are admitted in the first year of a given course. (See also enrolment).

Lead Time

With reference to high-level and middle-level manpower, the time required for their educational and training preparation is known as "Lead time".

Learning Curve

A course representing the rate of programme of an individual's or group's learning standard with increase in experience.

Levels of Education

The term is used to record the highest educational level

attained by a person, e.g., post-graduation, graduation, matriculation. For a person who is still studying in a particular class, the highest level attained by him will be one that he has actually passed and not the one in which he is studying.

Literacy

The level of education where a person can both read and write with understanding in any language. A person is regarded as *literate* if he can with understanding both read and write a short simple statement on his everyday life. The percentage of literate persons in a population is the *literacy rate*.

Non-Formal Education

Non-formal education is an out-of-school type of education; its purpose is to provide training for certain skills for the people. Examples are adult education, on-the-job training etc.

Operations Research

An applied science that is devoted to describe, understand and predict the behaviour of man-machine systems. By assessing the overall implications of various alternative courses of action in a management system, it provides an improved basis for management decisions.

Opportunity Cost

The term as applied in manpower analysis refers to the earnings foregone by students while attending school. This is one of the components in the calculation of costs of education.

Outturn

The number of persons who on the completion of a course of study are declared by some competent examining body as having qualified in the respective examination.

Profession

An occupation requiring advanced education and involving intellectual skills (like medicine etc.)

Reference Period

The time period with reference to which data are to be collected or studies are to be made such as a specific week, month, or year.

Refresher Course

The course of study designed to refresh previously learnt skills and knowledge which may have been partly forgotten as a result of lengthy interruptions in occupational life (e.g., because of unemployment, military service).

Retraining

The training for acquisition of knowledge and skills required in an occupation other than the one for which the person was originally trained. It involves on the job training or accelerated vocational training of employees sometimes in order to absorb them if rendered surplus as a result of technological change.

Sandwich Course:

A course consisting usually of periods of full time study at a college or an establishment of further education alternating with employment or training in some factory/workshop.

Scientific Manpower

The persons holding a university degree or an equivalent qualification in fundamental or applied sciences and who are engaged or willing to be engaged in scientific activity are included in the category of 'scientific manpower'.

Training

Instruction and learning for the development of the attitude, knowledge and skill required by a person to perform adequately a given job. 'Specific training' is the training which enhances the future productivity of a trainee in the firm providing it. 'General training' raises the trainee's productivity irrespective of the firm he works for.

Training Course

A series of sessions linked organically to deal with a well defined training programme/scheme, with specific aims and objectives clearly stated.

Vocational Education:

Education designed to prepare skilled personnel for industry, agriculture, commerce, etc. which is usually provided on the upper secondary level. Programme of vocational education include general studies, practical training for the development of skills required by the chosen occupation and related theory. The proportions of these components may vary considerably but the emphasis is usually on practical training. These programmes may be full time in schools or other educational institutions or part time as supplementary education for apprentices or others receiving their practical training in employment.

Vocationalisation of Education

The reform of the general education curriculum by introducing practical, applied, project-oriented, and occupationally oriented elements from the lowest primary class through the highest secondary class. This is to be done in such a way as to integrate academic and vocational aspects.

Vocational Orientation

Instructions through theoretical lessons and/or practical exercises of short periods in a variety of occupations to young persons approaching school-leaving age for providing them a general understanding of the employment market and its job and career opportunities. These instructions help them in the choice of occupation.

Vocational Training

Activities which essentially aim at providing the skills and knowledge, required for employment in a particular occupation (or a group of related occupations) in any field of economic activity including agriculture, industry, commerce, public and private services, etc.

Waiting Period

The time lag between leaving an educational institution and finding a job.

Appendices

APPENDIX 1

EXTRACTS FROM DR. RADHAKRISHNAN COMMISSION REPORT

(University Education Commission 1984-49)

Chapter II

The Aims of University Education

2. *Universities as the Organs of Civilisation*

He indeed must be blind who does not see that, mighty as are the political changes, far deeper are the fundamental questions which will be decided by what happens in the universities. Everything is being brought to the test of reason, venerable theologies, ancient political institutions, time-honoured social arrangements, a thousand things which a generation ago looked as fixed as the hills. If India is to confront the confusion of out time, she must turn for guidance, not to those who are lost in the mere exigencies of the passing hour, but to her men of letters and men of science, to her poets and artists, to her discoverers and inventors. These intellectual pioneers of civilisation are to be found and trained in the universities, which are the sanctuaries of the inner life of the nation.

In simpler conditions of life, in primitive societies, the leader can follow the urge of his instinct and take us to the scene of his vision. In the complex organisation of modern life, any reform requires careful thought and planning. Our leaders must be capable of intellectual analysis and imaginative insight.

3. *Intellectural Adventure*

We must give up the fatal obsession of the perfection of the past, that greatness is not to be attained in the present, that everything is already worked out and all that remains for the future ages of the world is pedantic imitation of the past. When we are hypnotised by our own past achievements, when all our effort is to repeat a past success, we become fetish worshippers. If our cultural life is to retain its dynamism, it must give up idolatory of the past and strive to realise new dreams. We should think with the young men in the Latin poem that nothing is down while anything remains to do. All that man has yet done is very little compared to what he is destined to achieve. The present which moves backwards and forwards, which is a summary of the past and a prophecy of the future, is hallowed ground and we who tread on it should face it with the quality of reverence and the spirit of adventure. Universities are the homes of intellectural adventure.

4. *An Integrated Way of Life*

A life of strenuous for human betterment is not possible, if we are not persuaded that life has a meaning. Many of our popular writers today seem to be possessed by the one desire to escape from the world of meaning and teach us the essential purposelessness of life. They make us believe, with a good deal of cleverness and sophistry, that life is infinitely complicated and totally inexplicable. Many of our students are taught to assume that free-will and personal responsibility are illusions, that human beings are conditioned almost wholly by their physical make-up and the society in which they live, and that the only sense that the religious statements make is emotional and subjective. This is a generation which knows how to doubt but not to admire, much less to believe. This aimlessness, this indifference to basic issues, is to no small extent, responsible for the decline of standards, for the fading of ideals, for the defeat of human endeavour.

The purpose of all education, it is admitted by thinkers of East and West, is to provide a coherent picture of the universe and an integrated way of life. We must obtain through it a sense of perspective, a synoptic vision, a samanvaya of the different items of knowledge. Man cannot live by a mass of disconnected information. He has a passion for an ordered intellectual vision of the connections of things. Life is one in all its varied manifestations. We may study the factual relations of the different manifestations but we must have knowledge of life as a whole. It cannot be a collection of distracting scraps, but should be a harmony of patterns. The subjects we study must be taught as parts of a curriculum.

5. *Wisdom and Knowledge*

Our ancient teachers tried to teach subjects and impart wisdom. Their ideal wisdom (irfan) along with knowledge (ilam), jnanam vijnana-sahitam. We cannot be wise without some basis of knowledge though we may easily acquire knowledge and remain devoid of wisdom. To use the words of the Upanisad, we may be the knowers of texts (mantravit) and not knowers of self (atmavit). Plato distinguishes between factual information and understanding. No amount of factual information would make ordinary men into educated or 'virtuous' men unless something is awakened in them, an innate ability to live the life of the soul.

> Where is the wisdom we have lost in knowledge?
> Where is the knowledge we have lost in information?
> The cycles of heaven in twenty centuries.
> Bring us further from God and nearer to the dust.

The strength of the new 'faiths' among intellectuals is partly due to their to explain the universe. By professing to interpret all human activity in terms of a single thesis, they give to the modern educated men a sense of assurance and certainty formerly provided by religion. Since education is both a training of minds and a training of souls, it should give both knowledge and wisdom.

6. *Aims of the Social Order*

We must have a conception of the social order for which we are educating our youth. We know what Hitler did in six years with the German youth. The Russians are clear in their minds about the kind of society for which they are educating and the qualities required in their citizens. They tried to remake man in a new image. Our educational system must find its guiding principle in the aims of the social order for which it prepares, in the nature of the civilisation it hopes to build. Unless we know whether we are tending, we cannot decide what we should do and how we should do it. Societies like men need a clear purpose to keep them at stable in a world of bewildering change.

The outlines of the social philosophy which should govern all our institutions, educational as will as economic and political, are indicated in the preamble to our Draft Constitution. It reads :

WE THE PEOPLE OF INDIA, having solemnly resolved to constitute India into a SOVEREIGN DEMOCRATIC REPUBLIC and to secure to all its citizens :

JUSTICE, social, economic and political;

LIBERTY of status and opportunity; and to promote among them all FRATERNITY, assuming the dignity of the individual and the unity of the Nation;

IN OUR CONSTITUENT ASSEMBLY this............................
of..............................
(.... day of August, 1949 A.D.) do

HEREBY ADOPT, ENACT AND GIVE TO OURSELVES THIS CONSTITUTION.

We are engaged in a quest for democracy though the realisation of justice, liberty, equality and fraternity.

43. *The Need for Culture*

What holds a society together and gives the individual balance and perspective, is the possession of culture. Culture is intellectual alertness, receptiveness, to beauty, human feeling, social enthusiasm.

As the result of the vest expansion of the area of knowledge and the diversification of its content, the aim of teaching has become almost exclusively specialisation. It is the normal feature in professional colleges. Even in colleges for liberal arts and sciences, the tendency is to specialise and prepare for advanced study in one or the other special field. If society is not to disintegrate into an aggregate of individual specialists, we should endow the youth with a central core of values, transmit to them a cultural heritage. It alone can serve as a cohesive force in a society which is getting splintered by over-specialisation. It will confer a unity and consistency of aim on specialised vocational courses and make for a more abundant personal life and a freer social order.

44. *The Un-Indian Character of Education*

One of the serious complaints against the system of education which has prevailed in this country for over a century is that it neglected India's past, that it did not provide the Indian students with a knowledge of their own culture. It has produced in some cases the feeling that we are without roots, in others, what is worse that our roots bind us to a world very different from that which surrounds us.

A British historian of Indian education observes: "Our education has done far less for Indian Culture than for the material and political progress of India. She looks to our Schools and Colleges for equipment in the struggle for existence; for the secret of happy living, vivendi causae, she looks elsewhere."

45. *Cultural Unity of India*

Nations are not made chiefly by traders and politicians. They are made by artists and thinkers, saints and philosophers. National unity and progress require a deeper foundation than political and economic arrangements. It is the life of spirit that has shaped and unified our collective existence and has been the real bond of oneness among the Indian people. After centuries of stress and conflict India has gradually evolved a common civilisation, a collective consciousness which embraces wide varieties of temperament, tradition, ways of thought and belief. Our people belong to different provinces, speak their own language, preserve their own habits and customs. There are sharp differences of temper, tradition and dialect. Despite all these there is a fundamental unity which binds the people together as members of one society with the same cultural loyalities.

Indian culture is like a palimpsest in which new characters do not entirely efface the old. In a single social pattern fragments of different ages are brought together. It would be impossible to think of an India where no Moghuls ruled, where no Taj was built, where no Macaulay wrote his Minute on education. Indian culture is like a living organism growing in richness and content. Primitive cultures are marked by extreme conservatism where social groups follow the same path of custom and convention with irrational persistence. Living cultures are dynamic and maintain their cultural concern by a continuous effort of individual and social discipline.

46. *Conflict in India's Soul*

Two contradictory impulses have attracted Indian intellectuals. One is a jealous pride in Indian genius and tradition wholly distinct from those of the West. The other is the no less jealous desire to profit by the example of the West.

A revolutionary period is not generally inclined to respect the wisdom of the past, but to cultivate this disrespect would be to forgo out spiritual heritage. There are treasures of spirit which may not be of any conceivable use in the struggle for material comfort, but if we are to be qualified to assist or resist the dominant tendencies of our age, we cannot afford to ignore the standards and ideals built by the austerity and abnegation of our ancestors across the centuries. The chief course of spiritual nourishment for any people must be its own past perpetually rediscovered and renewed. A society without a knowledge of the past which has made it would be lacking in depth and dignity.

47. *Critical Study of the Past*

This is not to romanticise the past filling the gaps of memory from the resources of imagination. India has suffered on account of her great weaknesses, her spirit of reaction and narrow-mindedness. We must be critical and selective and use the past to illumine the present. We should not blindly give up the great values of our past nor should we cling to beliefs simply because they are ancient. We should accept so much of ancient thought as is sympathetic to us.

Even in the darkest days of degradation, the light of India's culture never failed. It may have flickered but it was never extinguished. There were loving hands which cherished and tended it. Today it is burning with a renewed glow. If it is to become a consuming flame, we must became aware of its past greatness and its contemporary value.

Chapter IV

Standards of Teaching

VII. *Causes of Low Standards, Low Percentage of Passes, and Suggested Measures of Reform*

There are several causes which contribute to the low average quality of our graduates and the low percentage of passes at the B.A. and the B.Sc. Examination, but principal ones are the following:

27. *Overcrowding in Colleges*

During the last 10 to 15 years there has been a growing pressure of an increase in the number of admissions at the universities, but unfortunately, this wide and eager demand for university education is not proportional to the capacity to profit from such an education. The size of a college or a teaching university is determined by the number of students who can be accepted without a lowering of standards. Whatever may be done, in a burst of public enthusiasm, to expand university education, nothing should be allowed to lower the quality of work at the universities, and size, beyond a certain point, undeniably lowers the quality. A college or a university is like a living cell; once it reaches a certain size, it must either divide or die. The admission of a large number of students in response to popular demand without the necessary staff, class-room and hostel accommodation and equipment has made it impossible for most colleges and universities to give full education to their inflated undergraduate population. This factor, more than any other, has undoubtedly been responsible for the lovering of our standards. To quote Abraham Flexner, "bigness is almost necessarily fatal to greatness".

28. *Resulting Evils*

Some of the colleges we have visited have on their rolls five to ten times the number of students they could properly educate. They have neither adequate class-room space nor laboratory accommodation. The staff is miserably paid and we found that several teachers lectured at two or three colleges to eke out a living wage. In one of the colleges the management was saving 1.75 lacs a year on the running expenses of the college. This is an extreme case but we have found that with notable exceptions, there is a widespread tendency in colleges and universities, specially private colleges, to increase their enrolment in order to augment their fee income.

One of the harmful results of large number of the average low quality of undergraduates in the first degree classes is that the abler and more capable students suffer; they fail to get the educational opportunities they deserve. Teachers have to teach down to the level of the average; in justice to the majority they are unable to raise questions or employ methods designed to call forth mental effort from those students who are capable of being highly trained; consequently the more promising are kept back by the less intelligent and there is much waste of good material.

29. *Reduction of Numbers Recommended*

Every college in an affiliating university and every teaching university should deliberately fix a maximum limit to the number of students it admits every year. This maximum limit will vary according to the size of the building, the number of teachers, laboratory space, hostel accommodation, etc., but the limit must be fixed and adhered to, if the quality of education is to be raised. It is the duty of the affiliating universities to fix and to enforce these limits on their colleges, and for the teaching universities to fix these limits to maintain proper standards.

30. *Limitation of Number of U.P. Universities and Colleges*

We heard with satisfaction that at a recent meeting of the Vice-Chancellors of the universities in U.P., it was decided that the teaching universities of Lucknow and Allahabad should not have more then 3,000 students in their Arts and Science faculties, while degree colleges affiliated to the Agra University should not have more than 1,000 students. We commend this move to other universities and colleges. For the present, however, the maximum number of students in an affiliated college will have to be 1,500 for some years.

VIII. *Working Days and Vocations*

31. *Insufficient Number of Working Days*

The number of actual working days in the year in most colleges and universities is insufficient. At one university the number was as low as 120, which meant that students and teachers worked only for one-third of the year. Further, on account of the large number of stray holidays during the session, the continuity of work is broken and consequently the total output of work by teachers and students remains low. While it is necessary to close the colleges and the universities at most places for ten weeks during the season of intense heat, we must make the best use of the remaining 42 weeks of the year. In American universities, most of which work on a two semester (term) basis, each semester consists of about 91 working days and 12 examination days, so that there are more than 180 working days beside examination days during the year. Generally, the only holidays they have are 15 days of Christmas, one Thanksgiving day, 10 days of spring recess and 13 to 14 weeks of summer vacation. The following table gives the numbers of working days, besides examination days, at some of the American universities during the session 1948-49:

Harward	172 working days
Pennsylvania	174 working days
Michigan	182 working days
Johns Hopkins	188 working days
Vanderbilt	216 working days

32. *Minimum of 180 Days, Exclusive of Examination Days*

We recommend that the university session be divided into three more or less equal terms, each of 10 to 11 weeks' duration, separated by two short vacations of two or three weeks each and one long vacation of ten to thirteen weeks. All casual holidays during the currency of each term should be severely curtailed. Every college and university should so arrange its sessional work as to ensure a minimum number of 180 working days, exclusive of examination days.

33. *Maximum Utilisation of Working Days*

Not only should there be an increase in the number of working days, but it is also necessary that each day should be utilised to its maximum. There are teachers and students who attend the university only for two to three periods (100 to 150 minutes) a day. While there are conscientious teachers who keep their lectures up-to-date by reading and research, there are quite a number of others who deliver the same lectures, prepared years previously, year after year. It is these latter who give a bad name to the profession of a university teacher and lead to the criticism that university teaching is soft job. At one of the universities we were told that every teacher has to be on duty at the university for 6 hour a day—he may either teach or work in the library or laboratory. This may be repugnant to some of the teachers but there is no doubt that some kind of check is necessary for teachers who do not realise their obligation to engage in research and keep themselves up-to-date in their knowledge.

APPENDIX 2

Extracts From Kothari Commission Report, 1964-66

Summary of Recommendations

Chapter I

Education and National Objectives

1. The most important and urgent reform needed in education is to transform it, to endeavour to relate it to the life, needs and aspirations of the people and thereby make it a powerful instrument of social, economic and cultural transformation necessary for the realization of the national goals. For this purpose, education should be developed so as to increase productivity, achieve social and national integration, accelerate the process of modernization and cultivate social, moral and spiritual values. 1.20 (6)*

2. **Education and Productivity**

The following programmes are needed to relate education to productivity :

(1) *Science Education.* Science education should become an integral part of school education and ultimately become a part of all courses at university stage also. 1.23-24 (6-7)

(2) *Work Experience.* Work experience should be introduced as an integral part of all education.

(3) Every attempt should be made to orient work experience to technology and industrialization and to the application of science to productive processes, including agriculture. 1.25-33 (7-9)

(4) *Vocationalization.* Secondary education should be increasingly and largely vocationalized and in higher education, a greater emphasis should be placed on agricultural and technical education. 1.32 (9)

---

* The figures at the end of each recommendation indicate respectively
1. The number of the chapter;
2. The number of the paragraph (in international numerals); and
3. The number of the page (in brackets).

3. *Social and National Integration*

The achievement of social and national integration is an important objective of the educational system and the following steps should be taken to strengthen national consciousness and unity.

(1) *The Common School.* The common school system of public education should be adopted as a national goal and effectively implemented in a phased programme spread over 20 years. 1.36-38 (10-11).

(2) *Social and National Service.* Social and national service should be made obligatory for all students at all stages. These programmes should be organized concurrently with academic studies in schools and colleges.

(3) *Language Policy.* The development of an appropriate language policy can materially assist in social and national integration.

(4) Mother tongue has a pre-eminent claim as the medium of education at the school and college stages. Moreover, the medium of education in school and higher education should generally be the same. The regional languages should, therefore, be adopted as the media of education in higher education.

(5) The UGC and the universities should work out a programme for the adoption of these recommendations suitably for each university or a group of universities. The change-over should be completed within ten years.

(6) Energetic action is needed to produce books and literature, particularly scientific and technical, in regional languages. This should be made a responsibility of universities assisted by UGC.

(7) All-India institutions should continue to use English as the medium of education for the time being. The eventual adoption of Hindi should, however, be considered in due course, subject to certain safeguards.

(8) The regional languages should also be made the languages of administration for the regions concerned as early as possible so that higher services are not barred to those who study in the regional medium.

(9) The teaching and study of English should continue to be promoted right from the school stage. Encouragement should be given also to the study of other languages of international communication. The study of Russian needs special attention.

(10) It would be desirable to set up a few institutions, both at the school and university level, with some of the important world languages as media of education.

(11) English will serve as a link language in higher education for academic work and intellectual inter-communication. It is, however, equally obvious that English cannot serve as the link language for the majority of the people. It is only Hindi which can and should take this place in due course. As it is the official language of the Union and the link language of the people, all measures should be adopted to spread it in the non-Hindi areas.

(12) In addition to Hindi, it is essential to provide multiple channels of inter-State communication in all modern Indian languages. In every linguistic region, there should be a number of persons who know the other modern Indian languages and some who are familiar with their literature and able to contribute to them. For this purpose, there should be adequate arrangements, both in schools and colleges, for teaching different modern Indian languages. In addition, steps should be taken to establish strong departments in some of the modern Indian languages in every university. At the B.A and M.A. levels, it should be possible to combine two modern Indian languages. 1.49-62 (13-16)

(13) *Promotion of National Consciousness*. Promoting national consciousness should be an important objective of the school system. This should be attempted through the promotion of understanding and re-evaluation of our cultural heritage and the creation of a strong driving faith in the future towards which we aspire.

(14) There is no contradiction between the promotion of national consciousness and the development of international understanding which education should simultaneously strive to promote.

(15) The educational programme in schools and colleges should be designed to inculcate democratic values. 1.63-68 (16-17)

4. *Education and Modernization*

(1) In a modern society knowledge increases at a terrific pace and social change is very rapid. This needs a radical transformation in the educational system.

5. *Social, Moral and Spiritual Values*

The education system should emphasize the development of fundamental social, moral and spiritual values.

6. *Education about Religions*

It is necessary for a multi-religious democratic State to promote a tolerant study of all religions so that its citizens can understand each other better and live amicably together.

1.74-80 (19-21)

Chapter II

The Educational System :

Structure and Standards

7. *Structure and Duration*

(1) The standards in any given system of education at a given time depend upon four essential elements: (a) the structure or the division of the educational pyramid into different levels or stages and their inter-relationships; (b) the duration or total period covered by the different stages; (c) the quality of teachers, curricula, methods of teaching and evaluation, equipment and buildings; and (d) the utilization of available facilities. All these elements are inter-related, but they are not of equal significance.

— The structure which may be regarded as the skeleton of the educational system, is of the least importance.

— The duration or total period of education plays a more significant role; but it becomes crucial only when the available facilities are utilized to the full and no further improvement can be expected without the addition of time.

— The quality of different inputs is even more important and with an improvement in these, it is possible to raise the standards considerably without affecting the structure or increasing duration.

— But probably the most important is utilizing available facilities and obtaining the maximum return at the existing level of inputs.

(2) The immediate efforts on which attention should be concentrated at the school stage are two: increasing the intensity of utilization and improving the quality of inputs, other than time. With these, it is possible to add about a year of content to the school course. In addition, it is also necessary to increase the duration of

the higher secondary stage to two years under a phased programme which will begin in the fifth plan and be completed by 1985.

(3) The new educational structure should consist of

— One to three years of pre-school education;
— a ten-year period of general education which may be subdivided into a primary stage of 7 to 8 years: (a) lower primary stage of 4 or 5 years and a higher primary stage of 3 or 2 years and lower secondary stage of 3 or 2 years of general education or one to three years of vocational education (the enrolment in vocational courses being raised to 20 per cent of the total);
— a higher secondary stage of two years of general education or one to three years of vocational education (the enrolments in vocational education being raised to 50 per cent of the total);
— a higher education stage having a course of three years or more for the first degree and followed by courses of varying durations for the second or research degree.

2-01-2 (23-32)

Transfer of the Pre-University Courses

(1) The pre-university course should be transferred from the universities and affiliated colleges to secondary schools by 1975-76 and duration of the course should be lengthened to two years by 1985-86.

(2) The UGC should be responsible for effecting the transfer of all pre-university or intermediate work from university and affiliated colleges to schools.

(3) Simultaneously higher secondary class or classes should be started in selected schools by State Education Departments, as self-contained units, and assisted with adequate recurring grants.

(4) Boards of Secondary Education should be reconstituted to accept the responsibility for the higher secondary stage also.

2.22-24 (32-33)

Lengthening the Duration of the Higher Secondary Stage

(1) In the fourth plan, efforts should be concentrated on securing a better utilization of existing facilities, on making the necessary preparation for implementing the programme and on

lengthening the duration of the course in a few selected institutions as pilot projects.

(2) The programme of lengthening the duration of the higher secondary stage should begin in the fifth plan and be completed by end of the seventh plan. 2.25-29 (33-35).

Reorganization of the University Stage

(1) The duration of the first degree should not be less than three years. The duration of the second degree may be 2 to 3 years.

(2) Some universities should start graduate school with a three-year Master's degree course in certain subjects.

(3) Three-year special courses for the first degree which begin at the end of the first year of the present three-year degree courses should be started in selected subjects and in selected institutions.

(4) Suitable bridges should be built between the existing courses and the new (longer) courses.

(5) Incentives in the form of scholarships, etc. should be provided for those who take the longer courses.

(6) In Utter Pradesh, the lengthening of the first degree course should begin with the establishment of three-year graduate schools in selected subjects and in selected universities. The first degree courses in other colleges should be raised to 3 years in a period of 15-20 years. 2.30-32 (35-36)

Chapter III

Teacher Status

Intensive and continuous efforts are necessary to raise the economic, social and professional status of teachers and to feed back talented young persons into the profession. 3.01-02 (46)

Remuneration

The most urgent need is to upgrade the remuneration of teachers substantially, particularly at the school stage. 3.05 (47)

Chapter IV.

Teacher Education

The professional preparation of teachers, being crucial for the qualitative improvement of education, should be treated as a key area in educational development and adequate financial provision should be made for it, both at the State and national levels. 4.01 (67)

Removing the Isolation of Teacher Training

In order to make the professional preparation of teachers effective, teacher education must be brought into the mainstream of the academic life of the universities on the one hand and of school life and educational development on the other. 4.03 (68)

Chapter V

Enrolments and Manpower

A National Enrolment Policy

During the next twenty years, the national enrolment policy should have the following broad objectives:

- to provide effective general education of not less than seven years' duration to every child, on a free and compulsory basis; and to expand lower secondary education on as large a scale as possible;
- to provide higher secondary and university education to those who are willing and qualified to receive such education, consistent with the demands for trained manpower and the need to maintain essential standards; and to provide adequate financial assistance to those who are economically handicapped;
- to emphasize the development of professional, technical and vocational education and to prepare skilled personnel needed for the development of agriculture and industry;
- to identify talent and to help it grow to its full potential;
- to liquidate mass illiteracy and to provide an adequate programme of adult and continuing education; and
- to strive continuously to equalize educational opportunities, beginning with the elimination of at least some of the more glaring inequalities. 5.02 (89-90)

Raising the Educational Level of the Average Citizen

High priority should be given to programmes of raising the educational level of the average citizen —

(1) by providing five years of effective primary education to all children by 1975-76 and seven years of such education by 1985-86;

(2) by making part-time education for one year compulsory for all children in the age-group 11-14 who have not completed the lower primary stage and are not attending schools. The aim will be to make these children functionally literate and stop all further additions to the ranks of adult illiterates; and

(3) by developing programmes to liquidate adult illiteracy.

5.03 (90)

Future Requirements of Educated Manpower : The ISI/ISE Estimates

We broadly accept the estimates of future requirements of educated manpower given in the ISI/ISE Paper. This will, however, have to be continually revised in the light of the best data available and kept up-to-date. The table given on page 95 (Table 5.3) shows the estimates of the required workers, stock and out-turn of educated persons during the next twenty years.

Educational Implications of the Estimates

The following are the main policy implications of these estimates:

— to restrict the unplanned and uncontrolled expansion of general secondary and higher education, if massive educated unemployment is to be avoided;
— to make special and intensive efforts to vocationalize secondary education and to develop professional education at the university stage; and
— to devise suitable machinery, both at the national and State levels, which will relate the estimates of manpower needs effectively to the output of the educational system so that, by and large, there is some assurance that a suitably trained person would be available for every job to be done and every educated person would find a job appropriate for his education and professional training.

5.26 (97)

Education and Employment

We should move in the direction of giving every graduate an offer of employment along with his degree or diploma. From this point of view, the system of one year internship now prescribed for medical graduates should be extended to other categories of graduates. 5.49 (105-106)

A Wider Perspective.

The basic problem of human resource development can be solved only against a wider perspective. From this point of view, it is necessary to formulate and implement integrated plans which will have three objectives: (1) to reduce the birth-rate by about half; (2) to bring about an expansion of employment; and (3) to provide such education as will qualify young people for specific jobs. Such integrated plans are needed at the national, State and district levels. 5.50-51 (106-107)

Chapter VI

Towards Equalization of Educational Opportunities

Fees in Education

The country should work towards a stage when all education would be tuition free. From this point of view :

(1) tuition fees at the primary stage should be abolished in all government, local authority and aided private schools as early as possible and preferably before the end of the fourth plan.

(2) lower secondary education should be made tuition free in all government, local authority or aided private institutions as early as possible and preferably before the end of the fifth plan. If necessary, a phased programme may be drawn up for the purpose.

(3) for the next ten years, the main effort with regard to fees in higher secondary and university education should be to extend provision of tuition free education to all needy and deserving students. As a first step, the proportion of free studentship should be increased to 30 per cent of the enrolment. 6.08-15 (109-112)

Other Private Costs

Other private costs in education have increased greatly in recent years and not necessarily for educational reasons. Efforts are needed to reduce them to the minimum.

(1) Free textbooks and writing materials should be provided at

the primary stage. Children freshly joining schools should be welcomed at a school function and presented with a set of books. Others should be presented with a complete set of books for the next year as soon as the results of the annual examinations are declared and before the long vacations for further study.

Education of Women

We fully endorse the recommendations of the three committees which have examined the problem of women's education in recent years: (a) The National Committee on the Education of Women under the chairmanship of Shrimati Durgabai Deshmukh ; (b) The Committee on Differentiation of Curricula between Boys and Girls under the chairmanship of Shrimati Hansa Metha; and (c) The Committee under the chairmanship of Shri M. Bhaktavatsalam which studied the problem in the six States where the education of girls is less developed. 6.53 (135)

Education of the Backward Classes

(1) The existing programme for the education of the scheduled castes should continue and be expanded.

(2) Greater efforts are needed to provide educational facilities for the nomadic and semi-nomadic groups.

(3) Hostels should be provided for the children of the denotified communities.

Education of the Tribal People

The education of the tribal people deserves great emphasis and attention. We broadly agree with the recommendations made in this respect by the Commission on Scheduled Areas and Scheduled Tribes under the chairmanship of Shri U.N. Dhebar and in the seminars on the Education and Employment of the tribal people organized by the Planning Commission and the NCERT. We invite special attention to the following programmes in this context.

Chapter VII

School Education :
Problems of Expansion

The entire pre-university period of education should be treated as one single and continuous unit. It may be subdivided into sub-standards such as pre-primary, lower and higher primary, and lower and higher secondary. But it has to be noted that the similarities between the problems of the different sub-stages are more significant than the differences. 7.01 (147-148)

Expansion of Primary Education

The objective of primary education should be to prepare individuals to be responsible and useful citizens.

The constitutional directive of providing free and compulsory education for every child up to age to 14 years is an educational objective of the highest priority and should be fulfilled in all parts of the country through the development of the following programmes :

(1) Five years of good and effective education should be provided to all children by 1975-76.

(2) Seven years of such education should be provided by 1985-86.

(3) Emphasis should be laid on the reduction of wastage and stagnation. The objective should be to ensure that not less than 80 per cent of the children that enter Class I reach Class VII in a period of seven years.

(4) Children who are not yet fourteen years old at the end of Class VII and who do not wish to study further should be retained in the educational system till they complete 14 years of age but should be provided with short vocational courses of their choice.

(5) Each State and district should be required to prepare a perspective plan for the development of primary education in its area in the light of the targets stated above and its local conditions. It should be given full assistance to move forward at its best pace; and care should be taken to see that its progress is not held up for want of financial resources. 7.08-11 (151-152)

Chapter VIII

School Curriculum

In recent years, the explosion of knowledge and the reformation of many concepts in science have highlighted the inadequacy of existing school programmes and brought about a mounting pressure for a radical reform of school curriculum. A unified approach should be taken to the framing of the entire school curriculum, a new definition of the content of general education and a new approach to the place of specialisation. 8.01-82 (183-184)

Essentials of Curricular Improvement

School curricula should be upgraded through research in curriculum development undertaken by University Departments of Education, training colleges, State Institutes of Education and Boards of School Education; (b) periodical revision based on such research; (c) the preparation of textbooks and teaching-learning materials; and (d) the orientation of teachers to the revised curricula through inservice education.

Chapter IX

Teaching Methods, Guidance and Evaluation

Teaching Methods : Discovery and Diffusion.

The continual deepening of the curricula should be accompanied by an equally vigorous improvement in the method of teaching and evaluation. The main factors responsible for the dull and uninspiring school teaching today are the rigidity of the educational system and the failure of the administrative machinery to diffuse new educational practices to schools. These weaknesses should be overcome. 9.02-03 (224-225)

Chapter X

School Education : Administration and Supervision

A sympathetic and imaginative system of supervision and administration is essential for initiating and accelerating educational reform. 10.01 (249)

A Nation-wide Programme of School Improvement

In view of the great need to improve standards of education at the school stage, a nation-wide programme of school improvement should be developed in which conditions will be created for each school to strive continually to achieve the best results to which it is capable. From this point of view, the following steps should be taken :

(1) Each institution should be treated as a unit by itself and helped to grow at its own individual pace. For this purpose, it should prepare its own development programme of optimum utilization and growth.

(2) The emphasis on these plans should be on motivating

human agencies to make their best effort for the improvement of education rather than on increasing physical resources. Physical facilities should be improved through the cooperation of the local community.

(3) The success of the programme will depend upon the degree to which the effort is sustained over a period of time.

(4) Evaluative criteria for schools should be worked out by each State and may be used by schools for self-evaluation and by inspecting officers for their annual and triennial inspections. On the basis of these criteria, the schools should be classified on a three-point scale, norms being defined at optimum and minimum levels.

(5) During the next ten years, at least 10 per cent of the schools at the primary stage and one secondary school in each block should be raised to the optimum level. At the lower primary stage, access to these schools will be for the children in the neighbourhood. At the higher primary and secondary stages, admission will be on the basis of merit. 10.24-32 (257-260)

Chapter XI

Higher Education Objectives and Improvement

Objectives of Universities

In broad terms, the functions of the universities in the modern world may be said to be the following.

- to seek and cultivate new knowledge, to engage vigorously and fearlessly in the pursuit of truth, and to interpret old knowledge and beliefs in the light of new needs and discoveries;
- to provide the right kind of leadership in all walks of life, to identify gifted youth and help them develop their potential to the full by cultivating physical fitness, developing the powers of the mind and cultivating right interests, attitudes and moral and intellectual values;
- to provide society with competent men and women trained in agriculture, arts, medicine, science and technology and various other professions, who will also be cultivated individuals, imbued with a sense of social purpose;

— to strive to promote equality and social justice and to reduce social and cultural differences through diffusion of education; and

— to foster in the teachers and students, and through them in society generally, the attitudes and values needed for developing the 'good life' in individuals and society.

11.02 (274-275)

Medium of Education

(1) The regional languages should be adopted as media of education at the university stage in a phased programmed spread over ten years.

(2) At the earlier stage of the under-graduate course, the bulk of the instruction may be given through the regional language while at the postgraduate stage, it may be in English.

(3) In due course, all teachers in higher education should as far as possible, be bilingual and postgraduate students should be able to follow lectures and use reading materials in the regional language as well as English.

(4) The maintenance of colleges teaching through the medium of Hindi in the non-Hindi areas or of Urdu in any part of the country where there is a resasonable number of Urdu-speaking students, should be permitted and encouraged.

(5) Centres of advanced study should be established for the development of all modern Indian languages including Urdu.

(6) The classical and modern Indian languages should be provided as elective subjects, no language being made a compulsory subject of study at the university stage.

(7) Adequate facilities should be provided in universities and colleges for the study of English. Special units for teaching English should be established in universities to give a good working knowledge of it to new entrants by the adoption of modern teaching techniques. It would also be an advantage to teach some English as part of the elective subject course in the first year of the degree course.

(8) The teaching of important library languages other than English should be stressed, in particular the study of Russian, on a larger scale. 11.58-61 (291-293)

Chapter XII

Higher Education : Enrolment and Programmes

Expansion of Facilities

The expansion of facilities in higher education should be planned broadly in relation to manpower needs and employment opportunities. On the basis of the present trends, it appears that the enrolments in under-graduate and postgraduate courses will have to be increased from about 1 million in 1965-66 to 4 million in 1985-86. Facilities in professional courses such as agriculture, engineering or medicine and those at the postgraduate stage will have to be specially expanded. 12.02-09 (229-305)

Selective Admission

Since the demand for higher education will be much larger then the provision that can be made for it or is needed on the basis of manpower needs, a system of selective admissions will have to be adopted. Three measures would have to be adopted from this point of view :

— the determination of the number of places available in an institution in relation to teachers and facilities available to ensure that standards are maintained at an adequate level;
— prescription of eligibility by the universities; and
— selection by the institution concerned of the best students from amongst those who are eligible and seek admission.

(1) While the use of examination marks as a major basis for admissions may continue until better selection methods are devised, their arbitrariness or lack of reliability should be compensated, to the extent possible, by making due allowance for the socio-economic handicaps of students so as to relate selection more directly to innate talent. The final selection should also take into consideration such factors as the school record and the proficiency of the student in fields not tested in the examination. This is especially important in border-line cases. In exceptional cases, the universities should have the right and courage to suspend the rules and give admissions to students whose talent has been identified but who may not have been able to fulfil the entrance requirements. The procedure proposed for selecting students on the basis of 'school clusters' for

the award of scholarship may also be adopted for making admission to quality institutions.

(2) Each university should constitute a Board of University Admissions to advise the university about all matters relating to admissions.

(3) The University Grants Commission should set up a Central Testing Organization for the development of appropriate selection procedures for different courses of higher education.

12.10-20 (305-308)

Part-time Education

Opportunities for part-time education (correspondence courses, evening colleges) should be extended widely and should include courses in science and technology. By 1986, about a third of the total enrolment in higher education could be provided through a system of correspondence courses and evening colleges.

12.21-22(308-309)

New Universities

The establishment of new universities is inescapable. The metropolitan cities of Bombay, Calcutta, Delhi and Madras should have, by the end of the fourth plan, two universities each which would supplement to some extent the work of each other. The demand from the States of Kerala and Orissa for additional Universities is justifiable. The proposals for the establishment of a university for the hill areas of the North-Eastern Region should be supported as a major measure for spearheading economic and social development in the areas.

In establishing new universities, the following principles should be kept in view :

(1) The establishment of new university can be justified only if it leads to a substantial improvement in standards and in the output and level of research.

(2) No new university should be started unless the agreement of the UGC is obtained and adequate provision of funds is made.

(3) Co-operative effort by postgraduate centres to provide facilities for postgraduate education should be developed as a first step towards the establishment of a university. A

new university should not ordinarily be establsihed in a place where a university centre has not been in operation for some time.

(4) Good university organization would be one in which a university has a strong core of teaching departments combined with about 30 affiliated colleges in close proximity.

(5) The UGC may explore the possibility of bringing together all universities in a State in a 'consortium' to operate all the affiliated colleges in the State.

(6) A time of two to three years should be allowed to elapse between the appointment of the first vice-chancellor and the direct commencement of the university's work, the vice-chancellor being assisted by a Planning Board during the period.

(7) Larger resources should be placed at the disposal of the UGC so as to increase the amount of Central assistance to all State universities on the basis of their performance and merit. 12.35-43 (314-317)

Chapter XIII

The Governance of Universities

Universities should evolve dynamic techniques of management and organization suited to their special functions and purposes. The UGC should encourage the formation of groups in universities to study the problem of educational administration and management of university affairs. 13.02 (325-326)

University Autonomy

The proper sphere of university autonomy lies in the selection of students, the appointment and promotion of teachers and the determination of courses of study, methods of teaching and the selection of areas and problems of research. 13.05 (326)

University Finances

(1) The State Governments should place adequate financial resources at the disposal of universities and simplify rules and procedures for operating them.

(2) The UGC should be able to give both development and maintenance grants to State Universities.

(3) There should be some reasonable sharing of developmental expenditure on universities between the UGC and State Governments.

(4) UGC should take steps to resolve problems faced by some universities on account of the non-payment of grants on committed expenditure by State Governments.

(5) The system of grant-in-aid from the State Governments to the universities should be reorganized on the basis of a suitable system of block grants.

(6) The finance of universities should be placed on a sound footing on the basis of advice given by the UGC to the State Governments and the universities after periodical review.

(7) Universities should be immune from direct governmental intervention and also from direct public accountability.

13.16-31 (330-334)

Chapter XIV

Education for Agriculture

A programme of education for agriculture will have to be based on an effective organic link between the three main elements of teaching, research and extension. 14.01-06 (348-349)

Agricultural Universities

At least one Agricultural university should be established in each State.

(1) Beginning with traditional agricultural specialities, these universities should gradually extend their scope of studies to cover a wide range of specialized course to suit the needs of the day.

(2) A clear delineation of responsibilities between Agricultural Universities and the State Departments of Agriculture is necessary. The former should take over all research, education and extension programmes.

(3) Postgraduate work should become a distinctive feature of the Agricultural Universities which should be staffed with adequately trained personnel. The intake at the postgraduate level,

particularly in the hitherto neglected areas, will have to be considerably increased. To ensure maintenance of standards however, this expansion should be related to available personnel and facilities and no institution should be allowed to undertake postgraduate instruction unless it has adequate integrated facilities for education and research.

Chapter XV

Vocational Technical and Engineering Education

(1) A concerted and sustained programme is needed to ensure that by 1986, some 20 per cent of all enrolments at the lower secondary level and some 50 per cent beyond Class X are in part-time or full-time vocational and professional courses.

(2) Vocational education courses at school stage should be predominantly terminal in character, with adequate opportunities for the exceptionally gifted child, to rejoin the main stream and move higher, through further study. 15.09-10 (370-371)

Training Semi-Skilled and Skilled Workers

(1) There should be a further expansion of facilities in ITIs, beginning by at least a doubling of available places in the fourth plan. The minimum admission age should be gradually lowered to 14, with suitable adjustments in courses.

(2) Junior Technical Schools should be renamed Technical High Schools and along with the existing Technical High Schools should offer courses clearly terminal in character. There should be greater use of available time to meet the requirements of the Apprenticeship Act. Enough flexibility and experimentation should be permitted in the organization of the various courses.

(3) Training in ITIs and technical schools must be production-oriented.

(4) Skilled workers' training courses with entry requirements below Class X should be attached to polytechnics to make better use of existing facilities.

(5) Facilities for vocational and technical training for school leavers entering employment should be greatly expanded on a part-time, day-release, correspondence, sandwich or short-intensive course basis. Rigidity of approach in the organization of these courses, should be avoided. 15.12-18 (371-372)

Technician Training

(1) The overall ratio of engineers to technicians should be raised from the present figure of 1 : 1.4 to 1 : 2.5 by 1975 and to 1 : 3 or 4 by 1986.

(2) Courses for the training of technicians should be revised in the light of periodic investigations to be carried out in cooperation with industry, aimed at job analysis and specifications in terms of levels and clusters of skills and responsibilities for technicians.

(3) Diploma training should be more practical, by including industrial experience. This practical training should be of a project or problem-oriented type.

(4) Polytechnics should be located only in industrial areas, while those already functioning in rural areas should develop courses allied to agriculture and agro-industries.

(5) Teachers for polytechnics should be increasingly recruited from industry, by relaxing, if necessary, academic admission requirements. Salaries should not be linked to academic qualifications only.

(6) To give training in as near realistic conditions as possible, vacations should be used by the students and staff to do production work on simple tools either for equipping secondary schools or for sale.

(7) Teaching of science and mathematics in polytechnics should be strengthened, particularly in the first two years. Technician courses should include introduction to industrial psychology and management, costing and estimation.

(8) Polytechnics should increasingly adopt sandwich type of courses in cooperation with industry.

(9) In view of low mobility of diploma holders in the country, the courses offered in polytechnics during the fourth and fifth plans should be designed largely with local requirements in view, keeping at the same time, a watchful eye on total national needs.

(10) Courses of special interest to girls should be offered in all polytechnics at both the certificate and diploma levels and girls completing the lower secondary course should be encouraged to take them up.

(11) Every effort must be made to reduce the present high wastage rated in polytechnics to a minimum and to expand existing polytechnics to their optimum size.

(12) Selected polytechnics should provide post-diploma courses for technicians with some years of experience in industry to qualify as higher level technicians. 15. 19-32 (372-375)

Other Vocational Education

(1) At the higher secondary level (Classes XI & XII), alongside the polytechnics, there is considerable scope for starting a range of interesting courses in commercial, scientific and industrial trades and in areas of special interest to girls. This should be fully exploited.

(2) Products of Technical High Schools and polytechnics should be encoraged to set up small enterprises of their own or to join together with others in creating small-scale workshops, industries and services needed in the community. 15. 33-36 (375-376)

Chapter XVI

Science Education and Research

General Principles

The progress, welfare and security of the nation depend critically on a rapid, planned and sustained growth in the quality and extent of education and research in science and technology. It is unfortunate that India today is almost at the bottom end of the ladder of GNP per capita as also of the ladder of per capita expenditure on education and research. In view of limited resources available, the following measures are needed to make rapid progress :

(1) A rigorously selective approach has to be adopted.

(2) In postgraduate studies and research, the standards of attainment must bear international comparison. The only way this can be done is through a most careful selection of subjects for advanced study and research, selection of the most able students for such courses, and by building a small number of centres of excellence and assigning to each of these, resources exceeding a certain critical size.

(3) In the utilization of our scientific manpower we must strive our utmost to achieve high efficiency—higher even than in the industrially developed countries. We should determine our priorities and programmes in education and research on the basis of hard 'indigenous' thinking and needs, and not follow the

fashion set by other countries whether highly 'advanced' or not so advanced.

(4) The development of science must derive its 'nourishment' from our cultural and spiritual heritage and not bypass it.

(5) The need from the earliest stage of science education for a proper understanding of the basic principles and the process of scientific abstraction and creative thinking must be emphasized.

16. 01-14 (389-396)

Science Education

(1) Apart from improving the standard of the postgraduate courses, the postgraduate enrolments in science and mathematics need to be expanded several-fold in the coming decades to meet the demands of rapidly expanding secondary and higher education and of research and industry. 16.22 (398)

Chapter XVII

Adult Education

Liquidation of Illiteracy

(1) Every possible effort should be made to eradicate illiteracy from the country as early as possible and in no part of the country, however backward, should it take more than 20 years. The national percentage of literacy should be raised to 60 by 1971 to 80 by 1976.

(2) As a first step to arrest the growth of illiteracy, the following measures should be taken :

(a) Expansion of universal schooling of five years' duration to the age-group 6-11 :

(b) Provision of part-time education to those children of age-group 11-14 who either miss scholing or drop prematurely out of the school.

(c) Provision of part-time general and vocational education to the younger adults of the age-group 15-30.

(3) For the liquidation of illiteracy a two-fold strategy comprising the selective approach and the mass approach should be adopted.

(4) Under selective approach, programmes should be adopted for specified groups of adults which could be easily identified,

controlled and motivated for intensive literacy work. All employers in large farms and commercial, industiral, contracting and other concerns should be made responsible, if necessary by law, for making their employees functionally literate within a period of three years of their employment. Big industrial plants in the public sector should take the lead immediately and set the pace in this important direction. Every development project should include, as an integral part, a plan for the education of its employees, more especially of those who are literate. Literacy programme should constitute an essential ingredient of all schemes launched by Government for economic and social developments.

(5) Under mass approach, all available educated men and women in the country should be mobilized for raising a force to combat illiteracy and utilize it in a well-planned literacy campaign. In the organization of mass campaign, the teachers and students and all educational institutions should be actively involved. The students in the higher primary, secondary, higher secondary, vocational schools and those in the undergraduate classes of the universities and colleges should be required to teach the adults as a part of compulsory national service programme. Teachers in schools of all types should be required to teach and participate in the campaign. Every educational institution should be given responsibility for liquidating illiteracy in a specified area. The school in particular should be transformed into a centre of community life.

(6) No literacy campaign should be launched without careful planning preparation. The various measures to be taken for this purpose have been discussed in the Report.

(7) In order to promote literacy among women, condensed courses for women sponsored by the Central Social Welfare Board should be adopted; appointment of 'village sisters' should be encouraged for teaching village women and organizing adult education among local communities.

(8) The mass media of communication should be effectively used as a powerful instrument for creating the climate and imparting knowledge and skills necessary for improving quality of work and standard of life.

(9) In order to retain the literacy achieved, literacy campaigns must have adequate follow-up including further education, the use of library, and the production of reading material. 17. 7-31 (423-431)

Chapter XIX

Educational Finance

Total Expenditure on Education

If education is to develop adequately, educational expenditure in the next 20 years should rise from Rs. 12 per capita in 1965-66 to Rs. 54 in 1985-86 (at constant prices.) This implies that the educational expenditure, which increased from Rs. 1,144 millions in 1950-51 to Rs. 6,000 millions in 1965-66, will further rise to Rs. 40,364 millions in 1985-86 and that the proportion of NGP allocated to education will rise from 2.9 per cent in 1965-66 to 6.0 per cent in 1985-86. 19. 21-24 (473-474)

Allocation of Funds

While the broad pattern of educational expenditure in the different sectors of education during the next two or three decades will be to devote two-thirds of the available reasources to school education and one-third to higher education, the relative emphasis on programmes should change from decade to decade as follows :

(1) From 1965 to 1975, the relative emphasis should be on a larger expenditure at the school stage. This will be necessary in order (i) to upgrade salaries of school teachers; (ii) to transfer the PUC and the Intermediate classes from the university to the school stage; (iii) to provide at least five years of effective education to all children; and (iv) to vocationalize secondary education.

(2) The programmes to be emphasized during the decade 1975 to 1985 will include the provision of seven years of effective primary education, the addition of one year to the school stage and vocationalization of secondary education. During this decade, emphasis should begin to shift in favour of higher education.

(3) After 1985, there will be increased emphasis on the development of higher education and research. 19.25 (474-476)

Sources of Educational Finance

(1) Although most of the responsibility for the support of education will be placed on government funds, a total centralization of all financial responsibility for education in the Government will not be desirable. Attempt should, therefore, be made to raise

contribution from local communities, voluntary organizations and the local authorities for this purpose.

(2) The assistance of the local community should be mobilized through the organization of school improvement conferences for improving the physical facilities in schools and the creation of school funds.

(3) In order to provide financial support to District School Boards, the Zila Parishads should raise funds for education by levying cess on land revenue. The State should prescribe the minimum rate of the levy and authorize the Zila Parishads to raise it to a certain prescribed maximum. In order to stimulate the collection of funds, the Government should give grant-in-aid proportionate to the additional revenues thus collected by the Zila Parishad. 19.14-20 (471-473)

Grant-in-aid to Zila Parishads

(1) The system of grant-in-aid from the State Government to Zila Parishads should be reformed on the following lines :

(a) 100 per cent grant for salaries and allowances to teachers and supervisory staff sanctioned by the Government. Definite norms regarding the number of teachers required and the administrative and supervisory staff needed should be fixed.

(b) For non-teacher costs, a block grant per child in attendance should be given. The amount of this grant should be fixed separately for each category of schools and should be revised after every 3 to 5 years.

(c) The resources raised locally by a Zila Parishad as well as the State grant thereon should be left with the Zila Parishad for such development programmes as it deems necessary; and

(d) Grant-in-aid for non-recurring expenditure should be given separately, preferably at about two-thirds of the expenditure.

(2) The amount of grant-in-aid given by the State Government to Zila Parishad should be allowed to be funded and not made to lapse at the end of the financial year. (Para 2, Supplementary Note I, p. 491)

Grant-in-Aid to Muncipalities

(1) It should be made obligatory for the Municipalities to bear a certain proportion of the cost of education. For this purpose, they should levy a cess on lands and buildings.

(2) For the purpose of Government grants, the Municipalities should be classified into groups on the basis of their wealth and the poorer Municipalities should be given grant-in-aid at a higher rate than others.

(3) All Corporations should be made responsible for supporting ar least primary education within their jurisdiction. The Government grant to them should be on a proportional basis so that the Corporations contribute a certain percentage of the expenditure from their own funds.

(Para 4, Supplementary Note I, pp. 491-492)

The Role of the Centre

The Central Government should assume a larger financial responsibility for education by expanding the Central and Centrally sponsored sectors. It should have the following characteristics :

(1) It should include programmes of crucial importance and national in character.

(2) In the Centrally sponsored sector, it should be possible for some programmes to vary from State to State according to their needs.

(3) Central assistance for programmes in the Centrally sponsored sector should be given for five years which may in certain cases be continued up to 10 years and not for plan periods only as at present.

(Paras 9-15, Supplementary Note I, pp. 493-496)

Economies and Utilization

Even with the mobilization of maximum resources for education, the funds will still be inadequate to meet even the minimum needs of educational reconstruction, if conventional techniques involving large wastage and stagnation continue. It would, therefore, be necessary to adopt measures for economy, for eradication of wastage and for most efficient utilization of funds. Some of these measures have been indicated in paragraph 20.44. These and all other measures, which promote economy consistent with efficiency, should be adopted 19.41 (486-487)

Research

Studies conducted in some other countries indicate the importance of education for economic growth, but no such studies have been conducted in India so far. In view of the importance of the subject, the UGC should encourage studies on the subject to be conducted in universities. 19.43 (487)

APPENDIX 3

Extracts from "Education Commission and After"

*By Shri J.P. Naik**

Chapter VII

Recommendations that were Opposed and Rejected

Selective Admissions in Higher Secondary and University Education

The Education Commission was not the first to put forward this idea. In fact, selective admissions of secondary and university education was a basic principle of education in the U.K. and the British administrators were always trying to impose it on Indian education, especially after 1900 when they realized that uncontrolled expansion of secondary and university education was leading to dissatisfaction against government and promoting the struggle for freedom. Indians, on the other hand, were stoutly resisting these attempts because they felt that the spread of secondary and university education would help to modernize the country. This struggle went on throughout the British period; and on the whole, the Indians won, especially after 1921, when education became a transferred subject. The last British attempt to impose selective admission on India was the Post-War Plan of Education Development (1944-84) which provided secondary education to one student out of every five who completed elementary education and university education to one student out of every fifteen who completed secondary education. Naturally, Indian public opinion rejected the plan outright.

In the post-independence period, a recommendation regarding selective admissions to the universities was again repeated by the University Education Commission (1948-49). It was not accepted but the subject was discussed almost continuously, especially as the problems of educated unemployment and student unrest began to grow. No effective decision could, however, be taken, especially because the backward classes opposed the proposal stoutly on the ground that selective admissions would affect them adversely and reduce their chances of vertical mobility.

* Written in 1979 and published in 1982.

The Education Commission made proposals for regulation of enrolments in higher secondary and university education. While making them, it did use man-power estimates as one criterion for determination of enrolment policies. This part of the argument came in for a good deal of criticism on the ground that the man-power approach to educational planning is neither desirable nor suitable, that the man-power estimates of the Commission erred on the side of exaggeration, and that it is not possible to link theoretically framed man-power estimates to practical day-to-day decisions in establishing institutions or determining their enrolments. Most of these criticisms were justified and on hindsight I find that the man-power approach has only a limited role in educational planning. This aspect of the problem is not however discussed here because it was only incidentally related to the actual recommendations of the Commission which would remain unchanged even if the man-power approach is entirely rejected.

The proposals of the Education Commission on selective admissions are not always fully understood; and it is, therefore, necessary to state them in some detail.

(1) The capacity of a society to expend educational facilities in terms of real resources sets up minimum targets (para 5.13). The Commission found that this salutary principle was generally ignored in practice and that enrolments were increased without increasing the facilities available. It was of the view that this attempt to expand education at the cost of standards was harmful and should be abandoned and recommended that enrolments in any institution should be limited to the actual facilities available therein.

(2) The public demand for secondary and higher education and even the desire to provide secondary and higher education to all talented students who deserve such education sets up high targets of enrolments which will be beyond our capacity to reach. The Commission, therefore, recommended that we should try to ensure that an enrolment policy is based on social justice and that secondary and higher education becomes available at least to the most talented students. (para 5.13).

(3) The present policy of open-door access has had several undesirable consequences: (a) dilution of standards; (b) over-production of some categories of personnel and under-production in others; (c) over-enrolment from urban families and upper and

middle classes; and (d) under-enrolment from the poorer sections (para 5.07). The Commission was of the view that these evils can be corrected only through a policy of selective admissions.

Against this background, the Commission made elaborate proposals for selective admissions which can be summarized as follows :

(1) The attempt to introduce selective admissions at the university stage only cannot succeed in isolation. It must be accompanied by adequate preparation at the secondary stage.

(2) Expansion is very difficult to control when secondary education is one undivided unit. The child is too young (aged 13 or 14) to be submitted to selection when secondary education begins (class VII or IX); and once admitted, he continues to remain in the school till he completes secondary education. This leads to unnecessary expansion. The Commission, therefore, divided the secondary stage into two sub-stages : (i) a lower secondary stage ending with class X where no principle of selection was introduced; and (ii) a higher secondary stage of classes XI-XII (where the child will be in the age-group 17-18) where selective admissions could and should be introduced.

(3) The higher secondary stage should be diversified and about 50 per cent of the students should be diverted into vocational and mostly terminal courses. This would greatly reduce the pressures on university admissions.

(4) Selective admissions are not an end in themselves; their objectives are two : (a) to relate the output of the educational system to man-power needs so that educated unemployment is reduced; and (b) to relate admissions to provision of facilities with a view to improving standards.

(5) Emphasis should be placed on proper planning of the location of higher secondary schools, colleges and universities and on fixing the maximum number of students that can be admitted to them in view of the facilities that actually exist. This will be a far more effective method of regulating enrolments than selective admissions as such.

(6) No selective admissions need be made where the number of applicants is already less than the number of seats available. But where applicants exceed the number of seats available, selection becomes inescapable and should be resorted to.
(7) Method of selection should be improved. Better selection tests should be devised and special emphasis should be laid on social justice.
(8) Selective admissions are meant for full-time institutions only. Side by side, the facilities for part-time and own-time education should be fully expanded so that no individual who is qualified and desired to study further need be denied education beyond class X.

The Commission pointed out that a policy of selective admissions exists even now, but it is in force only in a small core of institutions of higher education with prestige and quality. Here the net effect of selections is to convert these institutions into "elite" centres which are availed of mostly by the privileged groups. On the other hand an open-door access is provided in the vast bulk of the institutions of higher education which maintain indifferent standards and are mostly availed of by the common people. The Commission wanted this "dualism" to be reduced, if not eliminated altogether. From this point of view, it made two recommendations : (i) access to the good quality and prestigious institutions should be made available to talented students from the non-privileged groups through a programme of reservations, special facilities (such as personal guidance etc.), scholarships and placement; and (ii) the principle of selective admissions as described above should also be introduced in all the higher secondary schools and institutions of higher education where a policy of open-door admissions prevailed, mainly with a view to preventing an undeserved or inappropriate use of these resources.

There is no doubt that these proposals of the Commission were sufficiently realistic and moderate and that they carried the conceptualization of the problem a good deal further. But these never received a good hearing. The political climate was totally hostile and no party would touch the proposal with a pair of tongs. At the very beginning, the Committee of Members of Parliament rejected it outright and suggested that "every effort should be made to provide admissions to institutions of higher education to all eligible students who desire to study further". The backward classes were totally opposed. They welcomed the Commission's proposals to give them better access to the privileged and elite institutions. But they would not agree to any selective admissions below the M.A./M.Sc level. Their view was best represented by Shri Jagjivan Ram who told the Commission that he would launch a satyagraha and a nation-wide campaign if Government adopted selective admissions at the higher secodary or undergraduate stage. A State Education Minister told Dr. D.S. Kothari: "If selective admissions are introduced, the Vice-Chancellor will not have headaches. But if they are introduced, we (i.e., Government), who have to deal with the non-selected students, will have big headaches. Since we are in a position to make the decision, we shall pass on the headaches to you". The fate of the recommendation was, therefore, sealed at the very outset and there was no reference to it in the National Policy Resolution (1968). It was also pointed out earlier that an indirect reference to the proposal in the Maharashtra White Paper on Education created the highest storm against it and had ultimately to be deleted from the final version. Even today, there is no chance of an acceptance of the idea at the political level.

This political reluctance to support the principle of selective admissions at the higher secondary and university stages springs from, and is in turn strengthened by, several social factors among which the following may be mentioned:

(1) The hang-over of the pre-independence struggle against the British Government which wanted to restrict secondary and higher education is still too strong. We then developed a bias for a policy of open-door admissions which is more like that in U.S.A. Even though this policy is suited only to very affluent societies, we refuse to see the contradiction between our educational objectives and our financial capacity and persist in pleading for uncontrolled expansion of secondary and university education.

(2) From the social point of view, it is the advanced castes or groups that support selective admissions because they have come to realize they can hold their own in the competition. On the other hand the proposal is opposed

by the backward classes who fear that their vertical mobility will be adversely affected. In a hierarchical society like ours, education tends to percolate, over time, to castes and social strata which are lower down in the scale. At any given time, therefore, there will be some castes or social strata which will have advanced enough and will be willing to support selective admissions. At that very time there would also be other social strata and castes whose hopes have been aroused but which have not received adequate benefits from the system. They will tend to oppose such proposals tooth and nail. The line at which the fight for and against selections takes place varies from time to time, and hence the groups that support and oppose the proposals also differ over time. But there is no doubt that the social opposition to such proposals from some backward classes or the other will continue for a long time to come.

(3) The social situation has built-in problems for which selective admissions are no solution. For instance, what are these young men and women to do? They have completed secondary education. They cannot get a job and the age of marriage for girls is continually rising. They join higher secondary schools or colleges because there is nothing else to do and they cannot stay at home doing nothing. A system of selective admissions may solve a problem for the educational system but it does not solve the social problem they are actually facing. The social pressures will, therefore, see to it that selective admissions are not introduced.

(4) There is an innate distrust of the selective process itself. The public is convinced that all selection will be biased by considerations of caste, religion, personal loyalties and even corruption. There is some trust in selections where the process is remotely controlled at very high levels (i.e., the all-India examinations for IITs). But no one is prepared to buy the idea that selections to higher secondary schools, colleges and even universities will not be manipulated.

(5) A trend has grown to look upon the expansion of education itself as a major avenue for new jobs. As

unemployment increases, the case for selective admissions becomes stronger. But exactly for the same reason, the social and political opposition to the idea gains increasing strength.

The rejection of this recommendation should not be regarded as a defeat for the Education Commission. This concept is one answer to major social and educational problem, viz., how to control the growing volume of educated unemployment and to raise educational standards in spite of the limited resources available, without affecting the interests of the backward classes and their chances of vertical mobility. We have been struggling with this problem since 1921 and have neither been able to accept this solution nor to evolve any other suitable alternative. The stalmate has continued and will continue until we find an answer. The attempt to popularize this concept or to devise suitable alternatives to it will, therefore, have to continue.

Some important developments of the last twelve years which have a bearing on this problem and the various proposals that are being put forward to solve it deserve notice.

(1) State Governments are now less inclined to establish new colleges and universities. This is due partly to continuing pressure from the UGC and the Central Government and partly to lack of financial resources. It is also a fact that the rate at which new colleges and universities were being established has fallen; and even the rate of increase in enrolments at the university stage has gone down considerably. The growing unemployment among the matriculates and graduates has probably begun to dampen the zest for secondary and higher education to some extent.

(2) An idea has been put forward that a system of reservation (on the basis of population) may be introduced for backward classes or weaker sections of first generation learners etc., so that their fears about an adverse effect on their vertical mobility can be allayed. Although the suggestion is good, it has not yet become acceptable to the backward classes who do not accept selective admissions even with this sugar-coating. Needless to say, the proposal is totally opposed by the urban upper and middle classes whose access to the system will be adversely affected by it.

(3) The idea that fees should be increased to control expansion of higher secondary or university education has also been put forward. Two points are argued in favour of the proposals : (i) it will control expansion to some extent through monetary devices rather than through direct selection; and (ii) it will at least reduce the element of subsidy in such education. The proposals for raising fees are of a number of types : (i) a flat rate increase of a small amount every five years or so; (ii) relating fees to income; (iii) making fees pay an increasing share of the total cost, etc. Side by side, it is also proposed to give fee concessions to all poor and needy students (including those from backward classes in order to ensure that a rise in fees does not affect them adversely. None of these proposals has been found to be acceptable, and no Government seems to have the political courage to raise fees.

(4) The old idea that the Government should recruit all their employees at the end of the school stage and then train them, where necessary, in special institutions for any period from one to five years is often paraded before the public and the authorities. It has had no general acceptance and its claim that it will lead to a reduction in university enrolments is at best hypothetical.

(5) The idea of vocationalizing secondary education and diverting a large proportion of students into terminal courses to reduce pressure on universities was first put forward in 1882. It is being discussed continually ever since. The basic issue is that we have not been able to vocationalize secondary education on any worthwhile scale. Even if we do it, we are not quite sure that we will not be creating a problem of unemployment among those who have received vocational education without solving the problem of pressures on university admissions.

(6) The idea that degrees should be delinked from jobs is now being increasingly canvassed. But we do not know how to do this in practice, what further problems it would create and what precise effect it will have on reducing enrolments at secondary and university stages.

(7) Courses of part-time and own-time education are becoming increasingly popular, but they are still far below

the targets suggested by the Commission. Further work on them is, therefore, needed in three directions : (a) to extend their coverage, (b) to improve their quality, and (c) to make them really effective in controlling expansion of full time institutions.

It is a pity that we are caught in a dilemmma where we are helplessly converting uneducated rural (or urban) under-employment or unemployment (which is mute, unorganized and without any nuisance value) into urban (or rural) educated unemployment (which is vocal, organized and has a nuisance value). We are also continually being driven into a situation where an unemployment dole will have to be increasingly provided to control the explosive volcano of urban discontent. Selective admissions which could be an answer to this problem are not socially and politically accectable and we have not yet been able to devise any worthwhile alternative or alternatives. This is certainly not an enviable situation.

Of course, one knows the long-term and ideal solution of the problem. As the Commission observed, we need integrated plans of development at the national, State and district levels which will (1) reduce the birth-rate by at least half in a planned programme spread over 10-15 years, (2) bring about very rapid economic development so that there is a job for every young person who enters the labour force and (3) create an education system which will train every young person for some job needed in the society. How to do this is the main question; and one is not sure whether it can be done at all under a capitalist system or how to bring in socialism, even assuming that socialism can provide a better answer. At the moment, our options seem to be limited. But we are duty bound to explore all available options to the full and to search for an answer or answers that will be feasible and continually approximate to the ideal. This is yet another area in which there is immense scope for research and experimentation.

Seed-Farm Technology

The Commission held the view that if standards are to be maintained and continually improved, it is necessary to create high quality pace-setting institutions in every sector and at every stage of education. These institutions can generate excellence in the first instance and it can then be extended to others. By the time the entire system absorbs and internalizes this excellence, the pace-setting institutions would have climbed to a still higher level of excellence and set in motion another wave for spreading excellence of a higher order; and so on. The Commission described this process as the seed-farm technology and was of the view that the existence of high quality and pace-setting institutions at every stage and in every sector is an essential characteristic of the national system of education.

This concept, it must be admitted, is not new to Indian education. The British Government had introduced, as early as 1882, the concept of "model" institutions maintained by Government which would provide inspiration and practical guidance to other institutions to improve themselves. The Indian Education Commission (1882) had suggested that Government should maintain a high school in every district and a college or so in every Province as "models" and leave the rest of the field open for private enterprise. This idea was developed further by Lord Curzon in the early years of this century and, is some form or the other, survived till 1947. But Indian public and academic opinion never accepted this concept. They argued that the Government cannot have the monopoly of running model institutions, that the quality of many private institutions was far superior to that of government institutions, and that not infrequently a government institution, in spite of all the heavy investment made therein, can only be a model of what an educational institution of that type should not be. Secondly, it was argued that many of the so-called models set up were so costly that they were not repeatable at all. They were the Qutab Minars or Taj Mahals which had a place of their own; but they were planned to be unique or rare rather than multipliable things. Thirdly, the vast bulk of the institutions could not have the resources even to approximate the models they were supposed to imitate; and not infrequently, this improverishment of the average institution was due to the creation of the costly models themselves. Fourthly, it was argued that model institutions, even when successfully set up, tended to be linked to privilege and were generally availed of by students from the well-to-do and privileged classes only. All in all, the nationalist view was that the concept of model institutions to be maintained by Government was a cheap, futile device adopted by an alien Government which did not desire to invest adequately in education and that this device tended to lower the average standard of the education system rather than to raise it. In fact, the famous prayer of Fra Lippo Lippi was often quoted in this context with considerable effect: "Make no more giants, God ! Raise up the whole race at once."

The Commission had taken full note of this experience and criticisms. While recognizing all the negative features of the old concept of "models" the Commission still came to the conclusion that the creation of pace-setting institutions was essential and that the programme could be worked out in a way which would avoid the dangers into which the pre-independence experience of "models" had run. For instance,

- the pace-setting character of educational institutions should not be linked to their management only and that it would be wrong to assume that Central institutions were better than those of States, or that the latter were better than those of local bodies, or that government institutions were better than private ones. The pace-setting institutions could be under any management. They should be indentified by appropriate and objective criteria and should have the same level and type of financial support, irrespective of their managements;
- the difference between the pace-setting institutions and others should not be very wide—as between skyscraper and a hovel but should be small and bridgeable. In fact, the costs allowed by the Commission to the pace-setting institutions vis-a-vis the others were only of the order of 2 : 1;
- there should be definite mechanisms in the system whose main objective should be to strive to ensure that the excellence generated in the pace-setting institutions is extended to the others. Similarly financial and other support must be liberally available to every institution which has the potential and which is prepared to strive to reach the higher levels of excellence; and
- suitable measures can and should be adopted to ensure that the benefits of the pace-setting institutions go to the under-privileged groups and to society as a whole rather than to a privileged class. The programme of pace-setting institutions recommended by the Commission is to be understood against this background and subject to all these reservations.

Major Universities

Of the two recommendations of the Commission on the subject of pace-setting institutions, let us begin with that of major universities. The Commission recommended that we should strive to create, over the next ten years or so, five or six major universities which would:

— function on a national basis in the sense that they enrol talented students from all parts of the country (on the basis of scholarships provided) and recruit their faculty also on a national basis;
— use English and Hindi as media of instruction;
— make first-rate post-graduate work and research possible;
— maintain standards which are internationally comparable; and
— be closely linked to the university system as a whole, so that the transfer of the excellence generated therein to other universities is facilitated.

These major universities were not necessarily Central, although the Central Government should support them liberally through the UGC. In fact the Commission had turned down a proposal, frequently discussed in the Central Advisory Board of Education, that a Central University should be established in every State.

In the opinion of the Commission, creation of these universities would have several advantages : (1) They would help to improve standards at the post-graduate stage and thereby the standards in the education system as a whole; (2) they would supply the high quality staff needed for higher education as well as for other walks of life; (3) they would provide first-rate centres of post-graduate education and research in the country itself and thereby obviate the need to send students abroad in large numbers; and (4) they would help the country to develop an indigenous capability in research and restore its self-respect so that the centre of gravity of intellectual life which is now outside the country will be located within the country itself. The Commission also highlighted the point that the development of these universities was essential in the present state of higher education and that the proposal was in the larger interests of the country and democracy itself in spite of its apparently elitist character.

In spite of all the Commission's eloquent pleas for the proposal, it invited very strong opposition from all quarters. The use of the word "major" was unfortunate and a tactical blunder. But the proposal had no chance even if it had not been used. The Committee of Members of Parliament rejected it summarily. The Vice-Chancellors' Conference also threw it out, quite understandably because the Vice-Chancellors whose universities could not have been selected under the scheme were hostile and in absolute majority. Even academics who generally favoured a selective approach were not in favour of this particular reform; and needless to say, scholars like Dr. D.R. Gadgil, who opposed elitism in all its form, were extremely critical. He said :

"23. The Commission evidently believes that in academics excellence is achieved by massing resources : it also seems to think that these "major" universities will suffer from no problem of administration of personal relations or of hierarchical ordering. While it may be true that an isolated scholar with a heavy load of other work cannot develop his potentialities, a high concentration of a body of scholars is not absolutely essential for the best type of work. The newer departments in a large number of Indian universities are gradually establishing conditions in which a steady stream of good work should become possible. How large the concentration can be at any number of points depends on the size of the country and the availability of scholars. In our situation, high concentration at a few points can only be brought about by denuding others and it is a matter for judgement as to what type of distribution will give the best results. Personally, in this matter as in others, I am for relative dispersal. However, this need not be judged purely subjectively. We have today a high concentration of research personnel in the national laboratories; these are well equipped and have adequate resources. Further, there are many other large institutions of research and training run by government, by individual ministries or as autonomous corporations. There is a sufficient number of these in Delhi alone for the Commission to have carried out individual case studies with which to support its novel and revolutionary recommendation. I may be misinformed; but what I have heard regarding the functioning of a number of laboratories and institutions does not support the assumption that a concentration of resources and research personnel will automatically lead to a large volume of high quality research or that the higher the concentration the more is the institution free from administrative, hierarchical or personal problems.

24. How will the major universities contribute to the solution of the problems highlighted by the Commission? Let us recapitulate that these problems are of a lack of interest among teachers, of financial worries, of unsatisfactory physical conditions, of hierarchical concentration of authority and of intrigues, specially present in the weaker colleges and universities; among the students they relate to unsatisfactory home conditions and earlier training, to intellectual apathy, to the medium of instruction, to financial worries etc. There is nothing in the report of the Commission to indicate how the establishment of "major" universitites will help in the solution of these problems. The only suggestion which indicates a connection between the "major" universities and others is that the major universities would supply "a goodly portion of the outstanding personnel needed for the staffs of universities, colleges" etc. It would easily take ten years for these universities to get established and to rise from their present low standards into towering excellence. After that some of their products may flow out but if experience elsewhere is any guide the outstanding among them would soon flow back into the "major" universities.

25. The "major" university concept has thus no relevance to an improvement of existing conditions in our universities and colleges. However, it is possible to state with some confidence that the establishment of "major" universities will, on the other hand, surely worsen these conditions. At least three important effects of this step on the other Indian universities can be identified. Firstly, they will all suffer a diminution in the financial resources that will be available to them in future plan periods. In view of the grandiose writing of the Commission, I would put the diminution at the minimum of an average ten per cent. More seriously they will have to put up with the loss, now and continuously afterwards, of a large number of their best men in all subjects. Thirdly, they will suffer degradation. It is one of the merits of the present Indian situation that in our various systems of ranking and privilege there is as yet no established ranking among universities. We do not suffer from the psychological strain resulting from the classification of "bridge" and "redbrick". I can think of no greater disservice to Indian education than the deliberate, artificial of resources and of official patronage having the ability to create high standards of academic excellence.

But I have no doubt that immediately after their establishment teachers and students at the major universities will behave like snobs, and that others will be permanently afflicated with an inferiority complex.

26. I realize that the Vice-Chancellor of a University which has no obvious claims to be upgraded into a major university trends delicate ground in commenting on this subject. However, I feel it so important to protest against this monstrous idea that I am prepared to risk the misunderstanding. Also I have hopes that Poona can stand even this strian. This city has been the centre of activities of scholars like Shankar Balkrishna Dixit, Vishwanath Kashinath Rajwade, Dr. Ketkar and Dr. Sukthankar and knows that high standards of scholarship are compatible with limited resources. I hope I shall not be considered presumptuous if I claim that the tradition of these scholars has in recent decades been maintained, to the best of their ability, by their successors. Therefore, I feel confident that this University will continue to retain the services of at least a small number of devoted scholars and maintain high standards of work, whatever its external ranking.

27. I should like to make it clear that the Education Commission is not particularly to blame. It was doing no more than following the current fashion. This favours "elitism" and concentration of resources, all in the name of ultimate peace and plenty. I realize that I am the dissenter in this consensus. I dissent because I believe that socio-economic progress is indivisible in a real sense and because nobody has yet explained to me the magic through which the addition of skyscrapers at Nariman Point can help to transform the hovels, say, under Bandra bridge."

An attempt was made to save the proposal with some modifications. The main criticism of even those who accepted the principle of selective approach for qualitative improvement was that a "university" cannot be the unit for such development. They, therefore, argued that a Department, and not a university, should be taken as the unit, that all departments of all universities should be eligible for selection as Centres of Advanced Study, that specific and objective criteria should be laid down for the selection of departments for their elevation into Centres of Advanced Studies, and that resources should be found to elevate a fair number of the total departments into such centres. In this general policy, they were prepared to "cluster" a number of advanced centres into some selected universities where conditions were favourable. Such clusters of centres would naturally support each other and the universities having them might, therefore, be able to perform the task which the Commission had visualized for major universities. This argument was accepted by the Committee of Members of Parliament who supported it (para 57) and this modified proposal also found a place in the National Policy on Education (1968) which said : "Centres of Advanced Study should be strengthened and a small number of 'clusters of centres' aiming at the highest possible standards in research and training should be established" (sub-para 12 (d) of para 4 of the Resolution). But this victory was of no avail and no effective steps were taken to implement the proposal even in this modified form. During the past 12 years, even the idea of 'Centres of Advanced Study' has lost the prestige and glamour it had in 1966.

Chapter X

Lessons for the Future

4. Higher Education

The Education Commission makes a good contribution when it discusses the objectives of the university system and the role that the universities have to play in national development. It also presents a grand vision of the university as a community of scholars engaged in the pursuit of truth and excellence, and most of its recommendations are meant to create this model. Its insistence on making the remuneration of university and college teachers comparable to that of other major public services so that a reasonable proportion of the country's top talent goes into the university system was absolutely right. Its proposals to make the affiliated colleges academically and financially viable and to confer autonomy on them were sound, but probably not adequate to meet the situation. It did a yeoman's service to the adoption of regional languages as media of instruction, although all its proposals on the subject have yet to be fully worked out. The introduction of the National Education Service, though in a truncated form, was a corollary of one of its recommendations. And this is probably all that can be said in favour of the Report. Its recommendations for improving selection procedures and raising the quality of teachers have not been implemented nor has its proposal of selective admissions been accepted as yet. This should of course be blamed on implementation than on the Commission. But it cannot also be gainsaid that the inadequacies of the proposals of the Education Commission on the reform of higher education have been too significant to be ignored. What is probably worse, it does not present any deep analysis of the factors which are responsible for the continuing crisis in which the system finds itself and it does not therefore make adequate proposals to resolve it. It also ignores the imperative need, which will become more urgent as time passes, to diversify higher education and to create a variety of models among which the classical model (on which the Commission relies almost exclusively) can be one. This subject therefore also finds hardly any treatment in the Report of the Commission. On the whole, therefore, one is left with the feeling that in tackling the basic issues of higher education in the days ahead, in making it relevant or linking it closely with national development and raising its standards, the proposals of the Education Commission provide only a partial answer. This is also an area where a good deal of fresh thinking, research and experimentation is called for.

Among the major issues that will have to be tackled in higher education in the years ahead, the following may be mentioned.

(a) The programme of using regional languages as media of instruction has to be developed further, with all the ancillary reforms needed to maintain standards.

(b) Continued effort will have to be made to introduce improved selection procedures that combine merit with social justice.

(c) Programmes have to be decided to ensure that all university teachers and students do effectively participate in meaningful and challenging proposals of national and social service. The present N.S.S. proposal is only a poor answer to this need and a bolder attempt is called for.

(d) A much greater expansion of non-formal programmes of part-time and own-time education is needed. The target suggested by the Commission in this regard that about one-third of the total enrolment in higher education should be in these courses by 1986 (para 12.22) is still far from realized.

(e) There is no justification for the continuance of the "dual" system which we operate in higher education, i.e., there is a core of high quality and prestigious institutions which are mostly availed of by the privileged classes surrounded by a large penumbra of institutions which maintain poor standards and in which we offer "open door" access to the underprivileged groups and provide them a seat in some institution, however poor, and in some course, however useless. The Education Commission diagnosed a similar malady at the school stage and suggested the concepts of the neighbourhood school and the common school system. These cannot be extended to the university stage. But some other measures will have to be adopted to see that this dual system does come to an end. This problem was not highlighted in the Report of the Education Commission. But it does need careful study and close attention.

(f) In the present model of higher education, the two functions of (i) producing, conserving and diffusing knowledge and (ii) grading and certification, mainly for purpose of employment, are combined. It is this combination that creates several problems. Is this combination really essential? If it is not, how can we separate and organize the grading and certification function independently of the universities? This is really the programme of delinking jobs from degrees that is now widely and rather loosely being talked of. On the other hand, if the combination of these two functions is inevitable, how do we solve the problems arising therefrom?

(g) At present, the system of our higher education is almost exclusively dependent on the classical model (the agricultural universities are one recent exception). The higher education of the future will have to be provided through diverse institutional forms. This is another field where a good deal of fresh thinking and experimentation is needed and in which the Report of the Commission provides little guidance.

(h) The problem of raising standards in higher education still continues to baffle us. That concentration of resources is necessary for improving standards is readily granted. But how much to concentrate and where—this is still an unanswered question. Nor have we been able to strike a proper balance between policies of concentration and dispersal. We still know very little why institutions rise to heights and then decline; and above all we are not able to add substantially to the competent and dedicated leadership available in the university system and not even able to make the best use of whatever talent is actually available. In fact, the whole question of proper management of the educational system from the point of view of improving standards is wide open and this is an area on which we shall have to concentrate in the years ahead.

(i) The problem of students will become still more pressing as time passes, particularly the problems of students from the scheduled castes, scheduled tribes and other weaker sections who will come to the universities with several handicaps and who will need a good deal of remedial teaching. The students of the system of higher education have long ceased to be a homogeneous body and we will have to learn to divide them into separate groups and to deal with each group in accordance with their needs and potential. Student services are weak and the extent of student aid is limited at present. These will have to be strengthened and expanded; and the challenging programme of associating students with the governance of institutions of higher education will have to be developed further.

(j) There is a first-rate crisis of management in the universities which are not even able to do their routine jobs like holding examinations on time and wherein the basic educational process itself comes to a grinding halt all too frequently. Modernization and improvement of university administration is one of the major challenges of the future; and here also there is immense scope for fresh thinking and experimentation.

It is hardly necessary to illustrate the point in greater detail. What has been said already is enough to show that the proper development of higher education is one of the major tasks which face us in the creation of a national system of education. In this area, as well as in the development of secondary education we shall have to go far beyond the lead provided by the Education Commission.

APPENDIX 4

Challenge of Education—A Policy Perspective

(Ministry of Human Resource Development
Department of Education, Government of India,
New Delhi, August, 1985)

This is a summary of a document entitled Challenge of Education circulated by the Ministry for initiating a debate on certain facts, views and issue relevant to the formulation of a Policy for Education.

Education being a complex subject with wide ranging ramifications, definitive views of a new policy for it cannot be finalised consulting the decision makers in the States and Central Government, and the parliamentarians, educationists, intellectuals, partners, students, entrepreneurs etc. This document aims to provoke a discussion by stating various viewpoints in a forthright fashion. If people read it, comment on it and criticise it, it will have served the purpose for which it has been prepared.

While preparing this docoment, it has been borne in mind that India is standing on the threshold of the twenty first century. Those being born now will finish their elementary school at the turn of the century. They will be face to face with unprecedented opportunities and challenges. To prepare for these and also to create a national environment for peaceful and harmonious development, it is necessary to reshape the education system since only education can imbue people with the knowledge, a sense of purpose and the confidence essential for building a dynamic, vibrant and cohesive nation capable of providing its people with the wherewithal for creating better, fuller and more purposeful life.

India's Constitution envisages a just, equitable and fraternal society which would assure the dignity of the individual and the unity and integrity of the nation. Policy planners in India are unanimous that while economic strength and vitality determines the scope and quality of political freedom, for millions the availing of the benefits of freedom depends on its being accompanied by an equitable distribution of goods and services. This is possible through expansion, disposal and diversification of employment, which in turn implies equality of opportunity, particularly in access to knowledge and skills.

The Indian polity is characterised by a concern for the individual, not as a mere instrument of development but as an end in himself. This emphasises the importance of education for the development of self-confident individuals with a commitment to democratic values and national unity.

Education helps to bridge the chasm of disparities between people, socio-economic groups and regions and thereby reduces disintegrative tensions. It develops human resources, which has a multiplier effort on utilisation of all other resources. Thus it is an investment in development.

Elementary education is the most crucial stage of education because the foundation of the personality, attitudes, self-confidence, habits, learning skills and communication capabilities is laid at this stage. Universal elementary education strengthens the fabric of democracy. That is why it was set forth in Article 45 of all Constitution.

Vocational education is essential for providing manpower for economic growth. It provides the link between the production function, employment and educational processes.

Higher education provides ideas and men to give shape to the future and sustain other levels of education. It provides the historical and ideological perspective to society. In addition, it supplies a wide range of increasingly sophisticated manpower required in industry, agriculture, services and administration.

Education system cannot remove all the shortcomings of society. As a sub-system of society, it tends to imbibe the characteristics of the total environment: it cannot maintain its excellence or its democratic character unless it is deliberately supported in these thrusts.

Education planning can have social relevance only if its quantitative and qualitative objectives are spelt out by those responsible for national development.

Moreover, it acquires dynamism based on a national will to nurture the future generations for excellence, without unduly exposing it to the rough and tumble of the current populist pressures.

Educational goals are often postponed on the grounds of high cost of implementation. While deciding this, the social cost of a "no-change" option is seldom taken into account. At their best, the products of our schools, colleges and universities are comparable to the best scholars, technologists, doctors and managers in the world. Against this small minority, the preponderant majority has little to show by way of capacity for self-study, communication skills and a sense of social or national responsibility. Even the gifted do not always show evidence of the expected commitment to social responsibility.

The above situation is largely because of excessive emphasis on degrees and an examination system which tends to evaluate students at yearly intervals largely on the basis of rote learning. Examinations and grades have lost much of their credibility. Neither the public nor employers trust them. Students relate education exclusively to examinations and, in the process, education has tended to become dysfunctional, producing a large number of unemployable youngmen and women. The system of examinations could be one of the reasons why students and teachers find it difficult to resist progressive erosion of values. Unless this process is reversed by a reorientation of education, it will be difficult to contain exploitation, insecurity and violence. It is also necessary to counteract divisive forces arising from castes, religion and regional considerations which are straining the sense of national integration. Pride in national identity has to be rebuilt.

Education will have to be modernised to facilitate the modernisation of production, services and infrastructures. Besides, to enable young people to develop entrepreneurial ability, students will have to be exposed to challenges of new ideas and unfamiliar situations. To enable the teachers to do this, besides changing curricula and teaching methods, the attitudes and values of teachers will have to be changed through basic changes in teachers training.

India has made considerable progress since independence in terms of increase of all types of institutions, enrolment and the sophistication and diversification of education programmes. It has, however, not been possible to meet the nation's aspirations from the view point of overall coverage, equitable distribution and quality of education. In terms of literacy, India is still amongst the most backward countries with literates accounting, in 1981, for only 36.2% of the population, with women, Scheduled Castes and Scheduled Tribes still at the level of 24.9%, 21.4% and 16.4% respectively.

We are still very far from fulfilment of the goal of universalisation of elementary education, which was envisaged in the Constitution itself to be achieved by the year 1960. One of the principal reasons for this is the high drop-out rate (Classes I-VIII) which continues to be above 75%. This rate is much higher amongst girls, Scheduled Castes and Scheduled Tribes.

The number of children going to middle, high and secondary classes has increased from 22 lakhs in 1947 to 340 lakhs in 1983, and the country now has 175,000 schools for these levels as compared to 13,000 in 1947.

The number of girls and boys successfully completing the higher secondary stage has risen from 2.37 lakhs in 1960-61 to 8.40 lakhs in 1981-82. The most disquieting feature at this level of education is that, even after 8 or 10 or even 12 years of schooling substanital number of pubils do not acquire the capacity to understand their physical, cultural or socio-economic environment, or to think for themselves. They do not enter the employment market with sufficient confidence or competence or vocational skills. Nearly 83% of students passing out of the higher secondary stream seek admission in colleges and universities. Only 20% of these are able to find berth in professional or technical institutions.

If the Education Policy adopted by Parliament in 1968 had been implemented, 50% of the students at 10+ level of secondary education should have developed employment oriented vocational skill. By the year 1982-83 students intake in vocational courses at +2 level reached just 60,000 per annum.

At the time of independence, there were only 700 colleges and 20 universities in India with an enrolment of 4 lakhs. Now the country has 5,246 colleges and 140 universities with an enrolment of 33.60 lakhs of whom 9.76 lakhs are girls.

The Education Policy of 1968 sought to relate education more closely to life, expand educational opportunities, improve quality of education, emphasise development of science and technology and cultivate moral and social values. While some significant achievements have been recorded, by and large, these goals have remained unachieved. In the mean time, new learning needs have arisen due to the inexorable march of economic and social growth and progress in science and technology.

A new approach to education is necessary. In the new design, capacity to learn will be more important than what is learnt and continuing education will be emphasised. Social and moral values will receive much greater emphasis. Access, equity and quality of education will be ensured through rigorous planning. Before such a design can be prepared, it is necessary to evaluate the past experience, assess success and failures and examine as to how far mechanisms for formulating policies, allocating resources, ensuring inter-sectoral coördination, enforcing standards and monitoring and evaluation need modification.

It is apparent that the most important reason for slow progress has been an acute paucity of resources. Growth in enrolment and rise in prices have outstripped the increases in budgetary allocations. Expenditure per student has, over the years, declined in real terms. More than 90% of the expenditure is on teachers' salaries and administration. Practically nothing is available to replace blackboard or buy chalks, or charts and teaching aids or even minimum school amenities.

People are generally apathetic to an education system which does not appear relevant to them and which has little accountability to them. The school seems to have become a part of a gigantic bureaucratic set up which does not provide sufficient scope for intervention at local levels and is also frustrating for teachers with initiative. Consequently, the education system has largely become the responsibility of government. Greater involvement of the community predicates delegation of authority to enable it to keep an eye on the performance of schools and specially of the teachers. The sheer size of the system creates an environment for the teachers and individual schools, in which any kind of default or creativity fails to come to notice.

To enable girls and boys from poor families to receive the benefit of education despite their inability to attend school regular hours, new and non-formal approaches have to be adopted. These would, however, require much greater support in terms of instructional material and regular monitoring and appraisal.

In absolute terms, there were more illiterates in 1981 (437 million) than there were at the time of independence (300 million). Nonetheless, as a per cent of population, literacy has progressed steadily from 16.67% in 1951 to 36.23% in 1981. There is, however, great disparity in the progress made, not only between men and women but also between regions. Female literacy in rural areas varies from 64.7% in Kerala to 5.4% in Rajasthan. In Bihar, Madhya Pradesh and U.P., which account for 38% of the rural families in the country, female literacy percentages ranges between 8.99 and 10.77. This situation reflects the fact that the positive results from elementary and adult education are largely nullified by a high rate of growth of population.

There is a positive correlation between literacy and acceptance of family planning. Because of this, both elementary education and adult education should be assigned a high priority. In any case, if things continue as they are, in the year 2000 A.D. there would be 500 million illiterates in India.

There is also a definite link between adult literacy and children's participation in schools. UNESCO's studies have revealed that adult literacy level of 70% is critical thershold for universalisation of elementary education.

At the level of secondary education, today, only 22% of the students of the corresponding age group are in the schools. Of the few who come to the schools, very few have access to schools with proper buildings, laboratories, libraries or playgrounds.

According to all India Educational Survey of 1978, many primary and middle schools do not have even basic amenities. In so far as primary schools are concerned, 9% had no buildings whatsoever, 41.5% had no blackboards, 72% had no library facilities and about 53% had no playgrounds. In the rural areas, 89% primary, 70% of middle and 27% of secondary and 10% of higher secondary schools had no urinal/lavatory facilities.

Vocationalisation in the higher secondary stage was a major plank of the education policy of 1968. 50% of the students at +2 stage were to go into the vocational stream. The actual figure is too insignificant to deserve mention. This is largely because neither the physical facilities nor a detailed plan of action, complete with details of employment opportunities, nature of diversification required, apporopriate course curricula and teachers trained for vocational training are available at present. In addition, social values which denigrate even skilled manual work also stand in the way of vocationalisation.

College and university education has greatly expanded since independence. Taken as a whole the general condition of colleges and universities is a matter of concern. Many of these are known for rampant casteism, regionalism and inbreeding. Some of these are virtual battlefields in which political and other factions, backed by teachers and aided by other staff, often fight pitched battles for power and supremacy. Some Vice-Chancellors spend their entire terms of office behind barricades.

There is a widespread feeling that the present state of higher education is largely because of overt and covert interference by external agencies. This underlines the importance of real autonomy. However, attention has also to be given to the equally important aspect of accountability. Often the Vice-Chancellors, who are considered responsible for running universities, function in conditions of fact dwindling prestige of their office. They have to be at the doorsteps of government officials for funds required for running the university and they have to compromise to get the co-operation of university bodies.

The UGC has made an enormous contribution to establishment of academic norms and promotion of innovative programme. It is, however, debatable as the extent to which it has been able to uphold the standards of education or enforce a minimum level of performance on colleges and universities. This tends to become difficult because many a time a move to refuse or reduce grants to these institutions assumes the character of confronation between the State Governments sponsoring them and the Central Government funding the UGC.

To a great extent the quality and employability of college graduates is adversely affected by the fact that arts and humanities are offered as unilinear programmes of study unrelated to the requirements of real life, multifaceted development of personality and the reasoning and learning capabilities of students. In the case of sciences, courses are designed essentially to explain concepts without supportive arrangements in the form of laboratory apparatus, kits etc.

There is no gainsaying that technical education has made a significant contribution to India's economic development. However, the system is now facing serious problems of obsolescence of machinery and equipment and the lack of wherewithal for research and training in respect of new technologies. These inadequacies have been removed for sheer survival.

Other measures necessary for effecting improvement in institutions, of technical education are: finding ways to attract good teachers; increasing interaction with industry; involving the faculties in application of modern technology for the benefit of the common man in rural areas; reducing the disparities between State Colleges, Regional Colleges and IITs; and establishment of net woring arrangements between different types of institutions.

It is also argued that instead of subsidising education in engineering institutions at the cost of the taxpayer, the organised private sector, which absorbs the bulk of manpower emerging from it, should be made to support technical education to some extent.

The role of teachers is central to all processes of formal education since they interpret the policies and programmes as much though their personal example as through teaching learning processes. Unfortunately, enough attention has not been paid to the updating of curricula for their training. Teachers education, therefore, has little relevance to the needs of the day. This inadequacy is compounded by the fact that teaching is the last choice in the job market.

The participation of a section of teachers in party politics has had serious repercussions on education. It has led to the politicisation of teachers organisations, has affected discipline and their wholehearted application to their time-honoured role.

There is widespread concern, particularly amongst teachers themselves, about the manner of implementation of the merit promotion scheme for teachers. Many of them feel that once age and years of services rather than erudition and competence as teachers, becomes the basis of advancement in career ; not enough incentive will be felt for pursuit of excellence.

There are wide disparities in the system of education from the view point of access, equity and impact. Even though rural areas account for three-fourth of the population, they are getting much less resources for education. While the well to do, who have access to the privately managed "quality" institutions located in urban area, take away the lion's share of unreserved seats in professional institutions, children of rural areas are put to a great disadvantage because of the relatively poor quality of rural schools.

Girls, children from the Scheduled Tribes and Scheduled Castes have made considerable progress during the last decade. In spite of this, they still are at the lowest ladder of educational attainment. While girls suffer because of social prejudices and their commitments to the care of siblings and household chores, the children of Scheduled Castes and Scheduled Tribes suffer from disabilities which cannot be removed merely by reservation of seats. Majority of them, besides suffering from the limitations of first generation learners also suffer from the after effects of early childhood malnutrition, a sense of social isolation, unsuitable work habits and lack of self confidence in realising their academic potentials. They find it difficult to adjust to the general stream of students. To obviate the resulting psychological strain, special programmes are needed for enhancing their competence and facilitating their adjustment.

The interface between education and job market is characterised by lack of complimentarity. Jobs requiring general education are not increasing at the same rate as the availability of manpower. On the other hand, for many jobs requiring technical competence and manual skills, appropriately trained manpower is not available in sufficient numbers. The most glaring example of lack of work orientation is provided by the fact that in the I-V, VI-VIII, IX-X or 10+ stages of education, there is nothing in the school system to increase the student's proficiency for the unorganised sector in agriculture or related rural occupations.

It is true that from Rs. 114 crores in 1950-51, the expenditure on education went up to Rs. 2304.16 crores in 1976-77. However, it is also true that because of inflation and growth of the number of students, at constant prices of 1970-71, between 1950-51 and 1975-76 per pupil per annum expenditure went down, from Rs. 468.9 to Rs. 330.9 for college education and from Rs. 1640.4 to Rs. 890.1 for professional education, registering a marginal increase of 1.1% per annum in the case of elementary education rising from Rs. 41.9 to Rs. 55.2 respectively.

Despite the constitutional imperative for elementary education, within the plan outlays for education, its share declined form 56% in the First Plan to 35% the Second Plan, 34% in the Third Plan and 30% in the Fourth Plan. In the Sixth Plan its share was 36%. On the other hand, between the first and sixth plans, the share of university and college education has gone up from 9% to 16%.

The States provide around 70% of the overall plan expenditure for education.Their capacity being variable, children from poorer State like Bihar, U.P., Orissa, J&K, Madhya Pradesh and Rajasthan are at a great disadvantage as compared to better off States. Per capita budget expenditure on education in 1982-83 was as low as Rs. 40.5 in U.P., Rs. 49.4 in Madhya Pradesh and Rs. 51.2 in Bihar as compared to Rs. 100 in Punjab and the all India average of Rs. 68.2.

Education policy is an instrument for shaping the future. It has an impact on a whole generation. It can be framed by a few people on the basis of their own perceptions. It calls for the involvement of those dealing with or interested in education, in an open ended discussion of various viewpoints and issues.

Besides development physically, intellectually and aesthetically integrated human beings with a scientific temper and democratic values as well as social awareness, education has to imbue the pupils with a healthy attitude to hardwork and dignity of labour, commitment to principles of secularism and social justice and dedication to the integrity, honour and the development of the country. In addition to this, for economic development and employment, education has to equip young people with appropriate knowledge and skills.

Besides integrating the individual into the social system, education also reduces disparities between human beings. In view of this equal access to education for all citizens are justified in expecting.

Education provides support to all other spheres of development. In return, it must also receive support from them in its endeavours. No law and order system can survive if even educated people do not have respect for life or sense of right or wrong. Democracy and civic life becomes a casualty if education does not make them tolerant of a different point of view. A country cannot grow if a spirit of adventure and the confidence to innovate is not instilled in the children. No programme requiring participation of the masses in development can make a headway without the input of education.

There is widespread feeling that the system of education cannot be improved by marginal changes and that this is the time for attempting its radical transformation. There is also a feeling that purposeful education is an indispensable instrument for the overall transformation of society, curbing fissiparous tendencies, creating an atmosphere for equity and social justice and modernizing production. It is also recognised that the outreach and effectiveness of education can be enhanced dramatically by the use of new educational technologies.

Educational planners are convinced that a good policy gets checkmated during implementation if the attitudes of those involved in implementation or the constraints inherent in the environment are not kept fully in view. Inevitably any radical change in the education system will come in conflict with vested interests benefiting from the present state of education. Changes in the examination system, innovative approach to teaching, development of new curricula, enforcement of discipline, restructuring of management and decentralisation of the administrative authority will encounter strong resistance.

Depoliticisation too will be opposed not only by politicians who may lose their cadres but also by some of the academic and non-academic staff who will lose their capacity to hold institutions to ransom.

The present orientation of media, lack of trained manpower for software development, non-availability of a television channel committed to educational use and the absence of well established pedagogy for distance education will also, in the short run, operate as constraints.

The inherent difficulties faced by the poor with regard to participation in education has to be regarded as a major problem in universalisation of elementary education. Non-formal and part-time education for children unable to attend the school in regular hours is best conducted by voluntary agencies. In the absence of these, in many areas, this approach will run into difficulties.

In the context of the poor, the present orientation of research and development activities in technical institutions may also pose difficulties. It will not be easy to persuade them to pay special attention to the generation of relevant knowledge for rural and unorganised sector since, in term of widespread recognition and material benefits it will not offer the same rewards as working for the organised corporate sector.

Legal constraints are often more implicable than others. In the Indian situation, the implications of the constitutional amendment to make education a Concurrent Subject are still to be worked out. The Central Government will have to decide upon the parameters of intervention for influencing the National Education System—for a qualitative improvement in prioritisation and performance. Amongst others, it will have to be decided as to what measures should be taken to see that language does not remain a barrier to mobility in the India of tomorrow. In this context and also in relation to the objective of national integration, the need and means of establishing a uniform national core curriculum will have to be considered.

If the management of universities is to be restructured to align them to the realities of the day, Sate and Central governments will have to amend their laws. The much debated issue of whether or not the Central Government should assume some powers for depoliticising and modernising the universities will also have to be decided through consultations.

It is urgently necessary to think carefully of financial constraints because without adequate resources it will not be possible to fulfil the objectives of universalisation of elementary education, expansion of vocational training, removal of illiteracy, improvement of teaching, and establishment of institutions of excellence. How the necessary resources may be raised is a matter for urgent consideration. In this connection, perhaps, a Joint Commission of Centre and States could be set up to study the problem of resources for education and work out a strategy for mobilising these on a long-term basis.

Education is no more than a sub-system of the total societal system. It is, therefore, conditioned by the environment and it also, inevitably, displays its salient characteristics in its own functioning. Indian society does not always respond warmly to new initiatives and change oriented measures. The intellectual sophistication nurtured through centuries of philosophical debate is misused by the bureaucracy and the intellectual establishment to furstrate new moves, without appearing to do so, by circumscribing these with so many preconditions and qualifying clauses that the whole momentum is lost.

Two other characteristics need special mention. Firstly, the disinclination to delegate real power to lower formation will be an obstacle to the establishment of a meaningful nexus between the school and community. Secondly, the compartmental character of the system will create difficulties in establishing horizontal linkages between education and other interdependent development activities.

Taking an optimistic view of the success of measures for population control and also of the success of universalization of education it appears, on rough calculation, that the budgetary requirements for school education, at the same unit cost in 1990 will be four times the level of allocations of 1980-81. India will require 22 lakh additional teachers by 1990 over the number (21.7 lakhs) in 1981. These estimates are based on the quality of school education remaining unchanged. This, however, is unrealistic. Provision of a minimum physical facilities cannot be delayed.

Considering the above scenario and the constraints on

continuous participation in education beyond 11 years of age, some educational planners have suggested a model of universalisation of education which ties up the Anganwadis with primary schools and provide for pre-primary and primary education upto class V. It also advocates distance education through Open Schools on a large scale between classes VI to VIII and large scale diversion into vocationalisation at an earlier age than envisaged in the 10+2+3 system.

A strategy for the spread of education and improvement of its quality is unthinkable without establishing a learning society in which people of all ages participate in continuing education. Such an environment cannot be established without a massive thrust for adult education which will not be concerned with mere literacy but will seek to enhance economic performance as well as the quality of the life of participants. It has been recognised that women will have to be assigned a central place in the programmes of adult education. If they are convinced of the benefits of education, the programme of universalisation of elementary education in general and the participation of girls in particular, will be greatly strengthened. It will also provide dynamism to the programmes for family welfare, energy, conservation, prevention of deforestation, health care, immunisation, etc., besides expanding the base for democracy.

Particular emphasis has been placed on vocational programmes, as a part of the 10+2 stage of the secondary system and also before this stage and outside this system. An important conclusion in this is that vocationalisation should not be linked only with employment in industry. It should be aligned with agriculture, the services sector and various programmes of rural development as well. It should also prepare young people for self employment. It needs emphasis that vocationalisation is not an inexpensive programme since it often involves considerable expenditure on machinery, equipment and consumables. Therefore, it should be taken up after ascertaining the probability of finding jobs for those who are inducted into it.

Amongst the major constraints to vocationalisation are: resistance of certain castes and classes to vocational training; absence of vertical and horizontal mobility for those who go into the vocational stream ; and lack of clarity about the relationship between vocationalisation and professional education on the one hand and with production centres on the other.

Other ideas which have been highlighted are the relationship between all kinds of education and the social system. It has been suggested that all streams and stages of education would acquire much greater meaning if educational system is decentralised and its management is assigned to the community participating in or benefiting from it.

The community participation implicit in this has a particular relevance to school education which is sought to be placed increasingly in the hand of village committees, obtaining from them resources, assistance and guidance. District Education Centres would be the focal points for educational planning, training monitoring, extension and action research. Decentralization of the planning function will also ensure that the special needs of education for the handicapped and the specially gifted children will not be neglected.

As far as higher education is concerned, a strong body of opinion favours meaurses to divert those who do not have a scholastic bent of mind to vocational training. Some of the measures suggested in this connection are administration of scholastic aptitude tests for entry into colleges and universities and delinking of degrees and jobs.

Other measures proposed for improving the relevance and quality of undergraduate and postgraduate education are a purposeful move for granting autonomy to more and more colleges, culminating eventually in moving entirely away from the system of common examinations and affiliation between universities and colleges. It has also been suggested that courses in arts, science and humanities should be restructured on a modular pattern with much greater inbuilt flexibility to establish closer links with the pupil's interests, society and the world of work. In these, it will be possible to combine courses with orientation towards theoretical knowledge, languages, communication skills, culture, sports and programmes of a vocational character.

A moratorium has been proposed on the expansion of the traditional pattern of college, favouring the opening of only those colleges which have a vocational character and are linked with identified multi-disciplinary tasks. New colleges will bridge the world of work with the world of knowledge by offering integrated courses for: Agriculture and Home Education; Forestry and Land Water Development; Urban Planning and Transport Management; Public Management and Office Management etc.

It has been proposed that multipronged strategy for the New Education Policy should seek to integrate the requirements of universalisation of elementary education; production of sophisticated manpower to deal creatively with new technologies; diversified vocationalization; and the creation of an overall environment for development through adult and continuing education.

APPENDIX 5

FIVE YEAR PLANS

Chapter on **Education—An Extract**

Planning Commission, Government of India

"Education", Chapter XVIII, First Five Year Plan, A Draft Outline, 1951-56, the Manager of Publications, New Delhi, 1951.

This chapter deals with the scope of the Plan, defect of the existing system and objectives of the plan and covers basic education, secondary education, university education, technical education and social education etc. (pp. 219-225).

"Education", Chapter XXXIII, First Five Year Plan, 1951-56, the Manager of Publications, New Delhi, 1952.

The chapter deals with pre-school education, primary and basic education, secondary education, university education, social education, professional education, women's education, etc. Other educational issues, such as labour and social service by students, teachers' salaries and conditions of service, physical and mental health have also been described. The progress of education during 1951-56 has been discussed (pp. 525-568).

"Education", Chapter XIII, First Five Year Plan, Progress Report, 1953-54, the Manager of Publications, New Delhi, 1954.

The chapter entitled "Education" is concerned primarily with the working of the Five Year Plan during the year 1953-54, but opportunity has been taken to review, the achievements of the first 3 years in relation to the targets set for 1955-56. It covers, primary education including basic education, secondary education, training of teachers, technical and vocational education, social education, university education, scheme to relieve unemployment among educated classes and promotion of Hindi. (pp. 241-249).

"Education", Chapter X, First Five Year Plan, Progress Report, 1954-55, the Manager of Publications, New Delhi, 1956.

This chapter provides information for 1954-55 and opportunity has been taken to review the achievements of the first 4 years in relation to the targets set for 1955-56. It includes, primary education including basic education, secondary education, university education, training of teachers, technical and vocational education, social education, scheme to relieve educated unemployed, labour and social service by students, promotion of Hindi, help to public schools, education of the handicapped. (pp. 179-188).

"Education", Chapter XII, First Five Year Plan, A Review, the Manager of Publications, New Delhi, 1957.

The chapter entitled "Education" deals with the progress and development of education during the period 1951-56. It covers, elementary education, basic education, secondary education, university education, technical and vocational education, social education and literacy. Teachers' salary and the progress of education in rural areas have also been discusesed. Girls' education, education for handicapped persons and other development schemes have been dealt with (pp. 249-261).

"Education", Chapter XXIII, Second Five Year Plan, 1956-61, the Manager of Publications, New Delhi, 1956.

The chapter deals with the progress and development of education during the five years of its Second Plan. It includes: (i) introducation; (ii) elementary education; (iii) basic education; (iv) secondary education, (v) university education; (vi) technical education; (vii) engineering and technology; (viii) social education; (ix) teachers' education; (x) scholarships; and (xi) cultural and other programmes; etc. (pp. 500-521).

"Education and Scientific Research", Chapter XIX, Second Five Year Plan, A Draft Outline, the Manger of Publications, New Delhi, 1956.

The chapter, entitled, "Education and Scientific Research" deals with elementary education, secondary education, university education and social education, etc. Scholarships and technical education and scientific research have also been discussed. (pp. 183-194).

"Education", Chapter XXIII, Second Five Year Plan, Summary, the Manager of Publications, New Delhi, 1956.

The Chapter, entitled, "Education" deals with elementary education, secondary education, university education, technical education, etc. The issue regarding teachers and different schemes on education have also been discussed. (pp. 154-158).

"Education", Chapter XII, Second Five Year Plan, Progress Report, 1959-60, the Manager of Publications, New Delhi, 1962.

The chapter on education deals with the progress and development of education made during 1959-60 in various fields. The topics included in this chapter are : (i) elementary education; (ii) basic education; (iii) secondary education; (iv) university education; (v) technical education; (vi) social education; and (vii) other programmes. (pp. 130-137).

"Human Resources and Social Services", Chapter VI, Third Five Year Plan, A Draft Outline, the Manager of Publications, New Delhi, 1960.

This chapter deals with education and covers general education and technical education. General education includes such topics as elementary education, secondary education, university education and social education. Moral and social values in education have also been discussed. National Service and other programmes have been analysed (pp. 98-108).

"Education", Chapter XXIX, Third Five Year Plan, 1961-66, the Manager of Publications, New Delhi, 1961.

This chapter deals with the education and national development, its achievements, targets and outlays. Pre-school education, elementary education, basic education and other school activities have been dealt with. Community efforts, secondary education, university education, girls' education have also been included. This chapter covers scholarships, teacher's salary, scales and conditions of service, educational research and training of key personnel, textbooks etc. Examination reform, physical education, spot and youth welfare activities have also been discussed. Social education, adult education, cultural programmes, national integration programmes have also been covered. (pp. 573-604).

"Education", Chapter XII, Third Five Year Plan, Progress Report, 1961-62, the Manager of Publications, New Delhi, 1963.

This chapter deals with the progress and development of education during the first year of the Third Plan. The chapter on education covers elementary education, basic education, secondary education, and university education, multipurpose schools, technical education, cultural activities and other schemes. The problems regarding teachers' and craftsmen's training have also been analysed. (pp. 147-157).

"Education", Chapter XV, Third Five Year Plan, Mid-Term Appraisal, the Manager of Publications, New Delhi, 1963.

This chapter discusses the progress in carrying out the programmes and policies embodied in the Plan during the three years 1961-62, 1962-63 and 1963-64. The chapter on education covers general education and technical education. General education deals with elementary education, middle school education. etc. The problems pertaining to scholarships, training of teachers and adult literacy have also been discussed. (pp. 153-160)

"Education", Chapter X, Third Five Year Plan, Progress Report, 1963-65, the Manager of Publications, New Delhi, 1967.

The chapter on education deals with the progress and development of education made during the period 1963-65. It covers such topics as elementary education, secondary education, development of language, scholarships, and social education, etc. (pp. 147-154).

"Social Services", Chapter VIII, Progress of the Plan, A Short Survey of the Working of the Five Year Plan from April, 1951 to September, 1953, the Manager of Publications, New Delhi, 1954.

This chapter deals with development and implementation of programmes of education and covers the following topics: (i) progress of expenditure; (ii) pattern of expenditure; (iii) main development, such as (a) scheme to absorb the educated unemployed; (b) scheme of pilot projects in basic education; (c) report of the secondary education commission; (d) university education commission; (e) technical education; and (f) development of culture, etc. (pp. 87-91).

"Education", Chapter XVI, Fourth Five year Plan, A Draft Outline, Publication Division, Ministry of information and Broadcasting, New Delhi, August, 1966.

The chapter on education deals with the following topics; (i) pre-school education with the proposal to confine governmental attention to certain strategic areas, such as training of teachers, production of teaching materials and evolving methods suitable to Indian conditions; (ii) elementary education suggesting better organisation of schools, free supply of textbooks and extension of the mid-day meal programme envisaged to achieve the constitutional directive of free and compulsory education for all children upto the age of 14; (iii) secondary education covering efforts to improve the quality of teaching in secondary schools and evolve a system which will prepare students for entrance to the university and also afford facilitites for those who want to enter a definite vocation; (vi) girls' education covers the measures suggested include provision of teachers' quarters, special allowance for women teachers serving in rural areas, and building up a cadre of teachers from amongst adult women through the provision of condensed courses to upgrade their qualifications, recruitment of school mothers, construction of hostel, etc.; (v) university education proposed to take steps to slow down the number of persons enlisting for arts and commerce courses and expand facilities for science, agriculture, technical (particularly diploma level) and medical education. Facilities for post-graduate and research have been emphasised.

It is also proposed to link the Institutes of Rural Higher Education with development programmes in rural areas through suitable adjustment of courses and admissions; (v) teacher education includes the changing character of the school population and the development of democratic practice; (vi) technical education includes the progress and increase of annual admission of students at degree and diploma levels. The Commission also recommended to make up the deficiencies and consolidate the existing institutions by providing essential physical facilities like buildings, equipment and hostels, ensuring the availability of qualified teachers and bringing about closer integration of engineering education with industrial requirements. It suggested that there should be part-time and correspondence courses to provide opportunities for study to those who have had to leave full-time educational institutions to enter employment; (vii) social education deals with wide-spread illiteracy. Adult literacy should be made functional in character. In addition to those, the chapter discusses development of languages, preparation of textbooks, physical education, cultural and other programmes, scholarships, enrolments and service conditions of teachers and educational administration. (pp. 311.327).

"Education", Chapter XV, Fourth Five Year Plan, Draft, 1969-74, the Manager of Publications, New Delhi, 1969.

This chapter deals with the progress and development of pre-school education, elementary education, secondary education, girls' education, teachers' education, higher education, science education etc. Adult literacy, youth services, planning, administration and evaluation have been discussed. Technical education has been included. Scholarships, fellowhsips of students and cultural programmes in the educational institutions have also been dealt with. (pp. 278-289).

"Education", Chapter XV, Fourth Five Year Plan, Summary, 1969-74, Publication Division, Ministry of Information and Broadcasting, New Delhi, 1971.

Chapter XV deals with the expansion of all levels of education. It includes elementary education, secondary education, girls' education, teachers' education, higher education, scholarships and fellowships, adult literacy, youth services, employment and technical education, etc. In addition to these, the chapter also discusses other programmes of importance such as improvement of teacher education, expansion and improvement of science education, raising standards of post-graduate education and research, development of Indian languages and book production, especially textbooks, and the consolidation of technical education including reorganisation of polytechnic education and its closer linkage with the needs of industry and its orientation towards self-employment. The chapter also highlights that the percentage of children going to schools in rural areas and from the Scheduled Castes, Scheduled Tribes and other backward classes is very low. (pp. 111-119). (The report is available in the Library of CRRID, Chandigarh).

"Education and Manpower", Chapter XVI, Fourth Five Year Plan, Mid-Term Appraisal, A Summary, Publication Division, Ministry of Information and Broadcasting, New Delhi, 1972.

The first part of the Chapter XVI deals with education. It discusses the expansion of facilities for elementary education, particularly for girls and for backward areas and communities; consolidation and diversification of secondary and higher education so as to meet the needs of trained manpower of the requisite standard; improvement of teachers education; expansion and improvement of science education at all stages; improvement of Indian languages; production of quality textbooks; consolidation and diversification of technical education, especially polytechnic education, its closer linkage with the needs of industry and its orientation towards self-employment; streamlining, planning, implementation and evaluation of machinery at all levels; increasing the use of part-time and correspondence courses; and relating educational programmes increasingly to the social and economic objectives of the Plan. (pp. 99-105).

"Education", Chapter VII, Fifth Five Year Plan, 1974-79, the Controller of Publications, New Delhi, 1976.

This chapter deals with elementary education, secondary education, university education, non-formal education and technical education, scholarships, language problem, cultural and other programmes, and the progress of education, (pp. 75-78).

"Draft Sixth Five Year Plan", 1978-83, Vol II, Planning Commission, New Delhi, 1978.

This cyclostyled volume deals with the different aspects of education. The important were : elementary education and adult education. (pp. 109, 123, 158-159).

"Education", Chapter XXI, Sixth Five Year Plan, 1980-85, the Manager of Publications, New Delhi, 1981.

The chapter on Education deals with early childhood education, elementary education, adult education, secondary education, higher education, technical education, and youth development and culture. Non-monetary inputs to quality improvement have also been discussed. The Sixth Plan provides an outlay of Rs. 2,524 crore for development of education and culture. Provisions have been made separately for the hill area development plan as well us under the relevant sectors of agriculture, allied sciences and health for education in medicine and related fields. (pp. 352-361).

"Education", Chapter X, The Seventh Five Year Plan, 1985-90. The Manger Pub.

The chapter exhibit that the Seventh Plan provides for reorientation of the education system so as to prepare the country to meet the challenges of the next century. The main thrust areas in the

Seventh Plan world be: (i) achievement of universal elementary education; (ii) eradication of illiteracy in the age-group 15-35 years; (iii) vocationalisation and skill-training programmes at different levels of education; (iv) upgradation of standards and modernisation of all stages of education with effective links with the world of work and with special emphasis on science and environment and on value orientation; (v) provision of facilities for education of high quality and excellence in every district of the country; and (vi) removal of obsolescence and modernisation of technical education.

APPENDIX 6

NATIONAL POLICY ON EDUCATION 1986

Part I

Introduction

1.1 Education has continued to evolve, diversify and extend its reach and coverage since the dawn of human history. Every country develops its system of education to express and promote its unique socio-cultural identity and also to meet the challenges of the times. There are moments in history when a new direction has to be given to an age-old process. That moment is today.

1.2 The country has reached a stage in its economic and technical development when a major effort must be made to derive the maximum benefit from the assets already created and to ensure that the fruits of change reach all sections. Education is the highway to that goal.

1.3 With this aim in view, the Government of India announced in January 1985 that a new Education Policy be formulated for the country. A comprehensive appraisal of the existing educational scene was made, followed by a countrywide debate. The views and suggestions received from different quarters were carefully studied.

The 1968 Education Policy and after

1.4 The National Policy of 1968 marked a significant step in the history of education in post-Independence India. 'It aimed to promote national progress, a sense of common citizenship and culture, and to strengthen national integration. It laid stress on the need for a radical reconstruction of the education system, to improve its quality at all stages, and gave much greater attention to science and technology, the cultivation of moral values and a closer relation between education and the life of the people.

1.5 Since the adoption of the 1968 Policy, there has been considerable expansion in educational facilities all over the country at all levels. More than 90% of the country's rural habitations now have schooling facilities within a radius of one kilometer. There has been sizeable augmentation of facilities at other stages also.

1.6 Perhaps the most notable development has been the acceptance of a common structure of education throughout the country and the introducation of 10+2+3 system by most States. In the school curricula, in addition to laying down a common scheme of studies for boys and girls, science and mathematics were incorporated as compulsory subjects and work experience assigned a place of importance.

1.7 A beginning was also made in restructuring of courses at the undergraduate level. Centres of Advanced Studies were set up for post-graduate education and research. And we have been able to meet our requirements of educated manpower.

1.8 While these achievements are impressive by themselves, the general formulations incorporated in the 1968 Policy did not, however, get translated into a detailed strategy of implementation, accompanied by the assignment of specific responsibilities and financial and organisational support. As a result, problems of access, quality, quantity, utility and financial outlay, accumulated over the years, have now assumed such massive proportions that they must be tackled with the utmost urgency.

1.9 Education in India stands at the cross roads today. Neither normal linear expansion nor the existing pace and nature of improvement can meet the needs of the situation.

1.10 In the Indian way of thinking, a human being is a positive asset and a precious national resource which needs to be cherished, nurtured and developed with tenderness and care, coupled with dynamism. Each individual's growth presents a different range of problems and requirements, at every stage—from the womb to the tomb. The catalytic action of Education in this complex and dynamic growth process needs to be planned meticulously and executed with great sensitivity.

1.11 India's political and social life is passing through a phase which poses the danger of erosion of long-accepted values. The goals of secularism, socialism, democracy and professional ethics are coming under increasing strain.

1.12 The rural areas, with poor infrastructure and social services, will not get the benefit of trained and educated youth, unless rural-urban disparities are reduced and determined measures are taken to promote diversification and dispersal of employment opportunities.

1.13 The growth of our population needs to be brought down significantly over the coming decades. The largest single factor that could help achieve this is the spread of literacy and education among women.

1.14 Life in the coming decades is likely to bring new tensions together with unprecedented opportunities. To enable the people to benefit in the new enviroment will require new designs of human resource development. The coming generations should have the ability to internalise new ideas constantly and creatively. They have to be imbued with a strong commitment to humane values and to social justice. All this implies better education.

1.15 Besides, a variety of new challenges and social needs make it imperative for the Government to formulate and implement a new Education Policy for the country. Nothing short of this will meet the situation.

Part II

The Essence and Role of Education

2.1 In our national perception education is essentially for all. This is fundamental to our all-round development, material and spiritual.

2.2 Education has an acculturating role. It refines sensitivities and perceptions that contribute to national cohesion, a scientific temper and independence of mind and spirit—thus furthering the goals of socialism, secularism and democracy enshrined in our Constitution.

2.3 Education develops manpower for different levels of the economy. It is also the substrated on which research and development flourish, being the ultimate guarantee of national self-reliance.

2.4 In sum, Education is a unique investment in the present and the future. This cardinal principle is the key to the National Policy on Education.

Part III

National System of Education

3.1 The Constitution embodies the principles on which the National System of Education is conceived of.

3.2 The concept of the National System of Education implies that, up to a given level, all students, irrespective of caste, creed, location or sex, have access to education of a comparable quality. To achieve this, the Government will initiate appropriately funded programmes. Effective measures will be taken in the direction of the Common School System recommended in the 1968 Policy.

3.3 The National System of Education envisages a common educational structure. The 10+2+3 structure has now been accepted in all parts of the country. Regarding the further break-up of the first 10 years efforts will be made to move towards and elementary system comprising 5 years of primary education and 3 years of upper primary, followed by 2 years of High School.

3.4 The National System of Education will be based on a national curricular framework which contains a common core along with other components that are flexible. The common core will include the history of India's freedom movement, the constitutional obligations and other content essential to nature national identity. These elements will cut across subject areas and will be designed to promote values such as India's common cultural heritage, egalitarianism, democracy and secularism, equality of the sexes, protection of the environment, removal of social barriers, observance of the small family norm and inculcation of the scientific temper. All educational programmes will be carried on in strict conformity with secular values.

3.5 India has always worked for peace and understanding between nations, treating the whole world was one family. True to this hoary tradition, Education has to strengthen this world view and motivate the younger generations for international cooperation and peaceful co-existence. This aspect cannot be neglected.

3.6 To promote equality, it will be necessary to provide for equal opportunity to all not only in access, but also in the conditions for success. Besides, awareness of the inherent equality of all will be created through the core curriculum. The purpose is to remove prejudices and complexes transmitted through the social environment and the accient of birth.

3.7 Minimum levels of learning will be laid down for each stage of education. Steps will also be taken to foster among students an understanding of the diverse cultural and social systems of the people living in different parts of the country. Besides the promotion of the link language, programmes will also be launched to increase substantially the translation of books from one language to another and to publish multi-lingual dictionaries and glossaries. The young will be encouraged to undertake the rediscovery of India, each in his own image and perception.

3.8 In higher education in general, and technical education in particular, steps will be taken to facilitate inter-regional mobility by providing equal access to every Indian of requisite merit, regardless of his origins. The universal character of universities and other institutions of higher education is to be underscored.

3.9 In the areas of research and development, and education in science and technology, special measures will be taken to establish network arrangements between different institutions in the country to pool their resources and participate in projects of national importance.

3.10 The Nation as a whole will assume the responsibility of providing resource support for implementing programmes of educational transformation, reducing disparities, universalisation of elementary education, adult literacy, scientific and technological research, etc.

3.11 Life-long education is a cherished goal of the educational process. This presupposes universal literacy. Opportunities will be provided to the youth, housewives, agricutural and industrial workers and professionals to continue the education of their choice, at the place suited to them. The future thrust will be in the direction of open and distance learning.

3.12 The institutions which will be strengthened to play an important role in giving shape to the Natinal System of Education are the University Gants Commission, the All India Council of Technical Education, the Indian Council of Agricultural Research and the Indian Medical Council. Integrated planning will be instituted among all these bodies so as to establish functional linkages and reinforce programmes of research and postgraduate education. These, together with the National Council of Educational Reserarch and Training, the National Institute of Educational Planning and Administration and the International Institute of Science and Technology Education will be involved in implementing the Education Policy.

A Meaningful Partnership

3.13 The Constitutional Amendment of 1976, which includes Education in the Concurrent List, was a far-reaching step whose implications—substantive, financial and administrative—require a new sharing of responsibility between the Union Government and the States in respect of this vital area of national life. While the role and responsibility of the States in regard to education will remain essentially unchanged, the Union Government would accept a larger responsibility to reinforce the national and integrative character of education, to maintain quality and standards (including those of the teaching profession at all levels), to study and monitor the educational requirements of the country as a whole in regard to manpower for development, to cater to the needs of research and advanced study, to look after the international aspects of education, culture and Human Resource Development and, in general, to promote excellence at all levels of the educational pyramid throughout the country. Concurrency signifies a partnership which is is at once meaningful and challenging; the National Policy will be oriented towards giving effect to it in letter and spirit.

Part IV

Education for Equality

Disparities

4.1 The new Policy will lay special emphasis on the removal of disparities and to equalise educational opportunity by attending to the specific needs of those who have been denied equality so far.

Education for Women's Equality

4.2 Education will be used as an agent of basic change in the status of women. In order to neutralise the accumulated distortions of the past, there will be a well-conceived edge in favour of women. The National Education System will play a positive, interventionist role in empowerment of women. It will foster the development of new values through redesigned curricula, textbooks, the training and orientation of teachers, decision-makers and administrators, and the active involvement of educational institutions. This will be an act of faith and social engineering. Women's studies will be promoted as a part of various courses and educational institutions encouraged to take up active programmes to further women's development.

4.3 The removal of women's illiteracy and obstacles inhibiting their access to, and retention in, elementary education will receive overriding priority, through provision of special support services, setting of time targets, and effective monitoring. Major emphasis will be laid on women's participation in vocational, technical and professional education at different levels. The Policy of non-discrimination will be pursued vigorously to eliminate sex stereotyping in vocational and professional courses and to promote women's participation in non-traditional occupations, as well as in existing and emergent technologies.

The Education of Scheduled Castes

4.4 The central focus in the SCs' educational development is their equalisation with the non-SC population at all stages and levels of education, in all areas and in all the four dimensions—rural male, rural female, urban male and urban female.

(i) Incentives to indigent families to send their children to school regularly till they reach the age of 14;
(ii) Pre-matric Scholarship scheme for children of families engaged in occupations such as scavenging, flaying and tanning to be made applicable from Class I onwards. All children of such families, regardless of incomes, will be covered by this scheme and time-bound programmes targetted on them will be undertaken;
(iii) Constant micro-planning and verification to ensure that the enrolment, retention and successful completion of courses by SC students do not fall at any stage, and provision of remedial courses to improve their prospects for further education and employment.
(iv) Recruitment of teachers from Scheduled Castes;
(v) Provision of facilities for SC students in students hostels at district headquaters, according to a phased programme;
(vi) Location of school buildings, Balwadis and Adult Education Centres in such a way as to facilitate participation of the Scheduled Castes;
(vii) The utilisation of N.R.E.P and R.L.E.G.P. resources so as to make substantial educational facilities available to the Scheduled Castes; and
(viii) Constant innovation in finding new methods to increase the participation of the Scheduled Castes in the educational process.

The Education of Scheduled Tribes

4.6 The following measures will be taken urgently to bring the Scheduled Tribes on par with others :

(i) Priority will by accorded to opening primary schools in tribal areas. The construction of school building will be undertaken in these areas on a priority basis under the normal funds for education, as well as under the N.R.E.P., R.L.E.G.P., Tribal Welfare schemes, etc.

(ii) The socio-cultural milieu of the STs has its distinctive characteristics including, in many cases, their own spoken languages. This underlines the need to develop the curricula and devise instructional materials in tribal languages at the initial stages, with arrangements for switching over to the regional language.

(iii) Educated and promising Scheduled Tribe youths will be encouraged and trained to take up teaching in tribal areas.

(iv) Residential schools, including Ashram Schools, will be established on a large scale.

(v) Incentive schemes will be formulated for Scheduled Tribes, keeping in view their special needs and life styles. Scholarships for higher education will emphasise technical, professional and para-professional courses. Special remedial courses and other programmes to remove psycho-social impediments will be provided to improve their performance in various courses.

(vi) Anganwadis, Non-formal and Adult Education Centres will be opened on a priority basis in areas predominantly inhabited by the Scheduled Tribes.

(vii) The curriculum at all stages of education will be designed to create an awareness of the rich cultural identity of the tribal people as also of their enormous creative talent.

Other Educationally Backward Sections and Areas

4.7 Suitable incentives will be provided to all educationally backward sections of society, particularly in the rural areas. Hill and desert districts, remote and inaccessible areas and islands will be provided adequate institutional infra-structure.

Minorities

4.8 Some minority groups are educationally deprived or backward. Greater attention will be paid to the education of these groups in the interests of equality and social justice. This will naturally include the Constitutional guarantees given to them to establish and administer their own educational institutions, and protection to their languages and culture. Simultaneously, objectivity will be reflected in the preparation of textbooks and in all school activities, and all possible measures will be taken to promote an integration based on with the core curriculum.

The Handicapped

4.9 The objective should be to integrated the physically and mentally handicapped with the general community as equal partners, to prepare them for normal growth to enable them to face life with courage and confidence. The following measures will be taken in this regard :

(i) Wherever it is feasible, the education of children with motor handicaps and other mild handicaps will be common with that of others;
(ii) Special schools with hostels will be provided, as far as possible at district headquarters, for the severely handicapped children;
(iii) Adequate arrangements will be made to give vocational training to the disabled;
(iv) Teachers' training programmes will be reoriented, in particular for teachers of primary classes, to deal with the special difficulties of the handicapped children; and
(v) Voluntary effort for the education of the disabled, will be encouraged in every possible manner.

Adult Education

4.10 our ancient scriptures define education as that which liberates—i.e. provides the instruments for liberation from ignorance and oppression. In the modern world, it would naturally include the ability to read and write, since that is the main instrument of learning. Hence the crucial importance of adult education, including adult literacy.

4.11 The critical development issue today is the continuous upgradation of skills so as to produce manpower resources of the kind and the number required by the society. Since participation by beneficiaries in the development programmes is of crucial importance, systematic programmes of adult education linked with national goals such as alleviation of poverty, national integration, environmental conservation, energisation of the cultural creativity of the people, observance of small family norm, promotion of women's equality, etc. will be organised and the existing programmes reviewed and strengthened.

4.12 The whole Nation must pledge itself to the eradication of illiteracy, particularly in the 15-35 are group. The Central and State Governments, political parties and their mass oganisations, the mass media and educational institutions must commit themselves to mass literacy programmes of diverse nature. It will also have to involve on a large scale teachers, students, youth, voluntary agencies, employers, etc. Concerted efforts will be made to harness various research agencies to improve the pedagogical aspects of adult literacy. The mass literacy programme would include, in addition to literacy, functional knowledge and skills, and also awareness among learners about the socio-economic reality and the possibility to change it.

4.13 A vast programmes of adult continuing education will be implemented through various ways and channels, including—

(a) establishment of centres in rural areas for continuing education;
(b) workers' education through the employers, trade unions and concerned agencies of government;
(c) post-secondary education institutions;
(d) wider promotion of books, libraries and reading rooms;
(e) use of radio, TV and films, as mass and group learning media ;
(f) creation of learners' groups and organisations;
(g) programmes of distance learning;
(h) organising assistance in self-learning; and
(i) organising need and interest based vocational training programmes.

Part V

Reorganisation of Education at different Stages

Early Childhood Care & Education

5.1 The National Policy on Children specially emphasises investment in the development of the young child, particularly children from sections of the population in which first generation learners predominate.

5.2 Recognising the holistic nature of child development, viz., nutrition, health and social, mental, physical, moral and emotional development, Early Childhood Care and Education (ECCE) will receive high priority and be suitably integrated with the Integrated Child Development Services programme wherever possible. Day-care centres will be provided as a support service for universalisation of primary education, to enable girls engaged in taking care of siblings to attend school and as a support service for working women belonging to poorer sections.

5.3 Programmes of ECCE will be child-oriented, focussed around play and the individuality of the child. Formal methods and introducation of the 3 R's will be discouraged at this stage. The local community will be involved in these programmes.

5.4 A full integration of child care and pre-primary education will be brought about, both as a feeder and a strengthening factor for primary education and for human resource development in general. In continuation of this stage, the School Health Programme will be strengthened.

Elementary Education

5.5 The new thrust in elementary education will emphasise two aspects : (i) universal enrolment and universal retention of children up to 14 years of age, and (ii) a substantial improvement in the quality of education.

Child-centred Approach

5.6 A warm, welcoming and encouraging approach, in which all concerned share a solicitude for the needs of the child, is the best motivation for the child to attend school and learn. A child-centred and activity-based process of learning should be adopted at the primary stage. First generation learners should be allowed to set their own pace and be given supplementary remedial instruction. As the child grows, the component of cognitive learning will be increased and skills organised through practice. The policy of non-detention at the primary stage will be retained, making evaluation as disaggregated as feasible. Corporal punishment will be firmly excluded from the educational system and school timings as well as vacations adjusted to the convenience of children.

School Facilities

5.7 Provision will be made of essential facilities in primary schools, including at least two reasonably large rooms that are usable in all weather, and the necessary toys, blackboards, maps, charts, and other learning material. At least two teachers, one of whom a woman, should work in every school, the number increasing as early as possible to one teacher per class. A phased drive, symbolically called OPERATION BLACKBOARD will be undertaken with immediate effect to improve Primary Schools all over the country. Government, local bodies, voluntary agencies and individuals will be fully involved. Construction of school buildings will be the first charge on NREP and RLEGP funds.

Non-Formal Education

5.8 A large and systematic programme of non-formal education will be launched for school drop-outs, for children from habitations without schools, working children and girls who cannot attend whole-day schools.

5.9 Modern technological aids will be used to improve the learning environment of NFE centres. Talented and dedicated young men and women from the local community will be chosen to serve as instructors, and particular attention paid to their training. Steps will be taken to facilitate their entry into the formal system in deserving cases. All necessary measures will be taken to ensure that the quality of non-formal education is comparable with formal education.

5.10 Effective steps will be taken to provide a framework for the curriculum on the lines of the national core curriculum, but based on the needs of the learners and related to the local enviroment. Learning material of high quality will be developed and provided free of charge to all pupils. NFE programmes will provide participatory learning environment, and activities such as games and sports, cultural programmes, excursions, etc.

5.11 Much of the work of running NFE centres will be done through voluntary agencies and panchayati raj institutions. The provision of funds to these agencies will be adequate and timely. The Government will take over-all responsibility for this vital sector.

A Resolve

5.12 The New Education Policy will give the highest priority to solving the problems of children dropping out of school and will adopt an array of meticulously formulated strategies based on micro-planning, and applied at the grass-roots level all over the country, to ensure children is retention at school. This effort will be fully coordinated with the network of non-formal education. It shall be ensured that all children who attain the age of about 11 years by 1990 will have had five years of schooling, or its equivalent through the non-formal stream. Likewise, by 1995 all children will be provided free and compulsory education upto 14 years of age.

Secondary Education

5.13 Secondary education begins to expose students to the differentiated roles of science, the humanities and social sciences. This is also an appropriate stage to provide children with a sense of history and national perspective and give them opportunities to understand their constitutional duties and rights as citizens. Conscious internalisation of a healthy work ethos and of the values of a human and composite culture will be brought about through appropriately formulated curricula. Vocationalisation through specialised institutions or through the refashioning of secondary education can, at this stage, provide valuable manpower for economic growth. Access to secondary education will be widened to cover areas unserved by it at present. In other areas, the main emphasis will be on consolidation.

5.14 It is universally accepted that children with special talent or aptitude should be provided opportunities to process at a faster pace, by making good quality education available to them, irrespective of their capacity to pay for it.

5.15 Pace-setting schools intended to serve this purpose will be established in various parts of the country on a given pattern, but with full scope for innovation and experimentation. Their broad aims will be to serve the objective of excellence, coupled with equity and social justice (with reservation for SCs and STs), to promote national inteagrtaion by providing opportunities to talented children largely rural, from different parts of the country to live and learn together, to develop their full potential, and, most importantly, to become catalysts of a nation-wide programme of school improvement. The schools will be residential and free of charge.

Vocationalisation

5.16 The introduction of systematic, well-planned and rigorously implemented programmes of vocational education is crucial in the proposed educational reorganisation. These elements are meant to enhance individual employability, to reduce the mismatch between the demand and supply of skilled manpower, and to provide an alternative for those pursuing higher education without particular interest or purpose.

5.17 Vocational education will be distnct stream, intended to prepare students for identified occupations spanning several areas of activity. These courses will ordinarily be provided after the secondary stage, but keeping the scheme flexible, they may also be made available after Class VIII. In the interests of integrating vocational education better with their facilities the Industrial Training Institutes will also conform to the larger vocational pattern.

5.18 Health planning and health service management should optimally interlock with the education and training of appropriate categories of health manpower through health-related vocational courses. Health education at the primary and middle levels will ensure the commitment of the individual to family and community health, and lead to health-related vocational courses at the +2 stage of higher secondary education. Efforts will be made to devise similar vocational courses based on Agriculture, Marketing, Social Services, etc. An emphasis in vocational education will also be on development of attitudes, knowledge, and skills for enterpreneurship and self-employment.

5.19 The establishment of vocational courses or institutions will be the responsibility of the Government as well as employers in the public and private sectors; the Government will, however, take special steps to cater to the needs of women, rural and tribal students and the deprived sections of society. Appropriate programmes will also be started for the handicapped.

5.20 Graduates of vocational courses will be given opportunities under predetermined conditions, for professional growth, career improvement and lateral entry into courses of general technical and professional education through appropriate bridge courses.

5.21 Tertiary level courses will be organised for the young who graduate from the higher secondary courses of the academic stream and may also require vocational courses.

5.23 It is proposed that vocational courses cover 10 per cent of higher secondary students by 1990 and 25 per cent by 1995. Steps will be taken to see that a substantial majority of the products of vocational courses are employed or become self-employed. Review of the courses offered would be regularly undertaken. Government will also review its recruitment policy to encourage diversification at the secondary level.

Higher Education

5.24 Higher education provides people with an opportunity to reflect on the critical social, economic, cultural, moral and spiritual issues facing humanity. It contributes to national development through dissemination of specialized knowledge and skills. It is therefore a crucial factor for survival. Being at the apex of the educational pyramid, it has also a key role in producing teachers for the education system.

5.25 In the context of the unprecedented explosion of knowledge, higher education has to become dynamic as never before, constantly entering uncharted areas.

5.26 There are around 150 universities and about 5,000 colleges in India today. In view of the need to effect an all round improvement in these institutions, it is proposed that, in the near future, the main emphasis will be on the consolidation of, and expansion of facilities in, the existing institutions.

5.27 Urgent steps will be taken to protect the system from degradation.

5.28 In view of mixed experiences with the system of affiliation, autonomous colleges will be helped to develop in large numbers until the affiliating system is replaced by a freer and more creative association of universities with colleges. Similarly, the creation of autonomous departments within universities on a selective basis will be encouraged. Autonomy and freedom will be accompanied by accountability.

5.29 Courses and programmes will be redesigned to meet the demands of specialisation better. Special emphasis will be laid on linguistic competence. There will be increasing flexibility in the combination of courses.

5.30 State level planning and coordination of higher education will be done through Councils of Higher Education. The UGC and these Councils will develop coordinative methods to keep a watch on standards.

5.31 Provision will be made for minimum facilities and admission will be regulated according to capacity. A major effort will be directed towards the transformation to teaching methods.

Audio-visual aids and electronic equipment will be introduced; development of science and technology curricula and material, research, and teacher orientation will receive attention. This will require preparation to teachers at the beginning of the service as well as continuing education thereafter. Teachers' performance will be systematically assessed. All posts will be filled on the basis of merit.

5.32 Research in the universities will be provided enhanced support and steps will be taken to ensure its high quality. Suitable mechanisms will be set up by the UGC for coordinating research in the universities, particularly in thrust areas of science and technology, with research undertaken by other agencies. An effort will be made to encourage the setting up of national research facilities within the university system, with proper forms of autonomous management.

5.33 Resarch in Indology, the humanities and social sciences will receive adequate support. To fulfil the need for the synthesis of knowledge, inter-disciplinary research will be encouraged. Efforts will be made to delve into India's ancient fund of knowledge and to relate it to contemporary reality. This effort will imply the development of facilities for the intensive study of Sanskrit and other Classical languages.

5.34 In the interest of greater coordination and consistency in policy, sharing of facilities and developing inter-disciplinary research, a national body covering higher education in general, agricultural, medical, technical, legal and other professional fields will be set up.

Oper University and Distance Learning

5.35 The open University system had been initiated in order to augment opportunities for higher education and as an instrument of democratising education.

5.36 The Indira Gandhi National Open University, established in 1985 in fulfilment of these objectives, will be strengthened.

5.37 This powerful instrument will have to be developed with care and extended with caution.

Delinking Degrees from Jobs

5.38 A beginning will be made in delinking degrees from jobs in selected areas.

5.39 The proposal cannot be applied to occupation-specific

courses like Engineering, Medicine, Law, Teaching, etc. Similarly, the services of specialists with academic qualifications in the humanities, social sciences, sciences, etc. will continue to be required in various job positions.

5.40 Delinking will be applied in services for which a university degree need not be a necessary qualification. Its implementation will lead to a re-fashioning of job-specific courses and afford greater justice to those candidates who, despite being equipped for a given job, are unable to get it because of an unnecessary preference for graduate candidates.

5.41 Concomitant with de-linking, an appropriate machinery, such as a National Testing Service, will be established, in appropriate phases, to conduct tests on a voluntary basis to determine the suitability of candidates for specified jobs and to pave the way for the emergence of norms of comparable competence across the nation.

Rural University

5.42 The new pattern of the Rural University will be consolidated and developed on the lines of Mahatma Gandhi's revolutionary ideas on education so as to take up the challenges of micro-planning at grossroot levels for the transformation of rural areas. Institutions and programmes of Gandhian basic education will be supported.

Part VI

Technical and Management Education

6.1 Although the two streams of technical and management education are functioning separately, it is essential to look at them together, in view of their close relationship and complementary concerns. The reorganisation of Technical and Management Education should take into account the anticipated scenario by the turn of the century, with specific reference to the likely changes in the economy, social environment, production and management processes, the rapid expansion of knowledge and the great advances in science and technology.

6.2 The infrastructure and services sectors as well as the unorganised rural sector also need a greater induction of improved technologies and a supply of technical and managerial manpower. This will be attended to by the Government.

6.3 In order to improve the situation regarding manpower information, the recently set up Technical Manpower Information System will be further developed and strengthened.

6.4 Continuing education, covering established as well as emerging technologies, will be promoted.

6.5 As computers have become important and ubiquitous tools, a minimal exposure to computers and a training in their use will form part of professional education. Programmes of computer literacy will be organised on wide scale from the school stages.

6.6 In view of the present rigid entry requirements to formal courses restricting the access of a large segment of people to technical and managerial education, programmes through a distance-learning process, including use of the mass media, will be offered. Technical and management education programmes, including education in polytechnics, will also be on a flexible modular pattern based on credits, with provision for multi-point entry. A strong guidance and counselling service will be provided.

6.7 In order to increase the relevance of management education, particularly in the non-corporate and under-managed sectors, the management education system will study and document the Indian experience and create a body of knowledge and specific educational programmes suited to these sectors.

6.8 Appropriated formal and non-formal programmes of technical education will be devised for the benefit of women, the economically and socially weaker sections, and the physically handicapped.

6.9 The emphasis on vocational education and its expansion will need a large number of teachers and professionals in vocational education, educational technology, curriculum development, etc. Programmes will be started to meet this demand.

6.10 To encourage students to consider "self-employment" as a career option, training in entrepreneurship will be provided through modular or optional course, in degree or diploma programmes.

6.11 In order to meet the continuing needs of updating curriculum, renewal should systematically phase out obsolescence and introduce new technologies or disciplines.

6.12 Some polytechnics in the rural areas have started training weaker groups in those areas for productive occupations through a system of community polytechnics. The community polytechnic system will be appraised and appropriately strengthened to increase its quality and coverage.

Innovation, Research and Development

6.13 Research as a means of renovation and renewal of educational processes will be undertaken by all higher technical institutions. It will primarily aim at producing quality manpower capable of taking up R&D functions. Research for development will focus on improving present technologies, developing new indigenous ones and enhancing production and productivity. A suitable system for watching and forecasting technology will be set up.

6.14 The scope for cooperation, collaboration and networking relationships between institutions at various levels and with the user systems will be utilised. Proper maintenance, and an attitude of innovation and improvement will be promoted systematically.

Promoting Efficiency and Effectiveness at all Levels

6.15 As technical and management education is expensive, the following major steps will be taken for cost-effectiveness and to promote excellence :

(i) High priority will be given to modernisation and removal of obsolescence. However, modernisation will be undertaken to enhance functional efficiency and not for its own sake or as a status symbol.
(ii) Institutions will be encouraged to generate resources using their capacities to provide services to the community and industry. They will be equipped with up-tp-date learning resources, library and computer facilities.
(iii) Adequate hostel accommodation will be provided, specially for girls. Facilities for sports, creative work and cultural activities will be expanded.
(iv) More effective procedures will be adopted in the recruitment of staff. Career opportunities service conditions, consultancy norms and other perquisites will be improved.
(v) Teachers will have multiple roles to perform : teaching, research, development of learning resource material, extension, and managing the instutions. Initial and in-service training will be made mandatory for faculty

members and adequate training reserves will be provided. Staff Development Programmes will be integrated at the State, and coordinated at Regional and National levels.

(vi) The curricula of technical and management programmes will be targetted on current as well as the projected needs of industry of user system. Active interaction between technical or management institutions and industry will be promoted in programmed planning and implementation, exchange of personnel, training facilities and resources, research and consultancy and other areas of mutual interest.

(vii) Excellence in performance of institutions and individual will be recognised and rewarded. The emergence of substandard institutions will be checked. A climate conducive to excellence and innovation will be promoted with full involvement of the faculty.

(viii) Select institutions will be awarded academic, administrative and financial autonomy of varying degrees, building in safeguards with respect to accountability.

(ix) Networking systems will have to be established between technical education and industry, R&D organisations, programmes of rural and community development, and with other sectors of education with complementary characteristics

Management Functions and Change

6.16 In view of the likely emergence of changes in management systems and the need to equip students with the ability to cope with them, effective mechanisms will be devised to understand the nature and direction of change per se and to develop the important skill of managing change.

6.17 In view of the integrated nature of the task, the Ministry of Human Resource Development will coordinate the balanced development of engineering, vocational and management education as well as the education of technicians and craftsmen

6.18 Professional societies will be encouraged and enabled to perform their due role in the advancement of technical and management education.

6.19 The All India Council for Technical Education will be

vested with statutory authority for planning, formulation and the maintenance of norms and standards, accreditation, funding of priority areas, monitoring and evaluation, maintaining parity of certification and awards and ensuring the coordinated and integrated development of technical and management education. Mandatory periodic evaluation will be carried out by a duly constituted Accreditation Board.

6.20 In the interests of maintaining standards and for several other valid reasons, the commercialisation of technical and professional education will be curbed. An alternative system will be devised to involve private and voluntary effort in this sector of education, in conformity with accepted norms and goals.

Part VII

Making the System Work

7.1 It is obvious that these and many other new tasks of education cannot be performed in a state of disorder. Education needs to be managed in an atmosphere of utmost intellectual rigour, seriousness of purposes and, at the same time, of freedom essential for innovation and creativity. While far-reaching changes will have to be incorporated in the quality and range of education, the process of introducing discipline into the system will have to be started, here and now, in what exists.

7.2 The country had placed boundless trust in the educational system. The people have a right to expect concrete results. The first task is to make it work. All teachers should teach and all students study.

7.3 The strategy in this behalf will consist of:

(a) a better deal to teachers with greater accountability :

(b) provision of improved students' services and insistence on observance of acceptable norms of behaviour;

(c) provision of better facilities to institutions; and

(d) creation of a system of performance appraisals of institutions according to standards and norms set at the National or State levels.

Part VIII

Reorienting the Content and Process of Education

The Cultural Perspective

8.1 The existing scheme between the formal system of education and the country's rich and varied cultural traditions needs to be bridged. The preoccupation with modern technologies cannot be allowed to sever our new generations from the roots in India's history and culture. De-culturisation, de-humanisation and alienation must be avoided at all costs. Education can and must bring about the fine synthesis between change-oriented technologies and the country's continuity of cultural tradition.

8.2 The curricula and processes of education will be enriched by cultural content in as many manifestations as possible. Children will be enabled to develop sensitivity to beauty, harmony and refinement. Resource persons in the community, irrespective of their formal educational qualifications, will be invited to contribute to the cultural enrichment of education, employing both the literate and oral traditions of communication. To sustain and carry forward the cultural tradition, the role of the old masters, who train pupils through traditional models will be supported and recognised.

8.3 Linkages will be established between the university system and institutions of higher learning in art, archaeology, oriental studies etc. Due attention will be also paid to the specialised disciplines of Fine Arts, Museology, Folklore etc. Teaching, training and research in these disciplines will be strengthened so as to replenish specialised manpower in them.

Value Education

8.4 The growing concern over the erosion of essential values and an increasing cynicism in society has brought to focus the need for readjustments in the curriculum in order to make education a forceful tool for the cultivation of social and moral values.

8.5 In our culturally plural society, education should foster universal and eternal values, oriented towards the unity and integration of our people. Such value education should help eliminate obscurantism, religious fanaticism, violence, superstititon and fatalism.

8.6 Apart from this combative role, value education has a profound positive content, based on our heritage, national goals universal perceptions. It should lay primary emphasis on this aspect.

Languages

8.7 The Education Policy of 1968 had examined the question of the development of languages in great detail; its essential provisions can hardly be improved upon and are as relevant today as before. The implementation of this part of the 1968 Policy has, however, been uneven. The Policy will be implemened more energetically and purposefully.

Books and Libraries

8.8 The availability of books at low prices is indispensable for people's education. Efforts will be made to secure easy accessibility to books for all segments of the population. Measures will be taken to improve the quality of books, promote the reading habit and encourage creative writing. Authors interests will be protected. Good translations of foreign books into Indian languages will be supported. Special attention will be paid to the production of quality books for children, including text books and work books.

8.9 Together with the development of books, a nation-wide movement for the improvement of existing libraries and the establishment of new ones will be taken up. Provision will be made in all educational institutions for library facilities and the status of librarians improved.

Media and Educational Technology

8.10 Modern communication technologies have the potential to bypass several stages and sequences in the process of development encountered in earlier decades. Both the constraints of time and distance at once become manageable. In order to avoid structural dualism, modern educational technology must reach out to the most distant areas and the most deprived sections of beneficiaries simultaneously with the areas of comparative affluence and ready availability.

8.11 Educational technology will be employed in the spread of useful information, the training and re-training of teachers, to improve quality, sharpen awareness of art and culture, inculcate abiding values, etc., both in the formal and non-formal sectors.

Maximum use will be made of the available infrastructure. In villages without electricity, batteries or solar packs will be used to run the programme.

8.12 The generation of relevant and culturally compatible educational programmes will from an important component of educational technology, and all available resources in the country will be utilised for this purpose.

8.13 The media have a profound influence on the minds of children as well as adults; some of them tend to encourage consumerism, violence etc. and have a deleterious effect, Radio and T.V. programmes which clearly militate against proper educational objectives will be prevented. Steps will be taken to discourage such trends in films and other media also. An active movement will be started to promote the production of children's films of high quality and usefulness.

Work Experience

8.14 Work experience, viewed as purposive and meaningful manual work, organised as an integral part of the learning process and resulting in either goods or services useful to the community, is considered as an essential component at all stages of education, to be provided through well-structured and graded programmes. It would comprise activities in accord with the interests, abilities and needs of students, the level of skills and knowledge to be upgraded with the stages of education. This experience would be helpful on his entry into the workforce. Prevocational programmes provided at the lower secondary stage will also facilitate the choice of the vocational courses at the higher secondary stage.

Education and Environment

8.15 There is paramount need to create a consciousness of the environment. It must permeate all ages and all sections of society, beginning with the child. Environmental consciousness should inform teaching in schools and colleges. This aspect will be integrated in the entire educational process.

Mathematics Teaching

8.16 Mathematics should be visualised as the vehicle to train a child to think, reason, analyse and to articulate logically. Apart from being a specific subject, it should be treated as a concomitant to any subject involving analysis and reasoning.

8.17 With the recent introduction of computers in schools, educational computing and the emergence of learning through the understanding of cause-effect relationships and the interplay of variables, the teaching of mathematics will be suitably redesigned to bring it in line with modern technological devices.

Science Education

8.18 Science education will be strengthened so as to develop in the child well defined abilities and values such as the spirit of inquiry, creativity, objectivity, the courage to question, and an aesthetic sensibility.

8.19 Science education programmes will be designed to enable the learner to acquire problem solving and decision making skills and to discover the relationship of science with health, agriculture, industry and other aspects of daily life. Every effort will be made to extend science to the vast numbers who remained outside the pale of formal education.

Sports and Physical Education

8.20 Sports and physical education are an integral part of the learning process, and will be included in the evaluation of performance. A nation-wide infrastructure for physical education, sports and games will be built into the educational edifice.

8.21 The infrastructure will consist of playfields, equipment, coaches and teachers of physical education as part of the School Improvement Programme. Available open spaces in urban areas will be reserved for playgrounds, if necessary by legislation. Efforts will be made to establish sports institutions and hostels where specialised attention will be given to sports activities and sports-related studies, along with normal education. Appropriate encouragement will be given to those talented in sports and games. Due stress will be laid on indigenous traditional games. As a system which promotes an integrated development of body and mind, Yoga will receive special attention. Efforts will be made to introduce Yoga in all schools; to this end, it will be introduced in teacher training courses.

The Role of Youth

8.22 Opportunities will be provided for the youth to involve them in national and social development through educational institutions and outside them. Students will be required to participate in one or the other of existing schemes, namely, the National Service Scheme, National Cadet Corps, etc. Outside the institutions, the youth will be encouraged to take up programmes of development, reform and extension. The National Service Volunteer Scheme will be strengthened.

The Evaluation Process and Examination Reform

8.23 Assessment of performance is an integral part of any process of learning and teaching. As part of sound educational strategy, examinations should be employed to bring about qualitative improvements in education.

8.24 The objective will be to re-cast the examination system so as to ensure a method of assessment that is a valid and reliable measure of student development and a powerful instrument for improving teaching and learning. In functional terms, this would mean :

(i) The elimination of excessive element of chance and subjectivity;

(ii) The de-emphasis of memorisation.

(iii) Continuous and comprehensive evaluation that incorporates both scholastic and non-scholastic aspects of education, spread over the total span of instructional time :

(iv) Effective use of the evaluation process by teachers, students and parents :

(v) Improvement in the conduct of examinations;

(vi) The introduction of concomitant changes in instructional materials and methodology;

(vii) Introduction of the semester system from the secondary stage in a phased manner; and

(viii) The use of grades in place of marks.

8.25 The above goals are relevant both for external examinations and evaluation within educational institutions. Evaluation at the institutional level will be streamlined and the predominance of external examinations reduced.

Part IX

The Teacher

9.1 The status of the teacher reflects the socio-cultural ethos of a society; it is said that no people can rise above the level of its teachers. The Government and the community should endeavour to create conditions which will help motivate and inspire teachers on constructive and creative lines. Teachers should have the freedom to innovate, to devise appropriate methods of communication and activities relevant to the needs and capabilities of and the concerns of the community.

9.2 The methods of recruiting teachers will be reorganised to ensure merit, objectivity and conformity with spatial and functional requirements. The pay and service conditions of teachers have to be commensurate with their social and professional responsibilities and with the need to attract talent to the profession. Efforts will be made to reach the desirable objective of uniform emoluments, service conditions and grievance-removal mechanisms for teachers throughout the country. Guidelines will be formulated to ensure objectivity in the postings and transfers of teachers. A system of teacher evaluation—open, participative and data-based will be created and reasonable opportunities of promotion to higher grades provided. Norms of accountability will be laid down with incentives for good performance and disincentives for non-performance. Teachers will continue to play a crucial role in the formulation and implementation of educational programmes.

9.3 Teachers' associations must play a significant role in upholding professional integrity, enhancing the dignity of the teacher and in curbing professional misconduct. National level associations of teachers, could prepare a Code of Professional Ethics for Teachers and see to its observance.

9.4 Teachers education is a continuous process, and its pre-service and in-service components are inseparable. As the first step, the system of teacher education will be overhauled.

9.5 The new programmes of teacher-education will emphasise continuing education and the need for teachers to meet the thrusts envisaged in the Policy.

9.6 District Institutes of Education and Training (DIFT) will be established with the capability to organise pre-service and in-service courses for elementary school teachers and for the personnel working in non-formal and adult education. As DIFTs get established, sub-standard institutions will be phased out. Selected Secondary Teacher Training Colleges will be upgraded to complement the work of State Councils of Educational Research and Training. The National Council of Teacher Education will be provided the necessary resources and capability to accredit institutions of teacher-education and provide guidance regarding curricula and methods. Networking arrangements will be created between institutions of teacher education and university departments of education.

Part X

The Management of Education

10.1 An overhaul of the system of planning and the management of education will receive high priority. The guiding considerations will be:

(a) Evolving a long-term planning and management perspective of education and its integration with the country's development and manpower needs ;
(b) Decentralisation and the creation of a spirit of autonomy for educational institutions ;
(c) Giving pre-eminence to people's involvement, including association of non-government agencies and voluntary effort ;
(d) Inducting more women in the planning and management of education ;
(e) Establishing the principle of accountability in relation to given objectives and norms.

National Level

10.2 The Central Advisory Board of Education will play a pivotal role in reviewing educational development, determining the changes required to improve the system and monitoring implementation. It will function through appropriate committee and other mechanisms created to ensure contact with, and coordination among, the various areas of Human Resource Development. The Departments of Education at the Centre and in the States will be strengthened through the involvement of professionals.

Indian Education Service

10.3 A proper management structure in education will entail the establishment of the Indian Education Service as an All-India Service. It will bring a national perspective to this vital sector. The basic principles, functions and procedures of recruitment to this service will be decided in consultation with the State Governments.

State Level

10.4 State Governments may establish State Advisory Boards of Education on the lines of CABE. Effective measures should be taken to integrate mechanisms in the various State departments concerned with Human Resource Development.

10.5 Special attention will be paid to the training of educational planners, administrators and heads of institutions. Institutional arrangements for this purpose should be set up in stages.

District and Local Level

10.6 District Boards of Education will be created to manage education up to the higher secondary level. State Governments will attend to this aspect with all possible expedition. Within a multi-level framework of educational development, Central, State, District and Local level agencies will participate in planning, coordination, monitoring and evaluation.

10.7 A very important role must be assigned to the head of an educational institution. Heads will be specially selected and trained. School complexes will be promoted on a flexible pattern so as to serve as networks of institutions and synergic alliances to encourage professionalism among teachers, to ensure observance of norms of conduct and to enable the sharing of experiences and facilities. It is expected that a developed system of school complexes will take over much of the inspection functions in due course.

10.8 Local communities, through appropriate bodies, will be assigned a major role in programmes of school improvement.

10.9 Non-government and voluntary effort including social activist groups will be encouraged, subject to proper management, and financial assistance provided. At the same time, steps will be taken to prevent the establishment of institutions set up to commercialise education.

Part XI

Resources and Review

11.1 The Education Commission of 1964-66, the National Education Policy of 1968 and practically all others concerned with education have stressed that the egalitarian goals and the practical, development-oriented objectives of Indian of an order commensurate with the nature and dimensions of the task.

11.2 Resources, to the possible, will be raised by mobilising donations, asking the beneficiary communities to maintain school buildings and supplies of some consumables, raising fees at the higher levels of education and effecting some savings by the efficient use of facilities. Institutions involved with research and the development of technical and scientific manpower should also mobilize some funds by levying a cess or charge on the user agencies, including Government departments, and entrepreneurs. All these measures will be taken not only to reduce the burden on State resources but also for creating a greater sense of responsibility within the educational system. However, such measures will contribute only marginally to the total funding. The Government and community in general will find funds for such programmes as : the universalisation of elementary education; liquidating illiteracy; equality of access of educational opportunities to all sections throughout the country; enhancing the social relevance, quality and functional effectiveness of educational programmes; generating knowledge and developing technologies in scientific fields crucial to self-sustaining economic development; and creating a critical consciousness of the values and imperatives of national survival.

11.3 The deleterious consequences of non-investment or inadequate investment in education are indeed very serious. Similarly, the cost of neglecting vocational and technical education and of research is also unacceptable. Sub-optimal performance in these fields could cause irreparable damage to the Indian economy. The network of institutions set up from time to time since Independence to facilitate the application of science and technology would need to be substantially and expeditiously updated, since they are fast becoming obsolete.

11.4 In view of these imperatives, education will be treated as a crucial area of investment for national development and survival. The National Policy on Education, 1968, had laid down that the investment on education be gradually increased to reach a level of expenditure of 6 per cent of the national income as early as possible. Since the actual level of investment has remained far short of that target, it is important that greater determination be shown now to find the funds for the programmes laid down in this Policy. While the actual requirements will be computed from time to time on the basis of monitoring and review, the outlay on education will be stepped up to the extent essential for policy implementation in the Seventh Plan. It will be ensured that from the Eighth Five Year onwards it will uniformly exceed to 6 per cent of the National income.

Review

11.5 The implementation of the various parameters of the New Policy must be reviewed every five years. Appraisals at short intervals will also be made to ascertain the progress of implementation and the trends emerging from time to time.

Part XII

The Future

12.1 The future shape of education in India is too complex to envision with precision. Yet, given our tradition which has almost always put a high premium on intellectual and spiritual attainment, we are bound to succeed in achieving our objectives.

12.2 The main task is to strengthen the base of the pyramid, which might come close to a billion people at the turn of the century. Equally, it is important to ensure that those at the top of the pyramid are among the best in the world. Our cultural well-springs had taken good care of both ends in the past; the skew set in with foreign domination and influence. It should now be possible to further intensify the nation-wide effort in Human Resource Development, with Education playing its multi-faceted role.

APPENDIX 7

Underwork in the University and at the College Level

A university teacher earns 12 months' salary by doing work for 2 or 2.5 months. The academic year practically consists of 187 days or so.

First term (since admission go on for 2 weeks even after college reopens) (1st August to 30th September)		2 months
Second term (10th October to 23rd December)		2 months & 1 week
Third term (8th January to 10th March)		2 months
Total		6 months & 1 week
i.e.	187 days	
Minus		
Sundays	26 days	
Univ. Holidays	20 days (may go up to 24)	
Off days (once a week)	26 days	
Discretionary Holidays i.e. Sports Day, College Day, etc.	4 days	
	76 days	
Leave :		
Casual Leave	10 days	
Earned Leave	12 days	
Half Pay Leave 20 (commutted to)	10 days	
Special Casual Leave	4 days (average)	
	112 days	
Total Working Days	75 in a year	
During 1980-81 Loss due to Strike	11 days	
Actual Working days	64 days	

Source : Report of the Committee to Enquire into the Working of the Central Universities, NCT (NIEPA), 1984.

Bibliography

Adiseshiah, M.S. (1975). Report of the *Education Finance Review Committee*, Madras (unpub.)

Aggarwal, B.L. (1977). 'Educated Unemployment in India', *Commerce*, Pamphlet 109.

Aggarwal, J.C. (1982). *Development and Planning of Modern Education*, Vikas Pub. House Pvt. Ltd.

——(1984). *Landmark in the History of Modern Indian Education*, Vikas Pub. House Pvt. Ltd.

Aikava, J. (1980). *Scheduled Caste and Higher Education*, Dastana Ramachandra & Co., Poona.

Anatharaman, M.S. (1979). "Performance Budgeting" in *Challenges in Higher Education Administration—Readings and Cases*, Subramaniam, M.K. and Joseph, M. (eds.), Vol. II, Administrative Staff College of India, Hyderabad.

Basargekar, S.A. (1978). Problems of Financial Administration of an Indian University; *University Administration*, Vol.V, No. 2, Dec. 1978, pp. 32-52.

Bhatnager, S. (1983). *Indian Education : Today and Tomorrow*, Loyal Book Depot, Meerut.

Blaug, M.P., R.G. Layard & M. Woodhall (1969). *Causes of Graduate Unemployment in India*, Allen Lane the Penguin, London.

Blang, M. and J. Mace (1983). *Financing Higher Education : An Economic Perspective* (Mimeo.)

Bowles, S. (1971). *Class Power and Mass Education*, Harvard University (Mimeo).

Carnoy, M., H. Levin, R. Nugent, S. Sunera, C. Torres and J. Unsicker (1982). 'The Political Economy of Financing Education in Developing Countries', in *IDRC*; 39-86.

Coombs, P.H. (1985). *The World Crisis in Education : The View from the Eighties*, Oxford, New York.

Das, B. (1976). *Financial Management, Evaluation and Planning for Development*, in S.C. Malik (Ed.).

Dhar, T.N., A.S. Ilchman and W.F. Ilchman (1976). *Education and Employment in India : The Policy Nexus*, Minerva, Calcutta.

Dutta, R.C. (1985). 'Schooling, Experience and Earnings : an Empirical Analysis', *Margin* (Jan.), pp. 60-73.

Education Commission (1966). *Education and National Development*, NCERT, New Delhi (Reprint 1971).

Fields, G.S. (1980) : 'Education and Income distribution in Developing Countries', in T. King (ed.) *Education and Income*, 231-315, Staff Working Paper No. 402, World Bank, Washington, D.C.

Frank, W. Banghart and Albert Trull, Jr. (1973). *Educational Planning*, The Macmillan Company, New York, pp. 6-7.

Goel, S.C. (1975). *Education and Economic Growth*, Macmillan, Delhi.

Gupta, L.D. (1983). *Education Administration at College Level*, Oxford & IBH Pub. Co., New Delhi.

Harberger, A.C. (1965). 'Investment in Men versus Investment in Machines : The Case of India', in C.A. Anderson and M.J. Bowman (Eds.), *Education and Economic Development*, Aldine, Chicago, pp. 11-50.

Hussain, I.Z. (1967). 'Returns to Education in India', in B. Singh (Ed.), *Education as investment*, Meenakshi, Meerut, pp. 141-56.

IRDC (1982) : Financing Educational Development, Ottawa.

Jimenez, E. (1986). 'An Economic Evaluation of a National Job Training System : Colombia's Servicio Nicional de Aprendizaje (SENA)', *EDT Discussion Paper* Series No. 24, The World Bank.

Joshi, K.L. (1976). Financial Management, Evaluation and Planning for Development, in Malik (ed.)

Kaur, Kuldip (1985). *Education in India* (1981-1985), CRRID, Chandigarh.

Kiranmay, Y.S. and Prasad, G. (1985) : 'Scientific Management Principles Absent', *The Hindu*, April.

Kothari, V.N. (1986). 'Primate Unaided Engineering and Medical Colleges—Consequences of Misguided Policy', *Economic and Political Weekly*, Vol. XXI, No. 14, April 5.

Kurrien, J. (1983). *Elementary Education in India*, Vikas Pub. House, Delhi.

Leitner, G.W. (1982). *History of Indigenous Education in the Punjab Since Annexation and in 1882*, Amar Prakashan, New Delhi.

Lockheed, M., Jamison, D. and Lau, L. (1980). 'Farmer Education and Farm Efficiency : A Survey', *Economic Dev. & Cultural Change*, 37-76.

Mathur, M.V. (1983). *Towards Improved Educational Planning and Administration*, Joy Madhathi Kunnel for Dialogue, New Delhi.

Mhendiratta, P.R. (1984). *University Administration in India and USA—Approaches, Issues and Implications*, Oxford and IBH Publishing Co., New Delhi.

Misra, A. (1962). *Education Finances in India*, Asia Pub., Bombay.

Misra, P.N. (1986). Quantification of Optimal Role of Government Expenditure on Education for Regional Development in Gujarat', in J.B.G. Tilak (ed.) *Education and Regional Development,* Yatan Pub. for Society for the Study of Regional Disparities, New Delhi.

Mohanty, J. (1983). *Indian Education in the Emerging Society* Sterling Pub., New Delhi.

Naik, J.P. (1979). 'Educational Development in India during the Next Twenty Years : 1981-2000; *IIE Bulletin 3,* (1982), pp. 12-20.

——(1982) : *Education Commission and After*, Allied Pub. Pvt. Ltd., New Delhi

Orivel, F. (1986). 'Economic Crisis and Educational Crisis : Looking Ahead', *Prospect* 16/2 : 197-204.

Padmanabhan, C.B. (1982). 'An Approach to Financial Management in Education—with Special Reference to Colleges in India', *Journal of Higher Education*, Vol. 7, No. 3, Spring.

——(1984). 'Towards Functional Financial Management in Universities', *University News*, 22/38, (October 8) 2-6.

Paliwal, M.R. (1984). *Social Change and Education*, Uppal Pub. House, New Delhi.

Panchmukhi, P.R. (1977). *Economics of University Finances*, Dharwal, Centre for Multi-disciplinary Research.

Pandit, H.N. (1976). 'Investment in Indian Education', Occasional Paper No. 42, Pan's IIEP.

Psachropoulos, G. (1980). Higher Education in Developing Countries : A cost-benefit Analysis', Staff Working Paper No. 440, Washingtion DC, World Bank.

Psachropoulos, (1984). To contribution of Education to Economic Growth : International Comparisons', in *International Comparisons of Productivity and Censes of the Slowdown* (ed.). John W. Kendrick Ballinger, 335-360.

Psachropoulos, G. and Loxley, W. (1985). *Diversified Secondary Education and Development : Evidence from Colombia and Tanzania*, Johns Hopkins.

Selowsky, M. (1967). 'Education and Economic Growth : Some International Comparisons', *Economic Development*, Report No. 83 (Cambridge, Harward University) Mimeo.

Sharma, B.R. (1976). 'Professionals in the Making : Their Social Origin', *Economic & Political Weekly*, February, pp. M5 -M10.

Singh, Amrik and Sharma, G.D. (1981). *University and College Finances*, Association of Indian Universities, Delhi.

Singh, P. (1982). *Financing of University Education*, B.R. Publishers, Delhi.

Tilak, J.B.G. (1979). 'Schooling, Experience and Earnings', *Margin*, 11(4), (July), pp. 82-88.

——(1987). *Economics of Inequality in Education*, Sage Publications (for Institute of Economic Growth), New Delhi.

——(1984). 'Political Economy of Investment in Education in South Asia', *International Journal of Educational Development*, No. 4, pp. 155-66.

Tilak, J.B.G. and N.V. Varghese, (1983). 'Resources for Education in India', *Occassional Paper No. 2*, NIEPA, New Delhi.

——(1985), 'Discriminatory Pricing in Education', *Occassional Paper No. 8*, NIEPA, New Delhi.

Varghese, N.V. (1982). 'Some Empirical Evidence', in *Report on Consultative Meeting*, New Delhi, NIEPA, (Mimeo).

——(1986 a). 'Higher Education and Unemployment Towards a Tentative Hypothesis', in J.B.G. Tilak (ed.), *Education and Regional Development*, Yatan, New Delhi.

——(1986 b). *Education and Labour Market : A Survey of Indian Evidence*, Study Sponsored by IIEP, Paris, NIEPA (Mimeo), New Delhi.

Walker, E.W. and Banghu, W.H. (1980). *Financial Planning and Policy*, Harper International, New York.

World Bank (1986). Financing of Education in Developing Countries, Washington, D.C.

DOCUMENTARY REFERENCES

Analysis of Budgeted Expenditure on Education 1984-85 to 1986-87, Ministry of Human Resource Development, Government of India, New Delhi, 1988.

Annual Report 1986-87 : Part I, Department of Education, Ministry of Human Resource Development, Government of India, New Delhi, 1987.

Annual Report 1987-88 : Part I, Department of Education, Ministry of Human Resource Development, Government of India, New Delhi, 1988.

Annual Report 1985-86, National Council of Educational Research and Training, New Delhi, 1986.

Annual Report 1986-87, National Council of Education Research and Training, New Delhi, 1987.

Challenge of Education—A Policy Perspective, Ministry of Education, Government of India, New Delhi, 1985.

Development of Education 1984-86 : National Report of India, National Council of Educational Research and Training, Ministry of Human Resource Development, Government of India, New Delhi, 1986.

Diagnostic Studies on Educational Management—Country Studies : India, UNESCO Regional Office for Education in Asia and the Pacific, Bangkok, 1984.

National Curriculum for Elementary and Secondary Education : A Framework (Revised Version), National Council of Education Research and Training, New Delhi, 1988.

National Policy on Education—1986, Ministry of Human Resource Development, Government of India, New Delhi, 1986.

National Policy on Education 1986 : Programme of Action, Ministry of Human Resource Development, Government of India, New Delhi, 1986.

National Policy on Education 1986 : Implementation Report, Ministry of Human Resource Development, Government of India, New Delhi, March 1988.

Report of the year 1985-86 : University Grants Commission, New Delhi, 1987.

Selected Educational Statistics 1984-85, Ministry of Human Resource Development, Planning, Monitoring and Statistics Division, Government of India, New Delhi, 1986.

Index